D1346089

TRY THIS AT HOME

TRY THIS AT HOME

ADVENTURES IN SONGWRITING

FRANK TURNER

HEADLINE

First published in 2019
by HEADLINE PUBLISHING GROUP

1

Cataloguing in Publication Data is available from the British Library

Hardback ISBN 978 1 4722 5785 7
Ebook ISBN 978 1 4722 5784 0

Typeset in Bell MT Std & Rosewood Std by
Palimpsest Book Production Ltd, Falkirk, Stirlingshire

Printed and bound in Great Britain by Clays Ltd, Elcograf S.p.A.

Headline's policy is to use papers that are natural, renewable and
recyclable products and made from wood grown in sustainable forests.
The logging and manufacturing processes are expected to conform
to the environmental regulations of the country of origin.

HEADLINE PUBLISHING GROUP
An Hachette UK Company
Carmelite House
50 Victoria Embankment
London
EC4Y 0DZ

www.headline.co.uk
www.hachette.co.uk

For Adam Duritz, John K. Samson and Jay McAllister

CONTENTS

INTRODUCTION

What kind of presumptuous fool volunteers to write a book about songwriting?

Well, this one, apparently. In my defence, I have been largely thinking about songwriting, almost to the exclusion of everything else, for most of my adult life. And while I haven't exactly had much in the way of chart hits with my work, I've written just shy of 200 songs, mostly alone, occasionally together with others. I've been touring those songs for twenty years, and making a living from them for around half of that time. It's the work of my adult life. So, in fairness, I do have some thoughts on the topic that might be worth sharing with the world.

I wrote another book, four years ago, about touring, called *The Road Beneath My Feet*. It was a sort of incomplete memoir of my time on the road. It did pretty well. But there was something of a philosophical gap in that tome; it didn't really have much to say about the songs I was playing through all those endless shows. I felt like it might be an idea to address that next time around. So here we are.

I should also say that I embarked on the previous work with no small degree of hubris. 'Writing a book can't be that hard!' I cried. 'I've written plenty of articles for magazines and the like before, it'll just be like about forty of those in a row!' Reader, how wrong I was. I'd like to take this moment to apologise to those of you who know more about writing books than I do and have more experience in the field. If it's any consolation, I discovered quite how wide of the mark I was pretty quickly. I've approached this work with much more humility, and with my sleeves well and truly rolled up.

All the same, I've gone and written another book that is essentially about myself — the one topic that doesn't require endless months of research in a library (though I have spent a lot of time going through notebooks and archives of recordings here to get this one right). Because this book is laid out chronologically, and because I have a tendency to write in a confessional first-person style, this book, like its predecessor, has an element of autobiography to it. It'll certainly help, as you read, if you're familiar with my music.

Having said that, I hope that there is a didactic angle here. Songwriting is both an art and a craft. While the art part remains appropriately mystical and out of reach, the latter craft side of it can be examined, dissected, practised and ultimately taught (although personally, I've never been to school for anything I'm about to write about). I hope that anyone who writes their own material might find some points of interest herein, a few tips and pointers. And, of course, I hope there's a lot here for people who aren't in the business of composing their own songs. Either way, this here is most of what I have to say about how to write songs, how I've written them in the past, and how I think it's best to approach the whole thing.

What exactly, then, are we talking about, when we talk about writing songs?

Art of all kinds is, in essence, a form of communication — perhaps the most complicated one that humans engage in, and one that seems to be universal to our various cultures. Friedrich Nietzsche once said, 'Without music, life would be a mistake.' That's certainly how it feels to me, though of course, I've encountered the rare incomprehensible curmudgeon, for whom music does nothing at all. I'm presuming, if you're reading this, that you're not one of them.

The corner of art, of music, that I inhabit and that I'm going to discuss is rock'n'roll. I'm not going to try to elucidate the entire history of the art form here (get on with it, man!), but I think I can safely say that this kind of music has long been something of an awkward stepchild within the wider family of the Arts with a capital A. That actually makes me more loyal to it. It's something that grew out of the demotic folk song traditions of the pre-industrial world, but which came into its own through the additions of electricity, mass popular culture, recording equipment, jazz, blues and the Folk Revival of the 1960s (and much more besides), until, by the end of the twentieth century, it was an established institution.

Rock'n'roll, and indeed my own music, is largely based on the guitar. The guitar is the great democratic instrument of modern times. Easy to play (unlike the accordion) and portable (unlike the piano), and full enough to accompany a solo performer (unlike the fiddle), it has dominated the arrangements of popular song for a long time for good reason. It's not the only basis for a song, of course, not even within my own canon, as we'll see. But it's at the middle of the picture. Much of our story is dominated by the timeless silhouette of the troubadour, the lone figure with the lone instrument, pouring out their truth in song for the rest of us to enjoy, absorb and apply to our own lives.

The songs we're talking about here tend to be short compositions. While punk has taken them down to a few seconds (well done, Napalm Death), and prog rock has stretched them to symphonic lengths (thank you, Genesis), for the most part, these songs hover around the three-minute mark. Intriguingly, there might be commercial and technological reasons for this. Apparently, in the post-war era, fast-food restaurants did market research to find out the average length of time it took an American to eat a cheeseburger – around three minutes. They also found out that, if a song finishes as you finish your food, you tend to get up and leave. The corporations encouraged the makers of records to manufacture a product that stuck to roughly that length of time, and the 45 single was born. Whether or not that's true (and I sincerely hope it is; it's cute), songs still last roughly 180 seconds or so. The removal of technological restraints with modern music making and listening equipment doesn't seem to have changed that.

Let's go deeper. A song is a blueprint, a genetic code. Normally it comprises a sequence of chords that provide a harmonic bed for a leading vocal melody, which carries a set of lyrics. Lyrics are not quite poetry, in that they're written within pre-existing musical constraints. Regardless, these instructions for music can result in very different end products from the same starting point ('With a Little Help from My Friends' sounds radically different in the hands of the Beatles and Joe Cocker, for example). The song can be stripped right back to its central, troubadour components, or it can be worked up in an arrangement to include walls of sound and symphony orchestras. Musicologists categorise different stylistic approaches into phylae that we know as 'genres', but I've always felt that songs tend to have more in common with each other than these artificial lines would suggest.

Songs can tell stories. They can shine a light on the inner workings of the author's troubled mind. They can deliver messages. They can incite riots. They can address a lover or the entire world. They can tell us things about ourselves, or they can make us sing along with meaningless but catchy ditties. In a time when pure poetry is a dying art, the lyrics to popular songs are, for most people, their most frequent and profound encounter with that end of literature.

And of course songs can be much, much more or infinitely less than all this. I've written here about my own work, so this is a necessarily limited, idiosyncratic exercise. I haven't written about every song I've written, that would have made for a book too long to read and too heavy to pick up. Any other songwriter could probably write a book on the same template and say the exact opposite of everything I have to say. As I mentioned earlier, songwriting is both an art and a craft. I remain sceptical whether the artistic part of it is something that can even be explained directly, let alone taught. Much of the time, when I'm trying to write, I feel like a fisherman, sitting by the edge of the water, dangling a hook into the stream and hoping that something bites. In some ways, there's not much more to say than that. But this book isn't really a lesson, it's more of a travel memoir of my own journeys through song; in that sense, I suppose it does have something in common with my first book. I hope you enjoy the journey.

Frank Turner, London, 2018

THE REAL DAMAGE

I woke up on a sofa in an unfamiliar house,
Surrounded by sleeping folks that I didn't know.
On failing to find my friends, I decided that it was clearly time to go.
So I made my way out of the door as quietly as I could –
There was no one there I knew to say goodbye.
Squinting in the sadly sobering sunshine of the Sunday morning light.

I started the night with all my friends and I ended up alone,
Oh yes I started out so happy, now I'm hungover and down.
It was about then that I realised I was halfway through the best years of my life.

I scanned the local landmarks, trying to find out where I was,
And maybe even find a bus back home.
I was longing for a shower, and for clean sheets, and a charger for my phone.
Suddenly it hit me – I got paid this Friday last,
So I rifled through my pockets for some change.
But all I found was a packet of broken cigarettes and a sinking sense of shame.

I had to ask myself, well,
Is it really worth it? Is any of this worth it?
Well the whole thing's far from perfect,
But I've yet to figure out a better way to spend my time.

Too many suits and dirty looks made me rack my brains –
The real damage started to sink in.
It'd been quite a heavy weekend but I could just about remember where I'd been.

Well I started the night with all my friends and I ended up alone,
Oh yes I started out so happy, now I'm hungover and down.
I stood on a street corner and I felt a little sick.
It was about then that I realised I was halfway through the first day of the week.

* * *

'The Real Damage' was far from the first song I ever wrote, but in a strange way, it feels like it *should* have been the first. It deserves that accolade, I think, because, in the process of writing it, I thought about songwriting for the first time, as an art form in and of itself.

Prior to the summer of 2005, I had, of course, made a lot of original music. On receiving an electric guitar starter kit for my eleventh birthday (*'guitar and amp – comes with strap and lead!'*), I set about learning chords for the songs then in vogue on my cassette player – well, the easier ones, at any rate. Almost immediately, I started messing around with those progressions, and claiming the resulting hybrids as my own. I remember changing the third chord of 'Knockin' on Heaven's Door' from an A minor to an A major (which actually completely recontextualises the melody, as it goes), and feeling like I'd written something. It sounds ridiculous now (though not as ridiculous as the fact that, at the time, I thought the song was by Guns N' Roses – tragic but true), but there it was, right at the start, a desire to make my own songs.

That said, I didn't really think of songs as coherent artistic entities then, or for a long time to come. I could identify songs I liked, of course, and learn how to play an approximation of them, good enough for a singalong on our family beach holidays in Devon and Cornwall. But they just existed as sections of music bolted together like a cut-and-shut job on a car; I can't remember thinking about any over-arching structures. The fact that the chorus reprised at the end of the song just meant there was one less bit to learn. A key change was a hassle because it meant the song required more chords.

This episodic, mechanical view of what songs were, and how they were put together, was given major reinforcement when I started getting into hardcore punk music. Hardcore songs (and I say this with affection) often tend to be built from an assortment of riffs laid out in a linear fashion, with little thought for overall coherence. The particular corner of the genre that captured my imagination in my teens actually made a virtue of this – bands like Cave In and Converge wrote long, rambling pieces that rarely came back to where they started. The only thing holding them together as 'songs' was the fact that they (usually) didn't stop dead for any length of time in the middle, they were listed as a single track on the CD, and maybe that there was a single set of lyrics over the top of the racket to give the whole thing some shape.

That approach to making music was very much at the heart of how my first serious band Million Dead operated. I remember us in dingy Holloway practice rooms, taking pieces of riffs that different people had contributed and trying to find ways to get them into the same song, the whole thing feeling more like an engineering problem than anything else. That's not to disown anything we did – I remain immensely proud of the music we made – it's just that I still wasn't really thinking about songwriting in any dedicated fashion.

Sometime around 2004 I started hanging out at a bar in north London called Nambucca. I've told that story in more detail elsewhere; for now, suffice to say that I encountered a new group of people who were making a new (to me) style of music. There was a lot of country and folk in the air, a lot of acoustic guitars, all of it centred around the Sunday night open mic called Sensible Sundays, which was hosted by Jay McAllister (who made music under the name Beans On Toast), who ran the bar along with Dave Danger.

We also used to do a lot of partying, staying up for days and getting wrecked. One particular weekend, a friend of ours took acid and was convinced he was being followed everywhere by very small Chinese soldiers. The following Sunday, Jay had a new song about 'Steve and the Secret Chinese Army'. The song was short, simple and funny – and a total revelation to me, on a number of levels. Firstly, the simplicity of the music was striking to someone who was lost in trying to overcomplicate things in the rarified atmosphere of a technical post-hardcore scene. Secondly, the lyrics were clear, direct and witty, and they told a simple story, which also told us something about ourselves as a group of friends. And most of all, the song was about something that had happened *last week* – *to us*. I was used to slaving over words for months at a time, putting complicated and deliberately obscurantist metaphors at centre stage. And yet it didn't have to be like that – and we could be the heroes of our own stories!

The seed was planted; this was a new way of making music, a new approach, something radically direct and simple. It felt *punk* to me, but also like it was real folk music. And at the heart of it all was the idea of a song, a thing in itself. I started to wonder, idly, if I could write that way too.

So it was that I started thinking about stories I could tell in a simple song format. The universe was not long in providing. As mentioned, my time in and around Nambucca was pretty debauched. There were a lot of drugs, and not much sleeping. One weekend, apropos of not very much, a friend (let's call him

Paulo) and I started a session at the bar of the pub that quickly got heavy. We went clubbing, came back, went upstairs, went to house parties, generally said yes to everything we could, and ended up getting very, very trashed. The details of our progress slowly faded to black, until the cloak of intoxication overtook me completely.

The next thing I remember is waking up on a sofa in a room I didn't know. Opening one eye at a time and squinting through smoky morning light and a headache, I saw that the floor around me was littered with comatose bodies, none of whom I could immediately recognise. It looked how I felt – like a bomb had gone off. I slowly gathered myself, realised I was still fully dressed, and had my phone and wallet with me (a relief – but then I was always a professional wreckhead), and decided to creep out without waking any of the strangers around me. Outside felt pretty challenging, but I set my mind to the most important task – getting back to my place in Finsbury Park for a shower and some proper sleep in my own bed.

I slowly figured out where I was by consulting local bus stops, and eventually got myself home, after enduring a journey studded by waves of nausea and the suspicious and judgemental glances of strangers – of whom there seemed to be rather a lot, given that it was, as I understood it, a Sunday. When I finally got back to my room, I was able to charge my phone, and to call Paulo, to try and piece together some of the missing hours. To my shock and horror, Paulo was at work. We had begun our adventure on a Saturday night, and it seemed reasonable to me to imagine that I'd passed out somewhere and woken up the following morning. Alas, no. I had actually somehow powered through an entire extra day, none of which I remembered. Paulo laughed at my predicament, while I felt pretty shady and shame-faced; as much as I enjoyed getting wasted, this was a new high – or low – in my career as a party animal, losing twenty-four hours. I still don't know where I was or who I'd been with, to this day.

A few days later, I'd recovered from my weekend, and decided that my only course forward was to see the funny side of it. In fact, I decided to try out the idea of using this escapade as the basis for a song. The inspiration for a set of words was in. Now I just needed some music to go with it.

I'd been listening to a lot of stuff like Ryan Adams, Springsteen's solo work and, in particular, Neil Young. The traditional country chord structures in the key of G that form the basis of songs like 'Comes a Time' had really taken my fancy; they were easy but satisfying to play, and in the key I know best. I started thinking of a melody and a chord sequence to underpin it, actively trying to keep things traditional. It begins with the root chord, G, working in the major scale*. The chorus starts on the IV chord (C major), which gives a feeling like the song is moving forward. The bridge section uses the III chord (B minor), which always sounds wistful to me. And then it all resolves again, back down to a I, a G major.

Over the top of all this, the lyrics fell into place. Again, I was trying to restrict myself, to hold back, and to make a virtue of simplicity by telling the story as it happened. That said, I felt like I wanted to make some kind of point with the song as well.

---

* A note for the uninitiated (and don't panic; this stuff is only barely comprehensible to me, after nearly two decades of playing music!). A normal scale has 8 notes, from the first note (or root) up to the same note, an octave above. In a given key (here, G major), the chords are named as roman numerals (to distinguish them from individual notes), so G major is I, A minor is II, B minor is III and so on. Using the numerals makes it easier to think about how the chords sound *relative* to each other. There are also rules for which chords in a key would be major, minor, diminished, and probably other, fancier things in other keys. But for now, that's what you need to know, when you start seeing me write about I, IV, V chords and so on.

I'd recently watched (and loved) the film *The Football Factory*. In a climactic scene, Danny Dyer's character asks the pertinent philosophical question, after going through the wringer of drugs and violence: was it worth it? 'Of course it fucking was!' comes the reply. I hadn't been in a fight on my lost weekend, but it kind of felt like it, and so the scene appealed to me. Despite the chaos and the damage done, it seemed like it had been worth it. After all, I had a story to tell, and now a song to sing.

The writing process was quick, and it was given extra impetus by the fact that I had a rare (at the time) solo show coming up. Towards the end of Million Dead's time, I did a handful of these solo sets, usually for charity shows. In this instance, our young label, Xtra Mile, had a night on at the Underworld in Camden coming up. Label stalwarts Reuben were headlining, and I'd been asked to play some music on my own beforehand. I decided to use this as an opportunity to try out my new song (previous such solo outings had largely comprised of covers), not least because I knew Paulo was coming to the show. I took the stage – sitting down, as I recall – and rambled through the song, somewhere in the set. It seemed to go down well; Paulo in particular found it hilarious, and all in all, the experiment was a success.

Over time, Million Dead came to an end. I never made a move to do something else seriously before the band was over, but we agreed to see out our existing touring commitments after the decision to split was made, so by then, I had another route that I could explore opening up before me. I'd played 'The Real Damage', and a handful of others, at Sensible Sundays over the summer. When Dave and Jay heard Million Dead was done (a band they'd never much liked, not being hardcore punk fans), they enthusiastically encouraged me to pursue this new line of songwriting.

*

I started booking shows around the country, travelling by train. But, as anyone at the bottom of the gig ladder will tell you, that's not easy to do without a demo of some kind. Using some very basic recording software on an old laptop, I knocked out some recordings of four songs, the lead of which was 'The Real Damage'. I kept the recorded version pretty simple – I tried double-tracking some guitars on the chorus, and adding a very simple piano line on the bridge – and started burning off CD-Rs to sell at shows. As time went by and things started to pick up, this song in particular became something of a crowd favourite (small as those crowds were). It moved from being my opener to being my closer, always the sign of a strong piece. I've probably played that song as much as any other in my catalogue.

Over time, two more versions were recorded. I did a bedroom session with a budding producer called Tristan Ivemy, who played some slightly more elaborate piano on the track; it was released on an Xtra Mile sampler CD, if memory serves. Later on, when we came to record *Sleep Is for the Week*, I tried to gather the best aspects of the previous recordings and get a definitive version down. The arrangement kind of works like that (although Matt Nasir, of The Sleeping Souls, has, over the years, added a much better piano part to the bridge). I have to say that, listening back now, the way I deliver the vocals sounds odd to me. It took me a long time to find a way to sing in the studio that matched how I delivered songs live. I also tend to slow down the broken-down final chorus when I play live. Ben Lloyd, as producer, later suggested we do that in the studio and I decided against it; not for the first time, he was right and I was wrong.

One point that I was specifically focusing on at the time was trying to sing in my natural English accent. Growing up listening to American punk rock and rock'n'roll, it's an eternal temptation to sing with a Yankee twang – I certainly did so in Million Dead from time to time. Now, however, I was dead set on delivering my words in the same way I'd say them. I think I succeeded at that, and it makes the finished item feel more honest.

The song became a single at one point, and so had a music video made for it. My idea was for it to be a businessman arriving late for work and giving a PowerPoint presentation of why exactly he wasn't on time, and what he'd been up to the night before. In the event, the plotline got kind of mangled by too many people trying to put their oar in – another lesson learned the hard way. It's a little cringe-inducing in places, but nevertheless, I kind of like it. We spent a night at Nambucca 'method acting' the party scenes, and the video contains shots of The Automatic (who I was touring with around that time), plenty of witnesses to the incidents that had given rise to Jay's song, and my terrible mini-afro haircut. A period piece, then.

At Nambucca for 'The Real Damage' video shoot with friends

'The Real Damage' stands as a successful first stab at writing a folk song, in my mind. I'd never tried anything like it before. There are parts of it that sound naïve to me now, but overall I still love it. It stands me in good stead to this day – in most parts of the world, especially in the UK, I can drag that one out for a setlist and guarantee myself a singalong.

NASHVILLE TENNESSEE

From the heart of the Southern Downs, to the North-East London reservoirs,
From the start, the land scaped my sound, before I'd ever been to America.

And if I knew anybody who played pedal steel guitar,
I'd get them in my band and then my band would get real far,
But I was raised in middle England, and not in Nashville Tennessee,
And the only person in my band is me.

A simple scale on an old guitar, and a punk rock sense of honesty.
I cannot fail, when I've come this far with no knowledge of Midwest geography.

And if I knew anywhere where I could drive in a straight line
For hours in the desert, I'd drive for hours at a time.
But I was raised in middle England, not in Nashville Tennessee,
And the only person in this car is me.

And yes I'm in four-four time, and yes I use cheap cheap rhymes,
But I try to make a sound my own.
I know I don't break new ground, many have travelled this sound,
But I try to make it sound like home.

Well I've been to Texas state, I didn't think it was that fucking great,
And Nebraska is just a bunch of songs,
Holloway and Hampshire where I belong.
And I don't know anybody who plays pedal steel guitar,

All the city roads are twisted and I do not own a car.
I was raised in middle England, not in Nashville Tennessee,
And the only thing I'm offering is me.

*   *   *

In January 2007, I did my first tour with a band – that is to say, my first shows with other musicians standing on the stage and playing with me. Nigel, Ben, Jamie and Tarrant, from the Oxford band Dive Dive, had volunteered to step up to the plate. I'd met them when I was crewing for Reuben in between Million Dead tours, at a time when it was becoming clear that the latter band was not going to last long. I'd started mulling over the idea of a solo career. I mentioned it to Ben, who told me that they (Dive Dive) had their own studio set-up in Oxford. If I ever needed a place to record, and indeed musicians to record with, they were game. I took him up on the offer for the *Campfire Punkrock* EP in 2006, and by the start of the following year we were on the road as an unnamed (as yet) ensemble.

The London show of that tour – as per usual, the biggest show – was at the Borderline in Soho, on 13 February 2007 (don't worry, I have my past shows written down on a list, I don't just remember them, contrary to popular suspicions about my feats of memory). While it was a good show – 270 of 275 tickets sold, which gets announced as 'sold out!' after the event – my lasting memory of the show is actually of a heckle. In the middle of the set, the Oxford boys departed the stage for a while, leaving me to play some solo numbers. At that point on that rainy Soho evening, someone at the back of the crowded room shouted, 'Lose the band!'

Back on that stage in 2007, it really pissed me off, and I vaguely remember responding slightly gracelessly, unpractised as I was in the art of dealing with hecklers. But the story raises a point about the format of what I've been doing that is worth addressing head on. Million Dead ended acrimoniously, and I felt at the time, whether justifiably or not, that I'd been let down by other people.* I wanted to make music under my own name and my own authority, to not be vulnerable to that kind of disappointment again. I began touring on my own, partly out of logistical and financial necessity, and partly out of sheer bloody-mindedness. And most of the very first demos I recorded were solo affairs, for the same reasons.

But it's a point of fact that I was never, at any time, intending to remain alone on the stage or on record for ever. My inspirations – Springsteen, Johnny Cash's *American Recordings*, Ryan Adams and so on – might have tended to be solo figureheads, but they all used other players. Coming, as I did, from a background much more rock than folk, I'm not sure I could have made an entire album without any drums. I learned quickly on the road that playing entirely alone is a great discipline in many ways – it teaches you how to ride the dynamics of your own playing and setlist, because you have to keep things interesting, given the instrumental limitations you're working with. But in a way that's the point – it *is* limited, and if you have ambitions towards making art, sooner or later you'll want to expand your available sonic palette.

So the fact of the matter is this; there was never really a golden solo age in my career, contrary to some of the more purist and backward-looking naysayers. Admittedly, I didn't much help matters by singing the line 'the only person in my band is me' on the song 'Nashville Tennessee'.

*

* I'm old and wise enough now to see that I should accept my share of the blame for what happened; water under the bridge.

I find it hard, most of the time, to pinpoint exactly when a song took shape, or was finished. Partly that's because, right here, we're talking about a song I wrote a long time ago, on the road, when I used to get drunk a lot. But it's also because some part of the process remains ethereal. When I finish a song, I feel like a sleep-walker who wakes up holding a bloody knife and surrounded by fresh corpses; I know I'm responsible for this, but I can't remember actually doing it.

At some point in late 2005, then, the song came together (though not, hopefully, too much like a somnolent killing spree). I was enjoying playing with simple chords and simple words, trying to find a direct line on what I wanted to say and a melody to say it with. This song was built around a simple riff, which is essentially an open G5 chord, strummed consistently, while my index and middle fingers pick out the ascending and descending first six notes of a major scale on the bottom two strings, in the bass. The higher strings and smaller fingers keep a drone of melody and rhythm over the top, so that it's almost like two parts, bass and rhythm, on the one guitar. Keeping that theme going, the second half of the verse riff makes a simple transition – from the IV (C major) to the V (D major) – more interesting by walking the bassline down the scale back to the resolve on the G. I was writing a lot of songs in that key at the time, so to top it off, I employed my new favourite tool, a capo,* on fret 2 to take the whole thing into A major. Having written a lot of songs that were more simply chordal, I was quite pleased with something approaching an actual riff – after all, I was raised on Metallica's James Hetfield's dictum that 'you ain't got nothing if you ain't got a riff'.

Sticking with the details of the musical form for a moment, we then get to a chorus. It's a pretty simple country turnaround, by

* Pronounced, my American friends, with a short 'a' – like 'happy'. Fact.

design, but I decided to complicate it a little. Admittedly, at the time, this was in part because I was still nervous about musical simplicity. Actually, there's nothing wrong with using traditional chord structures. The idea that two songs are 'the same' because they have the same chords in a given section shows remarkably little understanding of the nuances, overtones and shades that actually make up a complete song; and that's without saying anything about top-line melodies or, you know, lyrics. I digress. The chorus, as I say, has a conventional country feel, though I use similar but slightly different patterns on each repeat (something of a writing habit of mine, which tends to drive The Sleeping Souls to distraction). The bridge nods more in the direction of Counting Crows, one of my all-time favourite bands, and one whose songs I'd spent much of my youth learning. Thereafter the song hits a solo over a verse (a trick I learned from Nirvana and Weezer), returns to a chorus, and plays out. Pretty basic stuff, certainly not reinventing the wheel, but nevertheless pretty fresh territory for me as a songwriter at the time.

So far so predictable, in its way. The lyrics were another matter. So many of my influences in this new solo direction were American. But I was at pains, as I've mentioned, not to sound American, or to come across as trying to pass myself off as a Yank. My aim, then and now, was to filter my influences, wherever they might be from, through the prism of my own experiences. I loved hearing Tom Petty sing about Florida, or Springsteen about Jersey, but to be influenced by that meant that I had to sing about where I was from. And I was going to do it all in the simple, direct style I was developing. All these thoughts evolved, over time, into something of a personal manifesto, and somewhere in the sleepwalk I started putting that into rhyming couplets.

Back in 2005, my only direct personal experience of the USA was three short trips we'd made with Million Dead. Labels had flown us to New York and Los Angeles for (fruitless) showcases. And in March 2004 we flew to the South by Southwest (SXSW) festival in Austin, Texas, under our own steam, paying for the visit with T-shirt money, fudging our visa statuses and sleeping on some random guy's floor in the suburbs. We'd entered into that last trip with such enthusiasm and optimism, DIY warriors setting out to conquer the States. So it had been something of a let-down to play to about fifteen disinterested English industry types in a bar on a side-street. America remained resolutely unconquered, mysterious, unrequited. That experience found its way into the bridge of the song, though I was unaware, at the time, that the formulation 'Texas State' is generally used to refer to the university.

In terms of lyrical technique, three things spring to mind here for me. Firstly, the way the choruses vary within a set structure, in particular the resolve in the last chorus. A song has to take you somewhere (unless you're consciously circling back to where you started, and even then, the statement wants to feel recontextualised). Landing in the final play-out with an answer to the questions raised in the first two choruses was satisfying to write, to sing, and hopefully to listen to. Secondly, at this moment in time I was quite taken with sloganeering as a stylistic tool – the standout line that has sass and would look good on a T-shirt. Billy Bragg is one of the kings of that style ('How can you lie there and think of England / When you don't even know who's in the team?'), and I'd started listening to a fair bit of his stuff at the time.* I think it has some

---

* For the record, I was not particularly aware of Bill's work before I started playing solo shows. Reasonably quickly, people began telling me I reminded them of him, so I went and checked out his stuff – and loved it. I can count him as a friend as well as an inspiration these days, and we've shared a lot of stages. I get compared to him a fair bit, even now, and I'll take it as a compliment. But he wasn't on my radar until well after I'd started working out my style.

severe limitations as an approach; after a while it feels like a word game more than an expression of anything and it starts to grate. But saying things like 'the only person in my band is me!' fell into that category of writing, and it really did make for a fun shirt design in the early days. And finally, I was clearly quite comfortable with swearing, even back then, in my lyrics. It's something I've done a fair bit over the years, and some people regard it with distaste, or as an affectation of some kind. The truth is simply that I swear quite a lot when I talk, especially if I'm relaxed; I always have and there doesn't seem to be much I can fucking do about it. But it does, or can, raise the issue of radio edits . . .

I finished the song, added it to my live solo show, and it became a set highlight with the small but dedicated audience I was building straight away. However, more so than any song I'd worked on up to this point, I just knew, in my heart, that the finished version of the tune would be a full band arrangement. I was implying other instrumentation with the guitar parts that I was playing, and most of all I wanted it to be louder and heavier.

Before connecting with the Dive Dive folks, I was stuck for anyone to actually make these sounds with. I'd decided that I wasn't going to play with anyone from Million Dead or the scene around that band (in order to make a fresh start), but I didn't know too many players in the new style I was exploring, and those I did, didn't seem to have much interest in what I was doing just yet. So I sat down with my laptop and some cheap demoing software and started trying to build an arrangement on my own. Bass guitar and drums were an obvious starting point. The drums sounded obviously artificial – that technology has come on a long way since – but it was a demo, a sketch. I laid over some basic electric and Hammond organ parts and listened back. It wasn't a terrible start, but it also wasn't something I particularly wanted to share with the world. So it was slightly ironic that the demo version ended up being on a *Rock Sound* magazine cover-mounted CD not long afterwards, thanks to the faithful efforts of Xtra Mile, Million Dead's old label, who had agreed to start working with me on the new music I was making. I massively appreciated the extra exposure that brought me, but I was jarred by the low quality of the recording, and set about trying to improve that.

I took Ben up on his offer of a place to record and people to play with, and in February 2006 found myself at Tarrant's house in north Oxford, rehearsing three songs with those two and their drummer, Nigel, in the basement. Immediately it was clear that this would be the lead song for what would become the *Campfire Punkrock* EP. Their musicianship – not just the fact that they were real players, rather than algorithms – brought the song to a whole new level. We laid down the basics, Nigel added real keys parts, Ben played an instrument he found in a pile of junk that sounded like a mandolin but definitely wasn't,* and added vocals to finish it off. It sounded light years ahead of anything I'd put on tape to date, even if the lyric about being the only person in the band jarred in a way that became less funny and more uncomfortable as time went by. We also didn't find a pedal steel player for the bridge (until the first Lost Evenings festival in 2017, when Paul Sayer finally took that solo).

The EP was released in May 2006 and quickly sold better than expected. Not long afterwards I had an email from John Kennedy at what was then XFM, saying he was going to play the song on his show, and asking me in for a session. Steve Lamacq joined the clamour, even showing up in the front row of one of my shows

* I still have no idea what it was. An oud maybe?

at the Barfly in Camden, singing along with 'Nashville Tennessee' at the top of his voice – every word. I learned that I'd need to figure out an alternative, swearing-free lyric for radio perform-ances, and we mixed a clean edit of the song for the supportive DJs to play – not a move I regard as artistically compromised, incidentally; radio is a tool, it serves a purpose in getting people to tune in to the art you're making. Steve, John and Mike Davies at BBC Radio 1 gave me a lot of support and encouragement in this period, and I'm eternally grateful for their faith in what I was doing.

Eventually I had the wherewithal to put a live band together for that tour in 2007, and the Oxford boys – with Jamie, the singer of Dive Dive, valiantly playing a keyboard with two fingers – brought the song to life onstage. It sounded great, whatever that heckler might have thought, though we tend to play it a fair bit faster these days – a natural bit of evolution.

One final note on this song. I learned a lesson about taking care with my rhetoric thanks to 'Nashville Tennessee'. At a show somewhere in the UK, I casually introduced the song – by then a known entity for most of the crowd – as being about how I 'fucking hate Americans'. It's not a true statement, obvi-ously, and I just kind of threw it out there before launching into the tune for a cheap laugh, which it got, from the British audi-ence. However, after the event, I got an email from an American who'd been in the crowd, explaining how upsetting and alien-ating my quip had been, not least because it was one of their favourites. I was mortified, apologised profusely, and learned to try to be more precise – not to mention more forgiving – in the things I say into a microphone. As if to rub that in, I have, over the years, been nervous about playing this song in the USA, not least in Texas, a place known for its prevalence of gun ownership. I'm pleased to report that, contrary to what some of my London friends assume, I have never had anything more than a self-deprecating laugh, from even the toughest of Texan crowds.

SUNSHINE STATE

I remember the day – the day when I had to take you to the airport
And put you on a plane, and so you left me.
Left me alone on an empty tube train, deep under the ground,
While you were bathed in sunlight, high above the clouds.

I needed you here to be my sunshine in London Town.
California's had more than its fair share.

You left me to these small skies, and to rain-soaked concrete,
To Morrissey and Robert Smith and complicated streets I know,
On which you lost your patience and your way,
The way you always did on steel grey rainy days.

I needed you here to be my sunshine in London Town.
California's had more than its fair share
Of beating summer sun and shining seas,
But it doesn't have a shred of honesty.
I know the truth – Neil Young and Joni Mitchell were Canadians.
I guess that makes sense – they had their fill and then they moved away again.
You're not alone, we all sometimes use words that we don't understand.
Your 'love' was only just skin deep and in the end it gave me cancer.

You might have been my sunshine, but I'd rather have a rainy day.
Sunshine gets just what it deserves.

* * *

I have never thought much of myself as a guitarist. When the guitar-playing bug first bit me, aged ten or so, I had visions of a virtuoso future. After a few years of mangling Megadeth riffs and torturously learning the solos to Iron Maiden songs from a tab book, I was heartened to discover that I could play songs by Weezer, Nirvana, and most of all Counting Crows – simple songs with open, strummed chords. I have had two batches of lessons. The first was with the nineteen-year-old son of a friend of my mother's who lived in the next-door village, Mark Kippenburger, a big Satriani fan whose party trick was finger-tapping 'The Flight of the Bumblebee'. He started by telling me I was doing everything, not least holding my pick, completely wrong (and I still do); then he taught me a handful of metal solos which I still know (in theory at least), including Metallica's 'Fade to Black'. Eventually we both agreed that I was happier hammering away at the rudiments of the instrument alone, in my own cack-handed style.

A few years later, I had some lessons at school from Nigel Moyse, the resident guitar teacher. He was a genuinely excellent tutor, and I feel like I should apologise to him officially here, in print, for being a somewhat distracted pupil. I wasn't really interested in most of what he had to teach me; most lessons consisted of me showing up and playing him a record with a riff I wanted to learn (the riffs got heavier as the years passed, from Faith No More up to Converge), and he'd do his best to figure it out for me. There wasn't much in the way of a holistic approach to my instrument, and I hadn't yet figured out why you should learn scales (spoiler alert: you absolutely should). Sorry, Mr Moyse.

There is one technique in my armoury, however, which he did successfully impart to me. At some point I was cast in a very minor part in a school production of the play *Chips with Everything*. My role was basically to sit at the back of the stage, done up as an officers' mess, and play some guitar. I don't think I even had any lines. Clearly, the context didn't call for any thrash riffs, or even something off *In Utero*. I posed my dilemma to Mr Moyse, who taught me the rudiments of a style known as 'clawhammer' – essentially counterpoint finger-picking. I did not, at that stage in my life, have much appreciation for any music that actually used clawhammer, but the basics went in, and over the years I would absent-mindedly practise it from time to time.

When I started getting into more acoustic, country and folk music, this dormant skill came back to the forefront of my mind, and I realised, with pleasurable surprise, that I could handle the basics of quite a few Dylan and Cohen numbers already. As is usually the case, it wasn't long before I was experimenting with pushing the boundaries at the edges of the pieces I knew and coming up with my own.

One particularly satisfying musical figure emerged, which eventually became the song 'Sunshine State'. The guitar work is not really as complicated as it sounds – it's in standard tuning and simply plays two high strings on the offbeat while playing a lower melody line with the thumb – but if you do it fast enough, it sounds impressive. That gave me the basic verse, and for the chorus and bridge I merely cycled through the other basic patterns of clawhammer on the chords that made melodic sense.

All of this was actually taking place while I was still in Million Dead, so it wasn't intended to be an actual song, it was more something to do with my hands when I was holding a guitar and didn't have a pick. I was at university in London at the time and had started seeing a girl from San Jose, California, who was over in the Big Smoke doing a semester abroad. She was tall, blonde, with perfect teeth and the achingly healthy glow of the New World. I was quite impressed with myself for having pulled her, if I'm honest. Million Dead songs didn't really lend themselves, thematically, to the subject of romance, so I started toying with some words about her over this folky little guitar pattern.

Some songs take a while to come together, and if they're about a real, specific situation, the subject matter can evolve as the song is being written. My time with my girl from California was limited by definition – she was going home, one way or another, once the academic year was finished. So, after a simple love-struck beginning, the song took on a tinge of sadness. I did actually ride out to Heathrow with her once when she made a trip away, though not her final one, and that gave me the first verse. The chorus shifted to the past tense – from 'need' to 'needed' – and I actually finished a version in that vein, an unadorned and positive piece of work, which I believe my older sister still has a copy of somewhere.

The girl did eventually up sticks and head back to the West Coast, leaving me forlorn – but shortly thereafter, more information came to light. She had mentioned, on occasion, having a boy in consideration back home. What became clear to me after she left was that they had never officially broken up, and in fact he'd been in London for some of the time that I'd thought we were an item. With the benefit of hindsight and maturity, I suspect I was a little quick to gloss over any of her reservations about our official 'status', and as a Californian she had a pretty liberal attitude to these things anyway. Nevertheless, the revelation stung, and my fragile, twenty-one-year-old heart was cracked. I went back to the song, this gleaming thing I'd made for her, and like a scorned spouse slashing her husband's suits, I changed the second half of the song.

The new, and final, conclusion to the song dripped with sarcasm and hurt. This was inspired by events, of course, but also by some of my favourite songs – songs with a sting in the tail. 'Medication' by Damien Jurado springs to mind. Anyway, I'd mentioned

Morrissey and Robert Smith in the first half (which stayed the same); now I pointed out that many of the people she would cite as great Californian musicians were actually from Canada – thereby beginning a pattern of name-checking musicians I like in my songs, which has lasted through the years (and is occasionally perhaps overdone – everyone has their habits). The song actually builds to a point where I come close to comparing someone to a terminal disease. Looking back at it now, I'm slightly uncomfortable about that – partly because unkind songs are fierce, public things that tend not to go away, and partly because it's just a really mean thing to think, and I'm not sure, outside of the song, I ever actually allowed that thought to cross my mind. In the event, the thought stays in the realm of metaphor, but it's a close-run thing.

The joke is on me, in the final analysis, for a couple of reasons. Firstly, we ended up making a peace of sorts and became pen-pals for a while. Her razor-sharp and unforgiving parsing of my character was a constant reminder of my strengths and weaknesses; she never let me get away with anything. The friendship, such as it was, ended up becoming the subject of the song 'Jet Lag' (more on that later). And secondly, because I wasn't really in the mood for research, and because I was enamoured with the central metaphor of the song, I went ahead and released it as 'Sunshine State', only to discover, from many, many different helpful people, that the Sunshine State is actually Florida, not California.

THE BALLAD OF ME
AND MY FRIENDS

Everybody's got themselves a plan,
Everybody thinks they'll be the man, including the girls.
The musicians who lack the friends to form a band are singer-songwriters,
The rest of us are DJs or official club photographers.
And tonight I'm playing another Nambucca show,
So I'm going through my phonebook, texting everyone I know,
And quite a few I don't, whose numbers found their way into my phone,
But they might come along anyway, you never really know.

None of this is going anywhere –
Pretty soon we'll all be old,
And no one left alive will really care
About our glory days, when we sold our souls.

But if you're all about the destination, then take a fucking flight.
We're going nowhere slowly, but we're seeing all the sights.

And we're definitely going to hell,
But we'll have all the best stories to tell.
Yes I'm definitely going to hell,
But I'll have all the best stories to tell.

* * *

Probably the most popular and enduring song I wrote in this era was 'The Ballad'.* That's satisfying to me, because it was a quite conscious attempt to capture a place and a moment in time in amber; a feeling and an attitude that, even at the time, I knew was fleeting.

Jay Beans On Toast's approach to songwriting was rubbing off on me over the long nights and further days at Nambucca – not just ideologically, but stylistically as well. Jay's songs, particularly his early works from this era, tend to pick through simple chords in differing variations in a particularly sing-song way, skipping between bass notes on the lower strings and a mixture of drone and melody in the upper register. I suppose it's a ragged version of a pretty standard country guitar technique that you could trace back to Johnny Cash or earlier, but I essentially picked it up from Jay. More than one of my songs from this period of time use that right-hand approach, but this is the archetypal example.

Musically, the song uses both inversions of a very popular chord sequence – I / V / VI / IV, or otherwise VI / IV / I / V. To the less technically minded, that's a chord sequence like the one in Green Day's 'When I Come Around' and The Gaslight Anthem's 'Old White Lincoln', respectively. It's a chord sequence that has a natural drama to it, an internal narrative arc that is incredibly satisfying to the Western ear. It's been used as long as pop music has been around, but in recent decades (starting, I'd argue, with nineties pop punk) it has become ubiquitous to the point of cheesiness. Chris T-T has argued (to me, over a beer, in a bar, somewhere in Europe) that it's the modern version of the standard blues twelve-bar. I have mixed feelings about using

* Which many, many people perplexingly insist on spelling as 'Ballard'. Like J.G., I suppose?

it. On the one hand, a song is so much more than just a string of chords – the melody, the arrangement, everything else lies on top of this. On the other hand, this specific chord sequence has become a lazy shortcut to a halfway decent tune, in a way that often ends up feeling manipulative to me. In the end I can't really criticise because, as I say, I've used it myself here and there, not least in this song. But I always try to make sure I'm justified in using it, rather than just taking the easy road.

So the music is pretty simple, standard stuff: G chord shapes with a capo on the second fret, leaving us in the key of A – a key I find very comfortable to sing in, as my happy top note is a high A. Lyrically, the initial jumping-off point for me was actually the NOFX song, 'I'm Going to Hell for This One'. It's a typically acerbic piece of commentary on religion by Fat Mike, but the phrase (which doesn't appear in the song) struck me as tragically under-used in this instance. I decided to borrow it for myself. The rest of the phrase – 'all the best stories to tell' – fell into my lap, and I worked backwards from there.

I was trying to capture the vibe of those endless, formless, limitless nights in the pub. I think the creative process was eased by the fact that, as I worked on it, I was out of the country, on a ramshackle DIY tour of France. I was homesick for the bar, and managed to use that to inject some wistful nostalgia into a song about a scene that was, for the time being, still alive and kicking. There are a fair few gentle digs in the lyrics – Greg Nolan was the 'official club photographer' of FROG, the club Dave and Jay ran, and most of the singer-songwriter types (myself included) seemed to be belatedly trying to hire bands. And I really did spend my time texting any vaguely London-based numbers in my phone, even if I had no idea who they were, before one of my endless bar shows at that time.

It's quite a short song, which was a happy accident. It doesn't have much in the way of a verse or a chorus, it just runs through each section without repeating. I think I was planning on going back and assigning more traditional roles to each part – verse, bridge, chorus and so on – but when I got to the part where it now ends, it just felt finished to me. Nothing more needed doing. Sometimes the secret to songwriting is knowing when to walk away.

I played the song at the last show of that French tour, a weird open-air festival called Blagnac just outside Toulouse, with almost no one in attendance. I flew back to London the next day and arrived at Nambucca to find a party in full swing. Enthusiastically I joined in, my excitement heightened by the knowledge that I had this new song for everyone in my back pocket. I'd had the idea that I would record it late at night during a lock-in, rather than in a studio, and that very night the opportunity arose. Come about 4 a.m. everyone was out of their minds, so I explained the plan, taught them the singalong part, and recorded a version on Jay's laptop.

Nambucca again, for the 100th birthday party, with Jay
Beans and not much sleep

Unfortunately, on listening back a few days later, I realised I'd been very wasted and hadn't played the song all that well; it didn't feel up to standard for release (on what was shaping up to be *Sleep Is for the Week*).* So, a few months later, we tried again, at a show at the Barfly in Camden – also, by the by, the first proper headline show I ever sold out. Jamie Grime, my friend and touring partner at the time, recorded the song with the crowd singing along, and Ben Lloyd mixed it for the album† – the perfect finish.

The song very quickly became a staple of the live set, the guaranteed finisher. That lasted long after the tours for the album that contains it, and it got to a point where I found it a little restrictive. One night in New York I was, predictably, closing with the song, which was accompanied by a stage invasion sing-along that felt utterly routine, somehow false – and then someone managed to unplug my guitar cable while staggering around me, thereby unceremoniously ending the show with a damp squib. I started thinking about putting the song somewhere else (on Matt Nasir's first tour with us in 2008, we actually opened with it, which was cool). In the run-up to the big show I did at Wembley Arena in 2012, I decided that maybe that was a time to put the song to bed – not least because it was, on some levels, pretty incongruous to play that song in an arena. I sang it that night after announcing it would be the last time.

That's a line from the stage – one of very, very many – that

---

* The Nambucca 4 a.m. version did eventually surface, on the collection *Ten for Ten*, in 2015.

† We spent an annoying amount of time mixing out the drunken idiot – an acquaintance, I might add – who'd decided to try to spoil the one-off recording by yelling his girlfriend's name in the gaps between lines. I'm pleased to say we were largely successful in erasing him.

I've come to regret, over time. The song needed a break, and these days it's a special-occasion type affair – but it didn't need to be retired permanently. And so it hasn't been. In fact, for the *Songbook* sessions in 2017, I decided to finally record a studio version of the song, with Matt Nasir playing it on piano. And so she lives on.

I KNEW PRUFROCK
BEFORE HE GOT FAMOUS

Let's begin at the beginning: we're lovers and we're losers,
We're heroes and we're pioneers, and we're beggars and we're choosers.
We're skirting round the edges of the ideal demographic.
We're almost on the guestlist, but we're always stuck in traffic.
We've watched our close associates up and play their parts;
They're chatting up the It girls, and they're tearing up the charts,
While we were paying with coppers to get our round in at the bar.
We're the C-Team, we're the almost famous old friends of the stars.

Justin is the last of the great romantic poets,
And he's the only one among us who is ever going to make it.
We planned a revolution from a cheap Southampton bistro;
I don't remember details but there were English boys with banjos.
Jay is our St George, and he's standing on a wooden chair,
And he sings songs and he slays dragons, and he's losing all his hair.
Adam is the resurrected spirit of Gram Parsons,
In plaid instead of rhinestone and living in South London.
And no one's really clear about Tommy's job description,
But it's pretty clear he's vital to the whole damn operation.
Dave Danger smiles at strangers, Tre's the safest girl I know,
Zo and Harps will skamper up to victory in the city we call home.

We won't change our ways, we will proud remain when the glory fades.

I am sick and tired of people who are living on the B-list.
They're waiting to be famous and they're wondering why they do this.
And I know I'm not the one who is habitually optimistic,
But I'm the one who's got the microphone here so just remember this:

Life is about love, last minutes and lost evenings,
About fire in our bellies and furtive little feelings,
And the aching amplitudes that set our needles all a-flickering,
And help us with remembering that the only thing that's left to do is live.

After all the loving and the losing, the heroes and the pioneers,
The only thing that's left to do is get another round in at the bar.

* * *

Sleep Is for the Week was released in 2007, and, for a debut solo record on a small London indie label, it did OK. The band and I did a couple of tours around the UK, and I filled the intervening time playing solo shows pretty much anywhere anyone would have me, which included some early forays across the pond to the USA. It was by no means a bad way to live, but I was haunted by a slight feeling of disappointment. I remember that Jamie T, with whom I'd played plenty of Sensible Sundays shows, released his debut album, *Panic Prevention*, in the same month. He had posters *everywhere* around the country, was playing big shows and festival slots, and was all over the TV and radio. The album is an undeniable classic (it was eventually nominated for the Mercury Prize), and I don't want to come across as bitter, but in all honesty I was piqued by a touch of jealousy.

There were two obvious reasons for this disparity. Firstly, Jamie was signed to a major, Virgin Records. Xtra Mile were (and very much still are) wonderful and caring as a label, but they simply don't have the financial and logistical muscle of a major label. Secondly, Jamie's album was better – better written and better produced. I'm fortunate that my mother did her best to bring me up to use negative emotions as fuel for constructive action (I like to think); so in response to the situation, I resolved to sit down and write better songs. In many ways, the resulting album, *Love Ire & Song*, is a kind of do-over for my debut, in terms of style, arrangement and lyrical subject matter. Thankfully, the end result really was a vast improvement, to my ears.

A lot of people ask, about my songwriting, whether lyrics or music arrive first. The truth is, there's no hard rule. For the most part, I get snippets of inspiration from time to time – an interesting turnaround on the guitar, a catchy little melody, a fun way of phrasing an idea – and I write them down. Later on, I spend time sitting among these piles of ideas, picking up one piece and another and trying them out in combinations, like someone trying to build a car in a junkyard. That's the hard graft of songwriting, as far as my own 'process' goes, if you can call it that.

However, every now and again there's an exception to this, and these exceptions are the holy grail of my trade, the moments that every songwriter lives for. I call them the 'Yesterday' moments, after the story that Paul McCartney tells of waking up with that song pretty much fully formed in his head (the lucky bastard). Sometimes things just fall together in your lap (well, fingers and throat I suppose) as they arrive. Words, music, it all just kind of fits, and on the rare occasions that it happens for me, I feel more like an explorer uncovering an ancient text that has always existed than someone writing something new. The song feels like it has always been there.

Such a song is 'I Knew Prufrock Before He Got Famous'. Musically, I started with a set of chord shapes that ascend from a basic A major (with a capo on third, we're in the key of C). In fact, it's a structure that forms the basis of the Queen song 'Hammer to Fall' – the A string rings open at the bottom of each chord, anchoring the tonality, while the inversions climb slowly to more interesting places. If you keep that A string ringing at the bottom of a D major chord, that fits too. By cycling up the scale, through an E major, to an F# minor, and then to an E major with the third (G#) on the bass, I ended up building a sequence of chords that, like an Escher painting, always ascends but somehow ends up exactly where it started.

As this little escalator of a tune was falling together, words started to arrive at the same time. I'd recently started listening to a lot of The Hold Steady, and, like most, had fallen in love with Craig Finn's lyricism, his striking mock-opera portraits of the characters and vagabonds of the twilight. I felt like I hadn't quite captured the spirit of Nambucca on *Sleep Is for the Week* ('The Ballad' notwithstanding), so I decided to have another stab at that, guided by Craig's approach. I find it's often a good idea, if you're lyrically stuck, to take a moment to step back and lay out exactly what it is you're trying to say to the world. And just like that, I started humming to myself: 'Let's begin at the beginning . . .'

After a deceptively lackadaisical introduction, the song needed to pick up its pace a little. The right-hand strumming pattern in this song is one I've used a fair bit since (possibly a little too much!); it's a basic syncopation, with an emphasis on the one, four and seven in a count of eight. It has a rolling motion to it that kicks the song up a gear. Lyrically, I was trying to paint a picture of a specific occasion at the bar. Someone somewhere worked out when the anniversary of the completion of the building that housed Nambucca was, and decided to throw a two-day birthday party. On the first night, The Holloways headlined, the room full to capacity and more. On the second night, it was my turn. Ticket sales were distinctly less exciting, and the attendance was pretty thin – possibly a blessing in disguise, given the fact that no one had been to sleep the night before. But somewhere in the midst of that lost weekend was the spirit of that scene, and I tried to focus in on the important parts – not the buzz and hype that some of the bands were starting to generate, not the wannabe-famous hangers-on and starlet girlfriends queuing up for the afterparty upstairs, but the prelapsarian innocence of it all, the raw enthusiasm, the love and camaraderie.

Upstairs at Nambucca, in Kid Harpoon's room, trying out some songs

After a brief, initial crescendo, the song takes a breather, and momentarily steps out of the pleasing major scale by hitting a suspended B flat chord. Unusually, I wrote the song in a linear fashion, and it became clear early on that it was going to be structured like that as well. No chorus, not much in the way of repeats, just a steady build to some kind of climactic conclusion.

The second verse begins and we're back on track, very much

in Craig Finn territory, painting pictures of the people at the bar. I started with Justin (Hayward-Young). I met Justin in Winchester when he started playing solo folk shows as Jay Jay Pistolet. His songs were incredible, and we went on to share many stages around the UK. Before a show one time, in June 2006, to be precise, we had dinner together in a 'cheap Southampton bistro'* and talked about all the exciting new music coming around to Sensible Sundays. We both played regularly, but there was also Jamie T, Marcus Mumford (with a banjo) and Laura Marling, among many others. We talked about how maybe this new sound could take over the country, and then laughed at our hubris.†

From there, I mentioned Jay, of course (and I think he's still a little sore about the hair-loss comment: sorry, Jay), and then Adam Killip. Adam was the singer in a band called The Tailors at the time. They were a huge influence on me back then, as pretty much the first (alt) country band I'd seen up close. Adam's songs were amazing, and I have often told the story in the past of Adam teaching me about folk and country music on the roof of the bar one evening. He used to run a night in Brixton on Saturday nights called Sadder Days (geddit?), the best country music night in the capital. I met Emily Barker there for the first time, and for a long while my chief ambition was to get a slot on that bill (which, eventually, I did).

The character sketches speed up with the song. Tom was a resident DJ at Nambucca and Frog, the associated club night. He was (and is) an explosion of energy, positivity and good feeling, the word 'yes' made flesh, and decidedly vital to the atmosphere

---

* Everyone and their dog wants to know where. It was a Pizza Express, I think. Nowhere fancy.
† Justin is now the singer in The Vaccines, so I wasn't totally wrong about him making it.

in the bar. Dave Danger had to be mentioned, of course, with a sly reference to the old Million Dead song 'Smiling at Strangers on Trains', as well as Tre, another denizen of the scene who is still my tour manager today. Zoniel was briefly, at the time the song was written, part of the team, but moved on shortly after, thereby slightly spoiling a lyric for me. Kid Harpoon lived upstairs and was, there and then, the one person we all thought would be hugely successful. The line-up of his first live band was stunning, and I was most certainly taking notes for what I wanted from a band, stylistically. There's no justice, alas, so he didn't take over the world, though these days he does write hit songs for lots of other artists.

Here ended the (less than complete) cast of characters. I didn't spend all that much time thinking through who was and wasn't mentioned in the song, and it has got me into some hot (well, slightly warm) water over the years. In particular, Danny, an absolutely key character in the scene, missed his moment. When the song was released he was, I think, genuinely a little hurt, so to make it up to him, I wrote him a song all of his own for the next album, 'Dan's Song'. The song takes another little rest here, in terms of its upward climb, but does state what seems to me to be the central message of the song: once all the glitter and glamour has faded away, we'll still be here.* The first demo of the song uses the third person – 'they won't change their ways' – but in the end I decided to allow myself membership, and shifted it to the more inclusive first person plural – 'we will proud remain'.

And now, finally, we're into the last part of the ascent. The bassline has, to this point, been holding down the root note, the C, while the other instruments reach up from there. Here, the arrangement starts to gather, and the bassline detaches from the ground,

---

* And so we would be, no doubt, if the bar hadn't burned down in 2008.

rising up through the scale like a Zeppelin coming loose from its mooring. In earlier versions of the song, the chords also switched as implied at this point (to C, D minor, E minor, then F major); but I was learning taste and restraint in my writing, and in the finished version, that eruption is held for the last drop of the song, where the top piano line straightens out into eighth-notes and we arrive at last at the summit.

Thanks to the favour of the gods of songwriting, I was able to match this bombastic finale with words that could carry the weight. I remember them coming to me quickly, all in a flurry, and it was the best I could do to write it all down. Somewhere in the midst of it all, I wrote probably the most tattooed set of words in my catalogue: 'Life is about love, last minutes and lost evenings'. I've dined out, literally and metaphorically, on that phrase for many years. I suppose I should tell the story of where it came from here, for the record.

I was, at the time, vaguely besotted with a young lady from Cyprus, who lived in Nottingham. I met her after a show one night and left part of my heart in her hip pocket. A while later, I was hanging out in Leicester with my friend Tiernan, telling him all about this beautiful stranger. He pointed out that Leicester is a mere twenty-five miles from Nottingham, less than half an hour on the train. I set about trying to convince her to ditch her plans for the night and come join us, and at one point I texted her the now-immortalised line (though without the word love – I wasn't that romantically inept). In the end, nothing came of our dalliance, but I walked away with a killer line.

And so, with a deliberate bit of mock-heroic self-sabotage in the last line, the song comes to an end. As soon as it was done, I knew that I'd made something of a breakthrough as a writer. It felt better, more ambitious and yet more successful, than anything I'd attempted before. All that was left was to find a title.

For reasons that now seem obscure to me, I settled on a throw-away literary joke that had no reference point in the lyrics at all. I'm a T. S. Eliot devotee, and as a young man, 'The Love Song of J. Alfred Prufrock' haunted my every artistic venture. The poem is about greatness passing you by, hence the title is a joke – one that felt appropriate to the song, but which, in retrospect, could probably have been improved upon. I'd certainly spend less time explaining it to people after shows.

For the recording of the next album, Ben Lloyd and I put together a studio rig and drove down to Hampshire, to an outhouse on a farm where my best friend grew up, in the Meon Valley, which his parents were kind enough to lend to us. We put the songs together piece by piece, with Nigel on drums and piano, much as we had the previous record, but this time I felt much more in control of the situation. 'Prufrock' was the archetype of that – in laying down a guide guitar part over a click track, I knew instinctively where every little piece of the arrangement was going to fall. Jason Moulster, of Nigel's old band Unbelievable Truth, stopped in to say hello and ended up playing bass on the song. Strings and glockenspiels were added, and Tristan Ivemy mixed it in London.

I first played it live, solo, at a bar show in Bournemouth. The first band performance was in a sports centre in Oxford, on a day when Truck Festival got rained off. My initial excitement about the song was instantly reciprocated by both band members and audiences. This was something new for me, a definitive advance in my art. But at the same time, it was also an ending of sorts. Once 'Prufrock' was written, I knew I was finished with trying to immortalise the Nambucca scene – I'd done that as well as I was ever going to, so it was time, thematically, to move on. I like to think that I suspected that it was a song that would also take my shows out of that environment too, as more people started to pay attention. That expansion in a career is bittersweet for any artist, of course. But if I were to become too big to play Nambucca shows, I could be happy that I'd done it, at least in part, with a song about how magic that time was.

A short footnote for this song. I've always been pleasantly surprised with how much people connect with what is, to me, a very specific and personal song. There's a lesson in there somewhere about music showing us our common bonds over and above our differences. Or maybe there's just a lot of dive bars packed full of hungry vagabond musicians around the world. In playing the song on international tours, it can often be a bit surreal, seeing strangers sing back the names of my friends – I never thought to change them for the song. Sometimes people still do a double-take when I introduce them to Tre or Dave Danger. Once that scene was done, after the fire at the pub, people scattered to the four winds. So every now and again I have a lovely moment in playing this song, knowing that someone who was actually there, who knew what it all meant, is in the room again – like playing it in Malmö, Sweden, when Lotta and Emily might make it to the show.

But, thankfully, the song isn't only a piece of bravado, or solipsism. The connections people make with my songs are endlessly humbling and inspiring for me. One show, somewhere in America, sometime in the last decade, I was having a bad gig, and not enjoying slogging through the setlist, my mind elsewhere, feeling the drag of months on the road. And then we played 'Prufrock', and a man of (at a guess) fifty years of age or so, in the middle of the crowd, stood out to me. He stood perfectly still, closed his eyes, raised his hands, and sung every last lyric back to me, the words I wrote in a run-down bar on the other side of the world. And then it was clear why I still do all this. Thanks, man.

PHOTOSYNTHESIS

Well I guess I should confess that I am starting to get old;
All the latest music fads all passed me by and left me cold.
All the kids are talking slang I won't pretend to understand,
All my friends are getting married, mortgages and pension plans.
And it's obvious my angry adolescent days are done,
And I'm happy and I'm settled in the person I've become,
But that doesn't mean I'm settled up and sitting out the game;
Time may change a lot but some things they stay the same.

I won't sit down,
And I won't shut up,
And most of all I will not grow up.

Oh maturity's a wrapped up package deal so it seems,
And ditching teenage fantasy means ditching all your dreams.
All your friends and peers and family solemnly tell you you will
Have to grow up, be an adult, be bored and unfulfilled.
Oh but no one's yet explained to me exactly what's so great
About slaving 50 years away on something that you hate,
About meekly shuffling down the path of mediocrity;
Well if that's your road then take it, but it's not the road for me.

And if all you ever do with your life
Is photosynthesize,

Then you deserve every hour of your sleepless nights
That you waste wondering when you're going to die.

Now I'll play and you sing:
The perfect way for the evening to begin.

* * *

I've never really had a 'hit' as such. I haven't had singles in the charts, no songs included on compilation albums of recent smashes or anything like that. But the song I have probably played the most in my career overall is 'Photosynthesis'. It's still a staple of the live show (people get *really* irate if I don't play it), I've released three separate studio recordings of it, I know it's a lot of people's favourite in my catalogue to this day, and I could play it standing on my head in my sleep. None of that is meant to denigrate the song – I still love it dearly – but if I'm writing a book about songwriting, I should probably say something about it here.

Many words have been said, and much ink has been spilled, on the impact that the album *Nebraska*, by Bruce Springsteen, had on me as a writer in the transitional phase between being in Million Dead and my solo career, between hardcore punk and folk music. And that record did land pretty heavily with me; it was one of the first times I really understood that you can be heavy without having to take your shirt off and scream at people in the front row. But if I had to pick a Springsteen record as the most significant for me (if not perhaps my overall favourite), I'd pick *We Shall Overcome: The Seeger Sessions*.

Released in 2006, right at the start of my time playing songs on my own with an acoustic guitar, and not long after I'd really started paying attention to The Boss, it immediately turned my head. I didn't grow up listening to folk and country music, and at that point I spent a lot of my time trying to dig down and find ever more 'authentic' sounds. For the most part, I was just listening to the oldest stuff I could locate, and there's a lot of mileage in that approach. But this album really *felt* like a genuine country record; it sounds like Bruce and the Seeger Sessions Band were authentically capturing the spirit of old-time American music, and, as many of the reviews noted at the time, it sounded like they were having a lot of fun doing it. As soon as I got my hands on a copy, I listened to it on endless repeat, and it made a big impression on both my writing and my arrangement ideas. The song you can most obviously hear this on is 'Photosynthesis'.

The tune is based around a pretty basic chord sequence, open chords in the key of D, with a small flourish on the opening vamped chord (D major) which involves literally just taking your fingers off the strings for a moment. There's a touch of flavour in the verse, using an A minor chord instead of the more obvious A major, but otherwise it's in standard melodic territory. The structure of the piece is similarly traditional: verses, choruses, a solo and a bridge before a grand finale. So far so standard; and in fact often it's the simplest songs that have the longest life and the broadest appeal.

Where the song got more interesting for me was in the arrangement. By attempting to put together something old-sounding, but not quite knowing how to do that, I ended up with something, well, not exactly *new* as such, but certainly my own. The words 'folk punk' have been used around my music and the music of my friends to a degree that now definitely qualifies as overkill, but there is a kernel of truth in here. I learned to sing and play the guitar in bedrooms and small practice rooms, thrashing away through bad equipment to try and be heard. Moving now into more delicate, acoustic territory, I couldn't knock that physical approach to playing music out of me – not that I particularly wanted to. So the sound ends up being that of an overgrown punk rock kid making an enthusiastic but rough attempt at something out of his comfort zone – folk, or country. I could live a long and happy life without wasting more time getting into more arguments about the distinction between those two genre tags, but I have long thought that 'country punk' might be a better epithet for the early part of my solo output.

In practical terms, this meant that, down in Hampshire, Ben and I built the song around the acoustic guitar part and Nigel's brushed drums. Using brushes on the kit for what was, in my view, a more upbeat song felt exciting and weird to me, at the time. We added mandolins, harmonicas, an accordion (played by my friend Brian from Ireland via Copsale), Rachael Birkin on blistering form on the fiddle, and gang backing vocals and claps provided by The Holloways, passing through the Meon Valley en route to a show in Southampton. In the event it all fell together and felt easy in the studio, like we were onto something worthwhile – which, I think I can say without fear of overstating the case, we were.

Lyrically, the song actually grew from a strange beginning. As a teenager, I used to spend hours strumming away on a cheap acoustic guitar my parents bought me for my sixteenth birthday. I learned song after song by bands I was into at the time – Levellers, Counting Crows – as well as tunes that I thought might impress people at parties – Ocean Colour Scene, Oasis (forgive me). In between that schooling, I was also trying to write songs as well, but for the most part they were awful nonsense. One particular snippet survived in my memory though. The words I had were 'You play and I'll sing / the perfect way for the party to begin'. The chords and melody would be familiar to anyone who knows 'Photosynthesis'. There's a level on which much of what I've done with my adult music career is to try and recreate the atmosphere of singing songs around campfires on beaches with my sister – the point being that I wasn't so much performing songs, as leading the group in the collective act of singing (hence learning Oasis covers – sorry, again). That line seemed to capture that ethos, and it hung around.

Leading my friends in song in the pub in Cornwall, maybe 1997 or so

One day in 2007 or so (at a guess), the snippet came back to me, and I started kicking it around. I was thinking about how much had changed since my youthful guy-at-the-party-with-a-guitar days, and how much hadn't. Somewhere in the middle of all that, the idea of getting old became a theme, and the rest of the words slowly fell into place. Looking back, I actually wrote quite a lot of songs on that subject on my first few albums, between the ages of twenty-three and twenty-five – 'The Real

Damage' mentions being 'halfway through the best years of my life', a statement that is weird both philosophically and mathematically, in retrospect. A lot of (older) people at the time commented that it was a bit strange for someone so young to be thinking along those lines, and from my current lofty vantage point of my late thirties, I can absolutely see their point. The justification for it was that I *did* feel slightly old, and perhaps jaded, in my early twenties. I fell so hard in love with punk rock, and was so active as part of the UK hardcore scene in my late teens, that when I became disillusioned with it all, once the scene got violent and divided,* I felt like I'd lived through something complete already. There's a hefty dose of youthful hubris in that statement, I know, but it was sincere at the time. I really did feel like there was a fair amount in my rear-view mirror already.

The song, of course, is an attempt to reject those feelings, to be defiant and not accept a slide into mediocrity after an interesting adolescence. There was a fair amount of me shouting at my dad in there as well. I was old enough then to have heard him mutter about his disappointed dreams on many occasions, and it made me angry – he was born with so much privilege that the responsibility for an unfulfilled life lay, as I saw it, entirely with him. I was also getting a little tired of seeing very talented friends of mine from the scene back at Nambucca not amount to much because of their own lack of drive. Some young people join bands because they want an easy life, which has always struck me as ridiculous – being successful in music requires an awful lot of hard work. In short, I was tired of people making excuses for

* I had the shit kicked out of me by the singer in one of my favourite hardcore bands in around 2001, in response to me criticising his violent dancing at shows as being 'macho'; not perhaps the most well-thought-through response.

living their lives in ways they didn't want to, when no one was forcing that upon them.

My friend Ian once told me that one of the wages of sustained success was occasionally having to eat your own words, and I can attest that he's right. There's a fair amount in this song that now, as an older man, gives me pause. Some of it is humorous – I have a mortgage and a pension plan now, and, at the time of writing this, I'm engaged to be married soon as well. Referring to myself as 'happy and settled' at that age is, with the benefit of hindsight, fucking hilarious. And, as much as I deliberately put the words 'grow up' in quotes in the lyric sheet, it can be pretty frustrating, in an argument, having your own words quoted back at you when all you want to do is tell someone to grow the fuck up. It's also quite weird having a song named after a biological process about which I can remember very little from school – I was floundering for a title and picked the biggest word in the song, as far as I can remember.

The 'Photosynthesis' video shoot, at my mum's school in Winchester

More seriously, there is a legitimate criticism to be made of the piece, which has to do with privilege. It's an easy thing to criticise people for not grabbing life with both hands if you have the benefits of a good education and a financially stable family who, no matter how deep their disapproval of your career choices, wouldn't let you sleep rough or starve. During an early performance of the song, on the Softcore Tour in late 2007, I remember an audience member shouting out that I had a silver spoon stuck in my mouth for writing such a song. I don't think that's entirely fair, but I can see that some of my phrasing, more in talking about and introducing the song than in the actual words, was careless and inconsiderate. There is a valid point to be made about seizing the day, and not making excuses, and I like to think the song makes it, but on occasion it does keep me awake at night. I think about the (incredible) bridge to the full-length version of Pulp's 'Common People' – 'you will never understand how it feels to live your life with no meaning or control' – and I tend to take that anonymous heckler's point.

I am, no doubt and in keeping with my usual neuroses, probably massively overthinking this. Interestingly, such criticisms have never, ever, arisen in the USA, which I think says something about their attitude to class and aspiration. Regardless, it's a song that has been adopted as an anthem by a lot of people over the years, and I'm both proud of that and humbled by it. Well done, twenty-five-year-old me.

I have no way of actually tallying how many times I have played this song live, but I'd estimate it to be around the nine billion mark. People sometimes ask whether certain songs get boring, and the answer is, in the rehearsal room, yes. The Sleeping Souls and I will never, ever need to practise this song. But it's not boring to play live, for the simple reason that a live performance is a collaboration between performers and the audience. If I look out from a stage and see a room full of people getting off on a song I wrote, how could that ever be boring?

The song has changed over the years. There's a little guitar lick that I play in the chorus these days which evolved over time, and which I was actually astounded to hear was not on the record when I finally went back and had a listen a few years ago. Often, the business of touring a song will show up some easy and obvious lyrical fixes that I missed in the bustle of the studio. On the record, I sing 'yeah I won't grow up', which is clunky and slightly confusing; clearly it should be 'I will not grow up', as it has become on the road. Rachael's solo is such a thing of beauty (and complexity) that we don't usually try to recreate it live; instead Ben takes centre stage for a wild display of mandocaster dexterity (now *there's* a sentence).* The break before the final part of the song often gets vamped out while I make a speech to the crowd. We've had various mass participation activities in there over the years, from circle jigs to walls-of-hugs to mass sit-downs. Sometimes I get carried away with all the talking – at show 2000, I went on for about eight minutes, which, even I will concede, is a little much. My favourite live edit is the change, on second repeat, to 'We'll play, and everybody will sing'. It seems more in keeping with the original intention of the song, and somewhat makes up for me not mentioning my partners in crime in 'Nashville Tennessee'.

---

* A mandocaster, for those wondering, is an electric mandolin, based on a telecaster guitar.

LOVE IRE & SONG

Well a teacher of mine once told me
That life was just a list of disappointments and defeats
And you could only do your best.
And I said 'That's a fucking cop-out, you're just washed up and you're tired,
and when I get to your age, well, I won't be such a coward.'
But these days I sit at home, I'm known to shout at my TV,
And punk rock didn't live up to what I hoped that it could be,
And all the things that I believed with all my heart when I was young
Are just coasters for beers and clean surfaces for drugs.
So I packed all my pamphlets with my bibles at the back of the shelf.

Well it was bad enough the feeling, on the first time it hit,
When you realised your parents had let the world all go to shit,
And that the values and ideals for which many had fought and died
Had been killed off in the committees and left to die by the wayside.
But it was worse when we turned to the kids on the left,
And got let down again by some poor excuse for protest –
By idiot fucking hippies in 50 different factions
Who are locked inside some kind of 60s battle re-enactment.
So I hung up my banner in disgust and I head for the door.

Oh but once we were young, and we were crass enough to care.
But I guess you live and learn, we won't make that mistake again, no.
Oh but surely just for one day, we could fight and we could win,
And if only for a little while, we could insist on the impossible.

Well we've been a good few hours drinking,
So I'm going to say what everyone's thinking:
If we're stuck on this ship and it's sinking,
Then we might as well have a parade.
Because if it's still going to hurt in the morning,
And a better plan's yet to get forming,
Then where's the harm spending an evening
In manning the old barricades?

So come on, old friends, to the streets!
Let's be 1905 but not 1917,
Let's be heroes, let's be martyrs, let's be radical thinkers
Who never have to test drive the least of their dreams.
Let's divide up the world into the damned and saved,
And then ride to the valley like the old Light Brigade,
And straighten our backs, and we won't be afraid,
And they'll celebrate our deaths with a national parade.

So come on let's be young, let's be crass enough to care.
Let's refuse to live and learn, let's make all our mistakes again, yes.
And then darling, just for one day, we can fight and we can win,
And if only for a little while, we could insist on the impossible.

Leave the mourning to the morning:
Pain can be killed
With aspirin tablets and vitamin pills.
But memories of hope, and glorious defeat,
Are a little bit harder to beat.

* * *

Throughout my time as a (very minor) public figure, I've often been described by journalists as 'controversial', 'contrarian', or just plain old 'confused'. On some levels, I find that slightly perplexing – like most people, I have a reasonably well-defined view of the world and of myself, and I'm certainly not (usually) trying to be complicated for the sake of it. So perhaps it reflects a failure of communication on my part, a difficulty in expressing myself.

Another reason for the puzzlement has to do with the fact that I've been shooting my mouth off, in one more or less artistic form or another, in public for quite a long time now. I've had people email me to point out philosophical disparities between songs I wrote when I was nineteen and when I was thirty-five. The idea that I wouldn't have changed, in any way, in sixteen years, most of them spent on the road around the world, is silly, if not slightly insulting. I'd hope to change, to grow, over that kind of time and experience, and I have, quite a bit in fact. Arguably, I had started undergoing quite a profound process of change in my view of the world even before people started paying attention to anything I said. And so we come to politics.

I grew up in a socially conservative middle-class family with upwardly mobile aspirations, and I was sent (on a scholarship) to Eton College, one of the more famous English public schools. That exile to boarding school coincided with me discovering music – first metal, then grunge, then (hardcore) punk. The latter scene gave me the tools and the vocabulary to express what I found so distasteful about the social milieu I found myself in, as I came blinking into political consciousness. I started listening to a lot of bands with anarchist messages – Propagandhi, CRASS, Refused and so on. My exploration of the underground hardcore scene in London in my mid-teens was matched with an equally inquisitive and passionate foray into the world of anarchism, book fairs and squats, pamphlets and banners. The obvious injustice of private education gave me a lifelong commitment to egalitarianism, to treating each individual human as a being of equal worth, and an automatic distrust of authority and institutions. All of that still governs how I see the world now.

Handing out leaflets outside a McDonald's as an anarchist teenager

For many years, punk rock and anarchism were inextricably intertwined for me – they were basically the same thing. The image of Malcolm McLaren trying to blow up the music industry in a homemade shirt reading 'Be Reasonable, Demand the Impossible' was (and is) very inspirational to me. The first proper band I was in, Kneejerk, featured endearingly adolescent but achingly sincere lyrics about smashing the state, rejecting all authority, and 'throw[ing] up the old barricades'.* Of course,

---

* From the acoustic finale to a song called 'Everything Starts to Melt', the last track on our second album, *The Half Life of Kissing*; you can probably find it somewhere on the internet, and that little outro might sound a little familiar, in the context of this chapter.

over time, my idealism encountered cold, hard reality, and the crooked timber of humanity that makes up any group of people. I went to the London School of Economics for university, and my experience of the institutional leftists there was so disheartening as to be kind of funny – they were a ridiculous historical reenactment group trying to pretend it was 1968 *all the time*, their rage in directly inverse proportion to the seriousness of the issues they got angry about, and their ability to do anything about it. By the time Million Dead got started, my writings about politics were exclusively of the bitter and disillusioned variety. That band often got painted as being 'political', which always made me laugh, because the first song most people heard, 'Breaking the Back', was specifically about being bored of politics.

Bitterness turned out to be a rich seam of inspiration for me, which is telling in and of itself – as the old saying goes, scratch a cynic and you'll find a disappointed idealist. On my debut record, the song 'Once We Were Anarchists' put the case in a blunt and slightly artless way (and features what is still the dorkiest rhyme in my catalogue – 'bankers' with 'wankers', urgh). As I've said, much of the second album was an attempt to restate the ideas, both musical and lyrical, of my debut with better writing, better tools, better sounds. And so it is, finally, that we come to the song, 'Love Ire & Song'.

I had a teacher at school called Dr Steve Cullen. What on earth he was doing teaching at Eton I will never know, but I'm glad he was. He was a warm, sharp, iconoclastic man from Liverpool, and a self-described anarchist, albeit a deeply pessimistic one. I can't say for sure that he ever said exactly what the song alleges, but we certainly had conversations along those lines. I wanted to write in a conversational yet provocative style. The verses flowed out of me easily, as I remember. They don't exactly scan particularly well from a technical point of view, but they have their own flow over the guitar chords. I channelled all my frustration and disappointment with punk rock and anarchism into a pair of verses, accompanied only by an acoustic guitar, playing some pretty basic chords* in a country folk style.

The other driving idea for this song was to write a piece in two halves. At the time, I had a habit of putting songs into either a 'solo' or a 'full band' category. I came up with the idea of having a song that began as a solo piece, fooling the listener into thinking that it was settled into that arrangement (and letting them set the volume on their stereo accordingly), before dropping the rest of the band at the halfway point, and blowing everyone away. Once I reached the part of writing where I was working on the turnaround, the arrival of the band, it became clear that the lyrics had to shift as well. The song takes on a slightly more positive spin, though it's one that's much more in the realm of the romantic anarchism of McLaren than any kind of practical politics. The words of the first chorus drip with pessimism; by the time the band has arrived for the second one, we've switched it around into something else, simply by shifting a few tenses and pronouns, moving it from something nostalgic to something forward-looking.

There is a hefty dose of ambiguity to the lyrics of this song, which I like. It constantly shifts its meaning to me over time, and I've heard many different interpretations from listeners over the years. At the time I wrote it, the apparent optimism of the concluding chorus was dripping with sarcasm. The point about the 1905 Russian Revolution, as opposed to that of 1917, was

---

* There is a brief passing G major chord (a major second) at the end of the verse, which is momentarily more musically interesting – I'd been fascinated by the use of the major second by a lot of country writers, like Gram Parsons, at the time.

that it was a complete failure, even if it's one that is easy to glorify. When the revolution actually succeeded, it led to nearly a century of totalitarian oppression and murder. It's much safer and easier to glorify failure, not to have to test drive your ideas in the real world, and to coddle yourself with the notion that, had you succeeded, you'd have been great. 'Glorious defeat' sounds heroic and certainly caresses the ego, but it doesn't achieve any meaningful change in the world.

Once the song was finished, that level of sarcasm and bitterness made me slightly nervous. I wondered if the crowds at my shows, people who'd heard and enjoyed 'Thatcher Fucked the Kids',* would be insulted by the song. I remember setting off on tour opening for the Levellers in 2008. My friend Chris T-T told me I had to play this song for that audience; to hide it away would be cowardice. To my surprise, both the Levellers crowd and my own took it at first with good humour, and then with enthusiasm. It became apparent that it was possible to sing the whole song without being bitter, to take it as something joyous and hopeful. I firmly believe in the primacy of interpretation – it's not up to me to tell anyone what any song 'means' or not. And in this instance, my audience's take on this song started to affect my own, and I began to see it as something I could sing with pride and defiance. Over the years, my feelings about the song have switched back and forth, shifted partly by my own feelings and partly by the state of the world around me. I like that; it seems like the sign of a well-written song.

A final note about 'Love Ire & Song'. It has always struck me

---

* A song I had quickly stopped playing, as it brought out the very worst in the political music scene – intellectually fossilised old blokes (almost always blokes) who would praise you to high heaven for repeating their pre-existing opinions back to them in song, and crucify you for ever making them think.

as curious to have a song title that doesn't feature at all in the lyrics, especially if that song goes on to be the title track of an album. So perhaps it's worth me explaining the backstory a little bit here.

There's a Million Dead song called 'Father My Father'. As is often the case for me, I was originally working with a completely different lyrical idea over the chords and the melody of that song. I'd been thinking about Lenin's April Theses of 1917, which promised the Russian proletariat three things: peace, bread and land. Being a precocious twenty-year-old, I was trying to write a song about how that seemed to be a slightly dry, unimaginative (or at least unartistic) list of demands. So the line I had (which fits over the part that, in the final version, is 'Do as we say, not as we do, and don't ask') was: 'Peace, bread and land? Oh Vladimir, think big'.

I *know*. I couldn't really have been more of a caricature of the privileged, blinkered hipster leftist wannabe-situationist. What can I say? We all have our youthful foibles, and at least I had the sense to edit this one out before I got to the studio. Nevertheless, the follow-up suggestion of vital, necessary demands for life that I had (and I'm sure the Moscow proletariat during the Great War would have been positively *thrilled* to hear them) was: love, ire and song.

LONG LIVE THE QUEEN

I was sipping on a whiskey when I got the call,
My friend Lex was lying in the hospital.
She'd been pretty sick for about half a year,
But it seemed like this time the end was drawing near.
So I dropped my plans and jumped the next London train.
I found her laid up and in a lot of pain.
Her eyes met mine and then I understood
That her weather forecast wasn't looking too good.
So I sat and spun her stories for a little while,
Tried to raise her mood and tried to raise a smile,
But she silenced all my rambling with a shake of her head,
Drew me close and listen, this is what she said now:

'You'll live to dance another day,
It's just now you'll have to dance for the two of us.
So stop looking so damn depressed,
And sing with all your heart that the Queen is dead.'

She told me she was sick of all the hospital food,
Of doctors, distant relatives, draining her blood.
She said 'I know I'm dying, but I'm not finished just yet;
I'm dying for a drink and for a cigarette.'
So we hatched a plan to book ourselves a cheap hotel
In the centre of the City and to raise some hell,

Lay waste to all the clubs and then when everyone else is long asleep,
We know we're good and done.

Well I was working on some words when Sarah called me up.
She said that Lex had gone to sleep and wasn't waking up.
And even though I knew that there was nothing to be done,
I felt bad for not being there and now, well, she was gone.
So I tried to think what Lex would want me to do
At times like this when I was feeling blue.
So I gathered up some friends to spread the sad, sad news,
And we headed to the City for a drink or two,
And we sang:

'We live to dance another day,
It's just now we have to dance for one more of us.
So stop looking so damn depressed,
And sing with all our hearts, long live the Queen.'

* * *

I'm often asked for advice on songwriting – hence, to a large degree, me writing this book. And, as the length of this tome might imply, it's not a question with any short answers. Nevertheless, the context in which the question is asked often forces me to come up with something short, pithy and practical for the audience.

My usual answer to the question is pretty simple: learn from the greats. I learned how to play guitar mainly through a process of trial and error, using a chord chart from Bert Weedon's famous *Play in a Day* book and a cassette copy of the album *August and Everything After* by Counting Crows. This was something of an anomaly at the time; they weren't my favourite band (yet) by any stretch, as I was more into stuff like Metallica and Judas Priest.

But my sister loved the Crows, and their songs are much, much easier to play on a cheap acoustic. So I sat down, pressed play, and tried to play the first chord of the chart along with the song. Over an extremely long time, I worked out most of the chord sequences on the record (I was not aware that there was a music book for the album available at the time, dammit). I also developed, first, a lifelong obsession with those songs, which I still regard as some of the best ever written, and second, a methodological approach to looking at songs from the inside out that has served me well over the years.

If you learn to play a song that you like by someone else, even just learning the basic chord changes and singing the melody across the top, you get to see something of the mechanics of the piece in action – like standing behind the clock face of Big Ben. You get a clue as to how it is the middle-eight lifts out of the second chorus, and turns back around to land in a heightened third verse (for example). To this day, I learn as many songs as I can that I hear and enjoy – everything from Hot Snakes to Clean Bandit. I'm not learning them to cover them live (usually). I'm like a mechanic, taking a quick peek under the hood of a tasty-looking car.

The adjunct to this piece of advice is a list of songwriters who I think are worth examining, and that's a harder answer to give, because, of course, a lot of it comes down to personal taste. My ur-songwriters include Kurt Cobain, Townes Van Zandt, Rivers Cuomo, Nina Simone and many others, but it's really a question of investigating what you like. At the beginning, every writer is just a distillation of their own taste. All the same, I'd like to put in a solid vote for the late, great Tom Petty. Studying his writing is a masterclass all on its own. I was a little late to Petty, but I was fortunate to be introduced to his work in the ideal setting – driving along long, straight highways in the western half of the United States in a fast car, on tour with Jonah Matranga and Josh English in 2007.

One of Petty's greatest tricks, if you can call it that, is the single-chord-sequence song. The best example of that is the song 'Learning to Fly'. The guitar just plays four basic chords, in the same rhythm, round and round for the entire four minutes of the piece (with one brief exception, where he holds one chord, thus emphasising what he's up to). Even so, the song isn't in any way boring or monotonous, which raises the question of what, exactly, it is he's doing to keep our collective interest as listeners. The answer to that lies in the subtly evolving arrangement, and the way the melody raises itself up through the chorus, supported by the achingly beautiful backing vocals. I still get excited even thinking about the song.

I wanted to try my hand at writing using that approach. Quite a few of my earlier songs have an absolute mountain of chord changes (The Sleeping Souls complain particularly about 'My Kingdom for a Horse', which has about 8,000 of them). So around this time I started toying with a simpler, Petty-inspired vibe, a song that was based around four basic chords – A major, F# minor, B minor and E7 – a sequence that's firmly rooted in a traditional rock'n'roll sound.

The second piece of advice I tend to give to broad questions about songwriting is a little more nebulous and problematic, while also being more obvious. Write about what you know. I've always been pretty straightforwardly autobiographical in my writing, and there's a good reason for that. If you want to channel passion and meaning into your lyrics, you have to care about the subject at hand – if it goes well, you're going to have to sing the song over and over for many years to come, so it's best to make sure you're engaged with the topic. The easiest way to do that is to write from your own experience (in fact, I think writers who can channel meaning and emotion effectively through the prism of fiction are more impressive, in a way – I'll get into that in due course). I often get asked if the stories in my songs are true, and the answer to that is, almost always. But there are drawbacks to this approach.

I had a great friend called Alexa Burrowes. I met her on a Million Dead video shoot (for the song 'Living the Dream') where we asked fans to come down to the Barfly in Camden in glam outfits. Lexie, as she was always known, came down dressed up to the nines, and was the life and soul of the party at the shoot and afterwards. We became firm friends. Lexie was a breast cancer survivor, and not long after we met she put on an all-day benefit show in Colliers Wood, south London, called Lexapalooza. Sadly, after a few years of friendship, her cancer returned, and in September 2007 she passed away. I was on tour at the time, predictably enough, but I had managed to see her and say goodbye one last time in the hospital before she died.

Me and Lex, sometime around 2005

In a way that I found slightly ethically problematic both then and now, I'd been thinking about writing a song for her even before she left us. I felt guilty, knowing that the songwriting part of my brain was toying with an idea while she was still alive. It felt morbid, or even voyeuristic somehow. But by the time these ideas started floating around, the outcome was not in doubt. Our last meeting was as crushingly sad as these things usually are, but, true to her character, Lexie was adamant that we should enjoy ourselves at the funeral – no one was allowed to wear black – and indeed in our lives afterwards. When the news came through that she was gone, I was in Oxford with The Sleeping Souls, rehearsing. I headed into town for a drink. A little while later I was in Paris (I was seeing a Parisian girl at the time), and I walked up the hill in Montmartre to the church of Sacre Coeur, sat on a bench, and poured out the words that had been brewing in my mind for quite a while.

I suppose that my point here is that writing autobiographical songs necessarily (unless you're a hermit) requires writing about other, real people, and sometimes it's difficult to know where the lines of discretion and permission lie. Romantic songs have got me into my share of trouble in my time ('Substitute' garnered a whole cornucopia of angry phone calls from exes, some angry they'd been mentioned, one furious that she *hadn't* been; there's no pleasing some people). Writing about the passing of a friend felt fraught with emotional difficulty to me – not just because I wanted to get my own thoughts straight, but also because I was worried about how it would be taken by Lexie's family, not least her two young children. I don't have a hard and fast rule that solves this conundrum – in this case, I sent a demo of the song over to the family and was relieved to receive their blessing – but it is something that keeps me up at night. I have the right, perhaps even the duty, to be as honest as I can in my writing, but unless I put some kind of public disclaimer around my neck, I'm as yet unsure how that honesty relates to the other people in my life.

Using a simple chord sequence* and a slowly building arrangement, paired with the stream-of-consciousness outpouring of words from Paris, Ben and I put the song together in the studio in Hampshire. I think we knew at the time that we had something special on our hands, but of course it's hard to tell in the bunker mentality of the studio. As the album was being mixed, mastered, shared around the label and promoted, it was a song a lot of people tended to mention in their comments. Eventually, BBC Radio 1 DJ Sara Cox started playing the song on her daytime radio show, a massive deal for my career, and 'Long Live the Queen' took off, taking my career up with it.

In many ways it felt a little strange, enjoying a newfound level of success on the back of a song about someone else's tragic death. My worries and doubts returned, wondering if it was in some way exploitative. In the final analysis, though, I decided that Lexie would have been thrilled to know that I was doing well – after Million Dead broke up, my career fortunes had taken a pretty sharp dive at the start of my solo career, and she never lived to see me rise up beyond that. I did, over time, make a small adjustment. Lexie was a rock and metal girl through and through, and while she was always supportive of my music, I think she viewed my move into more acoustic territory with a dose of cynicism that verged on disappointment. I'm not sure how much she would have liked the soft, folky arrangement of her song, so eventually the Souls and I worked up a much heavier 'rock' arrangement of

* Well, it does change in the bridge, to a descending D major / A / C# major, B minor section, but then it goes back happily to Plan A.

the song, which we tend to play more often than the original to this day. I like to think she'd be much happier with that musical approach, and some days I like to think I can catch a glimpse of her in the mosh pit during the song.

JET LAG

I've heard it said the trick
Is to set your watch when you hit the plane;
And that way you can trick
The workings of a tired brain.
But sometimes I feel sick,
Sometimes I just feel so drained,
And cut down to the quick,
Longing for that voice again.

On the phone
You always ask if I'm OK,
But it's not the same as being happy.

I travelled 40,000 miles last year
And I'm working on the same again.
I fell for 15 different girls
And nearly lost all of my friends.
But while I am jet set, jet lag, jaded,
You're always 16 hours ahead,
Quietly reminding me how I used to be.

Airports make me sad;
I'm sure they shouldn't all be the same.
But they're just landing pads
For boring tourist shopping chains.

I remember times we had,
Drinking while we wait for your plane,
Feeling kind of bad,
Wondering which one of us has changed.

Because we used to be slick,
With supple young hips, romantic young kissable lips,
Unbearably sharp, unbreakable hearts,
Wide eyes and faith
That life could never pull apart if we were OK.
But distance kills the best of intentions.
I never intended to be this way.

I'm trying to remember how I used to be.
I used to be slick.

* * *

Sometimes, in songwriting as in any other creative endeavour, you get stuck. And when you get stuck, it pays to take a step back, take a breath, and try to re-evaluate the material you're working with, to find a new approach.

The song 'Jet Lag' came together from a few different sources. The music was mainly based around a couple of riffs on the electric guitar that I had left over from my time in Million Dead. I wrote about half the guitar parts for that band, and I had a certain style for so doing. The influences I drew on ranged from the aching open emo-tinged chords of bands like Mineral and The Promise Ring on the one hand, and the angular strangeness of Fugazi and At the Drive-In on the other. I really enjoyed the sound of weird suspended chords (chords with extraneous notes in that didn't have implications for the key of the song – extra seconds and fourths, like playing an A or a C in a G major chord), and the clashes of various ringing open strings in the midst of complicated fingerings higher up the neck. I had two riffs, both with slightly odd time signatures – one starting with an Fsus2 moving up to a Gsus2, with a melody overlaid on the top strings with my ring and little fingers, a bar of six followed by a bar of eight. Then I also had a lower piece structured around sliding fifths, starting with an A5, with the G string of the guitar ringing, also in bars of six.*

These pieces of jetsam had been lying around in my musical cupboard for a few years, so I started piecing them together, throwing in some more traditional-sounding 'country' chord sequences, until I had the basic musical structure of the song laid out in my head. The implied arrangement was very much in the vein of the American indie rock that I love so well – stuff like Jimmy Eat World, or even Q and Not U. The vocal melody was ready to go, so I began casting around for a lyrical direction to fit.

Between the ages of nineteen and twenty-one I was fortunate enough to attend the London School of Economics, studying modern history. Contrary to received wisdom (and the expect-ations of my parents), university was not a particularly profoundly affecting part of my life. It came and went in a blur, and I was already living in London and playing in bands on the hardcore scene at the time, so my memories of it are scant. That said, I had that brief relationship I've already written about with the

---

* I should add that working out how to write all of this down takes me a fair amount of time. My understanding of the music I write, and the theory that underpins it, is much more instinctive than schooled. Someone, probably Matt Nasir, will likely explain how some of this isn't technically correct. Whatever.

Girl from San Jose, which was deeply significant to me. She'd already earned herself one song, but it felt like it was time for another. In the intervening years, our short, sharp romance had assumed towering proportions of significance in my mind, even as we'd evolved into friends. She served as my lost love across the sea, someone who I believed knew me better than anyone. Whether or not that was actually true is debatable, but it infused and informed a lot of my thoughts and actions at the time, as well as playing neatly into the premature sense of nostalgia I've mentioned before. A song on the subject was thus unavoidable.

Incidentally, once upon a time I remember reading an interview with Blake Schwarzenbach of the band Jawbreaker. The interviewer remarked that, as the author of so many songs about women, he must be something of a Lothario. Blake replied, acidly, that clearly, all the songs were about the same person. The same is true of quite a lot of my own material.

Anyway. The theme of jet lag suggested itself early on, thanks to the disjointed nature of our communications, hamstrung as they were by an eight-hour time zone difference. I thought about times we'd spent at the airport, about how inappropriate, even vulgar, it felt to cry in these weird futuristic shopping malls. I thought about the cavernous silences in our phone conversations, and how they seemed only to emphasise the distance between us, both geographical and emotional, awkwardly covered over with the polite British platitudes that she found so infuriating. I was lonely, lovesick and mournful for the glowing few months in which we'd cut such a swathe through London together.*

There is, it's worth mentioning, a time zone-related joke in the

* I suspect that actually the reaction we most usually inspired would have been people pointing at us behind our backs and saying, 'How the hell is he with *her*?'

lyrics to this song, which only one person has ever got unprompted.* From the starting point of London, Greenwich Mean Time, it isn't actually possible to be sixteen hours ahead; that places you, in fact, somewhere on the coast of California, but eight hours behind, but sort of in the future. That captured the essence of distance, dislocation and memory for me.

Thus the words came together, and they fit the music as well. As with the other songs for this album, Nigel and I had worked up some basic ideas for drum parts on a day in Tarrant's basement in north Oxford (where we recorded the first EP and album). Once we got down to Hampshire, we laid the drum parts down and began layering the other instruments over the top.

It wasn't long before Ben and I hit a roadblock with the song. For some reason, it just didn't seem to hang together comfortably. The groove had something stuck in its throat, and we spent a long while throwing different arrangement ideas at it, trying to find a fix for the problem. Shakers, tambourines, different piano parts, extra guitars, nothing seemed to change the fact that the song felt like it was slightly lame, like it had one leg shorter than the other. While we did have a fair amount of time to luxuriate in sonic experiments, that time wasn't limitless, and there came a moment when the external pressures of finance and logistics started to suggest the easiest solution: ditch the song.

This, incidentally, is not something I've had cause to do too many times in my career, but it does raise an interesting angle on the age-old 'art-versus-commerce' debate. A simple fact of life for underground and independent artists is that resources are limited. There are many classic albums that could have sounded better or glossier with more money and time on their side. But,

* Take a bow, Chris Lucas – incidentally, the guitar player in Kneejerk, the band I was in at school.

as Steve Albini once perceptively noted, arguably all that a big studio and producer can ever really do is to make a bad record sound mediocre. If the songs are good, they'll shine through regardless.

Back to the story. I was loath to drop the song. The component parts were all of a high standard – I checked them all, individually. And yet for the life of me I couldn't work out how to make these ideas hang together and sing out like they did in my head. We didn't have time to recut the song from scratch, and I was depressed to think that this tune, which felt like a valuable piece of the album puzzle, was going to end up on the cutting room floor. Ben sensed my despondency, and, in his wisdom as producer, decided to try a last ditch, outside-the-box approach.

In the corner of the barn in which we were making the record was an old piano, which belonged to my friend's parents. It was something of an antique, early nineteenth century from memory. It was in reasonably good structural shape for its age, but there was a catch. While the piano was in tune with itself, it was not tuned up to concert pitch – the extra strain on the frame would have cracked the ancient wood. But neither was it tuned to something sensible, like a semitone down; it simply hung somewhere in the middle, a quarter tone or so below where it was supposed to be. That meant that, while the piano sounded lovely on its own, we couldn't use it on any of the songs for the record without putting everything else into an awkward quarter-step tuning. Ben and I had both been a little miffed to discover this, as one of the selling points of the location had been the presence of a real piano. The rest of the keys work on the album was done with an electronic keyboard with a decent digital instrument patch behind it.

The piano nevertheless occupied the far corner of the room, casting an imposing yet reassuring shadow across the other musical proceedings. As I lingered in a quagmire of inspiration,

Ben had the idea to see what would happen if I made an attempt to recast the song on the piano. As a pianist, I am very much in the amateur bracket. I scraped through Grade Two aged eleven or so, after which my piano teacher told me that clearly music wasn't for me, and recommended that I try my hand at something else. That fateful conversation took place at the exact moment when I discovered Iron Maiden, and thus rock'n'roll music in general. Insulted, I set about learning the guitar with the cold fury of a man slighted, and one might argue that a desire to prove her wrong about my musical propensities drove me to become the man I am today. Unfortunately, I still suck pretty hard at piano, despite all my rage.

The room in the Meon Valley where Ben and I made 'Love Ire & Song'

There is an upside to this gap in my talents, however. I'm primarily a guitar player, which means that most of my thinking about music and notes and their interrelations is based on the physical geography of the guitar. With a fair degree of effort, I can transpose guitar ideas onto the very different topography of the keyboard, and in so doing I can often stumble across new approaches to a piece, or even a fix for a problem. Ben made his suggestion, I sat down before the keys, and began trying to find a way to play 'Jet Lag' on the piano, torturously slowly at first. Ben kept exhorting me to dig deep and find the spirit of the song, to find a way of reaching the things that I thought were worth salvaging from this set of musical ideas. I had to shift the time signature to make it feel right, even if this left the timing of the verse in an extremely weird place, reminiscent of Radiohead's 'Pyramid Song'. I cut out the second chorus (as otherwise the piece would have been overly long), but then had to find a short cut in the lyrics to get from one spot to another. I fumbled my way around trying to replicate the suspended guitar chords on the white keys, holding down the sustain pedal to let the chords bleed into each other. I dragged my lazy left hand around the bottom end, finding the bass parts required to underpin the whole construction.

I did most of this with my eyes firmly tight shut, letting my fingers find their own way. After quite a while of plonking around on the antique instrument, I half-opened one eye and was surprised to see Ben very quietly arranging microphones around the piano as I played. Wordlessly, he motioned for me to continue my exploration, and with this encouragement, over the course of the evening, I found a version of the song for solo, slightly detuned piano that felt right. I wasn't competent enough to sing at the same time, but the wonders of recording technology allowed me to worry about that later. The studio that we'd thrown together didn't have much in the way of sound isolation, so once I reached a point of being able to attempt full run-throughs of the song, Ben retreated into the kitchen. Unfortunately for him, it took me significantly longer than either of us had expected to get a full take of the song that I was happy with. When I did, as the last chord rang out, I shouted out to him, 'That was the one!' Rather wearily, he emerged, confirmed that I was finished, and stopped the tape.*

Later that night we cut the vocal in a take or two, and so it was that we finally had a finished version of the song that I was happy with, which eventually made the final song on the album, complete with the conversation piece at the end. I'm very happy that Ben made me persevere with the song, it's the perfect end-piece for the album, and the concluding declaration – 'That was the one!' – seemed in keeping with the general feeling I had about the record as a whole. I've learned from experience that it's rash to predict too firmly how an album will be received while you're still actually making it, but there was a vibe around that session, a feeling that I was making a first definitive statement as a songwriter.

Ironically, towards the end of the time in the studio, in the last scraps of time available to us, Ben and I did eventually figure out how to make the original 'rock' arrangement hang together (it had to do with those tambourines). So we finished and mixed that version too, which was later released on *The First Three Years* as a rarity. Regardless, I feel like the piano version is in fact the right feel for the piece, and I'm glad that the creative road took me round the houses in trying to capture the spirit of this song and the relationship it commemorates.

* Well, pressed stop on ProTools on the computer.

LIVE FAST DIE OLD

I bought my soul back from the devil,
And now I'm keeping it all to myself.
I'm checking myself out of the program,
Because I know what's best for my health.

So why live the dream like you're running out of sleep?
I'm not playing to pass time, I'm playing for keeps.
We only just started and you're throwing the fight.
You'd rather burn out than fade away.
Well, why not both? I plan to stay.
So let's do this once and let's do it right.

I used to act like none of this mattered,
And I used to say that I didn't care,
That we wouldn't be doing this forever,
But then the truth is that I was just scared.

You put up a front to protect yourself,
But if we're down on the floor, why get back on the shelf?
You can't change your outfit once the night has begun.
We've still got the fuel and we still got the fire,
So me and you, Jay, let's never retire.
Let's keep on making mistakes till we're done.

It won't last, so be bold.

I'm going to live fast and I'm going to die old,
Going to end my days in a house with high windows
On the quiet shores in the South-West.
So you sort the tunes and I'll bring the beers,
And on my seventieth birthday I'll see you right here,
And together we will watch the sunset.

There's no one in my coffin, there's nothing in my grave,
And I'm tired of being damned, I'd rather be saved.
We can never sell out because we never bought in,
And if they build it back up then we'll swing back through town
And burn the whole thing down again.

It won't last so be bold:
Live fast, die old
Choose your path, show soul:
Live fast, die old

* * *

My writing process has always been a continual thing. I've been fortunate (to date!) to have a reasonably steady stream of ideas, snippets and suggestions that arrive in the time and manner of their own choosing. Of course there have been dry patches, moments of frustration and writer's block, and moments of inspiration dragged out of me by the wonderful expedient of that most helpful of assistants, the deadline. But, taking the long view, songs have come to me in measured procession.

Nevertheless, the niceties of the music industry in which I work, the traditions of my art form and the physical restraints of technology* require the grouping of material into bundles known as 'albums' every few years or so. There's a degree to which this massaging of songs into coherent artistic wholes is an artificial, ex post facto endeavour. But there is creativity in curation as well. The songs I wrote for *Love Ire & Song* were, roughly speaking, the ones that I wrote in the period between my first and third albums. But the presentation, ordering on the album, and indeed the choices of which songs made the cut, helps make the album a holistic piece (I hope).

It is, of course, one of my aims to make each album different from its predecessors. The most obvious way that happens is through recording a different bunch of songs (duh). Usually they are recorded in a different place, with different people working the technical angles. And I'm trying not to repeat myself, lyrically or musically, so things tend to head in fresh directions – that's the intent, at least. Other factors play into the development of songwriting over time. While I still tend to write in the same basic way, in a room with a guitar, the expectations of where and how I will record the song, and who will be playing it with me later, can subtly change the writing process. And the cycle of touring and promoting a record puts me in a different head space, helping to consolidate one group of compositions as a family, and leaving room for what comes next to change and grow.

All of which is a complicated way of saying that *Love Ire & Song* was my first reasonably successful album. By the time I had finished playing it in crowded rooms across the world, many things in my life had changed. The rooms in question were larger;

* Arguably much less so now that (most) people's preferred method of listening is digital; and yet, to date, the average lengths of songs and albums hasn't changed much, which might just be a case of old habits dying hard. Or maybe there really is something in that three-minute paradigm after all.

I had a settled line-up for my live band, with the permanent addition of Matt Nasir on keys. My creative horizons had expanded appropriately, alongside my musical palette. The material that became *Poetry of the Deed* was, arguably, just the next bunch of songs that I wrote. But the context in which I wrote them, and my thinking about the process of songwriting itself, had moved on.

In the event, this, my third album, is, for me, one of the more problematic entries in my back catalogue. There are a lot of strong ideas, material, even full songs on here, but there were a few creative missteps along the way which now, with the benefit of hindsight, give me pause for thought. Arguably, we arranged and recorded the album too quickly – we rehearsed up the songs over two weeks in Oxford and then went straight into the studio, leaving no time for reflection. The process of making demos was still not one I understood the value of at the time. I have some issues with the sound of the recording and the mix. I'll take the blame for its shortcomings – I was a man in a hurry back then. And I have always been reluctant to be critical, in public, of my own songs, as it always, without fail, turns out that I'm tearing down the favourite song of the person I'm talking to, which isn't particularly nice for anyone. But I'm trying to write an honest book about my own creative process here, so I will proceed, with appropriate caution.

Thus far in the book, I've mainly been celebrating my songwriting triumphs. I don't want to come across like I think that every idea I have is golden, like every song is a precious and perfect thing, so I thought I would write about a song that I struggled with for a long time, and that I don't think I ever quite got right, despite the strength of some of its ideas.

The single biggest new influence on my writing at this time

was The Hold Steady, a band I discovered while on the road in 2007, and whose place in my estimation had been ever rising. I instantly fell in love with every facet of their sound, starting with Craig's bar-room philosophical lyricism, as I've discussed. The arrangements they worked up on albums like *Boys and Girls in America* felt to me like a wonderfully fresh take on the traditional approach of the E Street Band, and I quite consciously wanted to follow them down that road, now that I had a great pianist, Matt, in the band with me. In fact, largely thanks to this influence, the horizons of my ambitions for complexity, both in song structure and in arrangement, had expanded considerably. I'll talk about that in more detail in due course, but 'Live Fast Die Old' is certainly an example of me pushing my own sonic boundaries at the time.

A particular example of that is the opening of this song. I spend a lot of time thinking about how an album will open, and for various reasons this song was always going to be the first track on album three. I think the opening lyric of an album is exceedingly important. As a writer, you set the tone for what is about to follow, you have to present yourself and the case you are making to your audience, and encourage them to jump in with you and follow your lead. But it's not just the lyric that matters; the actual first sound out of the speakers is important. I've thought about this on each of the records that I've made. My first album begins with a very traditional country guitar riff. My second opens with the lyric pre-empting the guitar. This time around I wanted to set the scene differently, to show people that I was aiming higher, musically. So the song, and thus the record, opens with a hi-hat pattern (drums first!), followed by a Roy Bittan-esque piano part, and then the whole band crashes in, with my acoustic guitar as merely one component. It's a carefully thought-through overture.

But what of the opening lyric? 'I bought my soul back from

the devil.' The success that had come to me after *Love Ire & Song* had led to a commensurate amount of public examination, both from critics and from fans. My words, and the view of the world that they propounded, had come under a lot of scrutiny – most of it positive, in the final analysis. Nevertheless, many people had picked up on the weird blend of early-onset nostalgia and glorified pessimism that characterises my first two records, in songs like 'The Ballad of Me and My Friends', 'I Knew Prufrock Before He Got Famous', and others. The fact that I was writing like the glory days were fading away in my early twenties had been noted. On top of that, I was keen to move beyond that set of preoccupations and say something new.

My chosen fresh direction was thrown open for me, in part, by a conversation I had with Jay. There is a low-budget (and frankly low-quality) early-years DVD, released through Xtra Mile, called *All About the Destination*. My friend Rachel Brook came on tour for some very hand-to-mouth shows in 2006, and caught me on camera chatting through some of my early songs. There's a section in the film where I talk about 'The Ballad', and make some passingly flippant comment about how all the scene around Nambucca was a passing thing, not destined to last for ever. I think my intention was to celebrate the ephemeral nature of our lives, but it came across sounding gloomy, and possibly a bit bourgeois – we won't be doing this for ever; it was, to use the phrase my parents tortured me with in my adolescence, 'just a phase'.

Jay took exception to this, and brought it up with me. He told me that he'd figured out who he was – a folk singer, a club promoter, a denizen of the underground world that we moved in – and he wasn't about to change anytime soon. His forthrightness brought me up short. That, combined with my newfound and unlikely popularity, made me rethink some of my preconceptions about my music, its shelf-life, the scene I was part of, and the possible future shape of my life. In the midst of all this I found a new defiant optimism about it all, and I wanted to channel that on the next album.

So it is that 'Live Fast Die Old' came together. Jay gets a mention in the lyrics, as a thank you for his input. The opening line bombastically reclaims my soul from the 'going nowhere'* of 'The Ballad', and the song as a whole puts value on the lifestyle that we'd chosen. We're here to stay, we're tired of being damned, show some soul, goddammit. Among other things, I wanted to leave behind my premature sense of ageing and celebrate life, and the fact that we could, in fact, do this for the rest of our lives, ending up on a beach in Cornwall somewhere, drinking beers, singing songs, and quoting Philip Larkin poems ('High Windows').

I actually remain largely happy with the words to this song. It is, in its way, somewhat naïve, but then that was kind of the point; trying to reclaim my own sense of youth and wonder at the world after two albums of moaning about it. There are a couple of quibbles – in point of fact, I was not aware that Ricky Gervais' character David Brent, in the TV show *The Office*, had used the expression 'live fast die old' in an episode. In the programme, this is used to highlight his priggishness, but I don't mind the association actually. As much as this is an earnest set of words, I think a sense of humour about yourself and what you do is crucial, in songwriting as much as in anything else. More cuttingly, my friend Ben Dawson, who'd been in Million Dead and, earlier, Kneejerk with me, pointed out that the line 'we can never sell out / because we never bought in' was playing a touch fast and loose with the

---

* There's a nice idea for a song lyric or title . . . Quite often, ideas will reoccur for me over time, though hopefully always in new configurations. Certainly, the subject matter of 'Going Nowhere' and 'The Ballad' are pretty far removed.

historical facts. Ben and I had been *very* serious about punk rock, hardcore and the related rules and ethics as teenagers; we definitely 'bought in' for a time there. I suppose my excuse would be to keep the terms of reference to my solo career.

So it's not the words to this song that trouble me now. It's the music. More specifically, it's the structure of the song. The individual sections each strike me as strong in their own way. The opening riff (and it really is a proper riff, for once), uses barre chord shapes on the lower four strings of the guitar, leaving the high B and E strings open, and descends down the scale from the V chord to the root, by way of a short detour through a G chord, which is out of the main key of E major. It's a cool riff. I was consciously trying to use chords and notes outside the root key of the song, to make things more interesting, melodically speaking. That's carried over in the bridge section – 'why live the dream like you're running out of sleep?' – which starts, again, on the G major, and throws in a C major and a D major for good measure. The chorus, while a simpler section, is strong, as is the verse. The whole thing is, in theory, tied together by a simple three-note motif, first on the piano, and then in the singalong backing vocals.

And yet, and yet . . . It doesn't quite hang together, for me. I have endless tapes and notes for this song of different possible structures. Starting with the verse, moving the chorus forward, bringing the motif in earlier, swapping whole sections around or cutting them completely. In the rehearsal room in Oxford, the band and I tried every kaleidoscopic calibration we could think of. The song takes an unusually long time to get to the chorus, but that's not, in itself, a problem, and it's partly because of the extended introduction, which I really like, and which I wanted to use to set the scene for the album as a whole. Even at the time, the song structure I went with didn't completely ring true for me, and I had a creeping sense that we settled where we did because we ran out of time for trying other things, rather than because it was the correct approach.

This is a problem that has arisen for me a few times as a writer. You find yourself holding a full hand of strong cards, and yet somehow you can't figure out how to play them in the right order. In most other instances where this has happened for me, I've been lucky enough to figure it out eventually. Quite often, this is one of the roles a producer can play in the studio – helping you dissect and reconstruct your own material (much more on that later). For this record, we only had a week to track all the music with the excellent Alex Newport, so there wasn't really time to get into the nuts and bolts of the song.

The rehearsal room in Oxford for 'Poetry Of The Deed',
and the list of songs for the album

I don't want to be overly down on this piece. As mentioned before, it's likely to be a favourite for at least some of the people reading this (I've seen the title tattooed more than a few times). And ultimately, as always, the interpretation of the song by the listener is of paramount importance. All the same, I feel a niggling discomfort about 'Live Fast Die Old'. Somewhere in there is an ever-so-slightly better song. In fact, in recent years, I've been known to play a completely different solo version of the song, in C major, which completely ditches the original arrangement, and simplifies the structure somewhat. It's still not quite right, but I think it's better. Maybe one day I will stumble across the perfect presentation of this piece.

Unfortunately, the nature of being a recording artist is such that, should I ever work it out, it will be too late. It has always struck me that there's something artificial about the whole process of recording songs. I regard songs as organic creations, living, breathing things, that can grow and change over time. They are, like people, centred on a basic unchanging skeleton, but, with that caveat, they can be short or tall, thin or fat, young or old. Recording is like taking a snapshot of someone; it's a great like-ness of that moment in time, but it doesn't, or perhaps shouldn't, define that person (or that song) for all time.

And so there it is. 'Live Fast Die Old' is a song that sticks in my mind more for what I believe it could have been than for what it is, on record. But maybe I'm the overly judgemental one, and other people can love it for what it is, with all its faults. And I'll be grateful for that.

THE ROAD

To the east, to the east, the road beneath my feet.
To the west, to the west, I haven't got there yet.
And to the north, to the north, never to be caught.
To the south, to the south, my time is running out.

Ever since my childhood I've been scared, I've been afraid
Of being trapped by circumstance, of staying in one place,
So I always keep a small bag full of clothes carefully stored
Somewhere secret, somewhere safe, somewhere close to the door.

Well I've travelled many countries, washed my feet in many seas,
I've drunk with grifters in Vienna and with punks in old DC,
And I've driven across deserts, driven by the irony
That only being shackled to the road could ever I be free.

I've felt old before my time but now I keep the age away
By burning up the miles and by filling up my days.
And the nights, a thousand nights I've played, a thousand more to go,
Before I take a breath and steel myself for the next one thousand shows.

So saddle up your horses now, and keep your powder dry,
Because the truth is you won't be here long, soon you're going to die.
To the heart, to the heart, there's no time for you to waste;
You won't find your precious answers now by staying in one place,
By giving up the chase.

To the east, to the east, the road beneath my feet.
To the west, to the west, I haven't got there yet.
And to the north, to the north, I never will be caught.
To the south, to the south, my time is running out.

I face the horizon, everywhere I go.
I face the horizon, the horizon is my home.

* * *

Poetry of the Deed was the first album I made with the (as yet unnamed) full band. Nigel, Tarrant and Ben had been part of the team and playing with me, both live and on record, for some years already. Beyond that core, I'd had a succession of different keys players, none of them permanent, for various different reasons, which had been frustrating. I'd had a picture of an ideal line-up for the band in my head since the very beginning, which was modelled on a pretty traditional country rock approach, on bands like Counting Crows, the E Street Band and The Band. I wanted a solid rhythm section, bass and drums, and then an electric guitar counterbalanced by both piano and organ or other keys, the whole thing topped up by a solid range of backing vocals. Of course, I'd used other instruments on the first two records, but that was the structural heart that I was aiming for.

While touring *Love Ire & Song*, we came across Matt Nasir – he was playing with Andy Yorke, who opened for us in March 2008. We got along famously, and he's a brilliant musician (piano is actually his third instrument!), so when a vacancy on the keys stool came up yet again, I asked if he'd be interested in filling in. From the very first show he did in the band – Leeds Cockpit, in October 2008 – it felt right, and we never looked back. When it came time to prepare for the recording of album number three,

I wanted to bring the band with me in the studio, playing on (almost) all the songs, reflecting our newfound confidence as a tight musical unit. Accordingly, I took the songs I'd written to the band, and we spent two weeks rehearsing and arranging them in a little room outside Oxford before hitting the studio with Alex Newport.

Having a solid line-up behind me gave my writing a new sense of confidence and vision. I wanted this record to be more sonically consistent, to sound like a band playing together, with me as the leader, as opposed to the piecemeal construction methods and results on its predecessors. As I've mentioned, there are moments on the album that, in retrospect, sound a bit rushed to me. But the overall vibe was good, and when we hit our mark, we sounded stronger than ever before.

As a writer, I've always been most influenced by the music and the people immediately around me. I think that's a good thing; my ears are like sponges, and, whether I want to or not, I'm almost always picking up on the sounds in the ether. I did a tour in early 2009 in the USA which had a big impact on my thinking about songs, and thus on my writing. My friend Chuck Ragan had invited me to play four shows on the Revival Tour the year before; this time, I did a full month, from northern California to Florida. The format of the Revival Tour is simple and inspiring. There's a house band on stage most of the night – this time around, it was John Gaunt on fiddle, Digger Barnes on upright bass and Todd Beene on pedal steel – and then a selection of 'name' performers. There are no individual sets as such, just one long night of songs, everyone joining in on everything else, one person vaguely leading the proceedings at any given moment, but with the traditional rock'n'roll sense of ego firmly pushed back into its seat. It would have been impossible not to be affected by such an onslaught of music, and I wasn't trying to fight it either. Playing with Chuck, Jon Snodgrass, Jim Ward, Audra Mae and others every night got under my skin.

The most obvious result of this was the song 'The Road'. On the Revival Tour run, we played twenty-two shows in as many days, and covered vast distances across the USA. I wanted to commemorate that, and the restless life I was living more generally. I chose a harmonic palette very much in keeping with Chuck's style, centred around a traditional-sounding country pattern in A minor. The verses begin with that chord, vamping around with some time-honoured country licks, before heading off into a long, eight-bar chord sequence. The chorus uses the same chords in a different order, keeping the musical theme but turning it around. When I reached the bridge (which I remember writing in a youth hostel in Vienna, on tour with Chris T-T), I found different inversions of the verse chords, higher up the neck and in a more 'post-hardcore' guitar style. To go with these, I halved the time signature (in a move popular in hardcore punk songs) to more of a 'beatdown' feel, and pushed the vocal melody higher and harder to accompany that. Finally, the music of the song winds back around to a concluding chorus, and an outro tail (using the second half of the chorus chord sequence in yet another inversion).

It's worth acknowledging that, at the time, I had something of a taste for the solo reprise in my writing. More than a few of the songs on my first few records do this, restating the original idea of the song in a defiant-but-exhausted mood at the end of the song. It's a neat trick, but it can be overdone, and I suspect I may be guilty of that. That's one of the reasons the coda of this song doesn't always get played live these days (the other being that it often sounds good to run straight into the next number – keep that energy up!).

On the Revival tour, learning songs with Jim Ward

Another point to dwell on, momentarily, is an expression that has been used around my music for many years now, but with which I don't have much of an emotional connection. On some levels, the term 'folk punk' is fine, as I've touched on before. I learned my musical rudiments in loud punk bands, and now I play something akin to folk music, it's a fair cop. I try not to spend too much time thinking about genre tags anyway. They serve a purpose up to and until the moment everyone in the conversation has heard the music being discussed, after which it's just material for arcane and pointless geek arguments on the internet. Yet it's also a pretty reductionist take on what I do, the influences I bring to bear on my music. And it has lumped me in with a wide and varying group of bands, some of whom I love, and some of whom I know and care nothing about. Having said all of that, the 'beatdown' half-time bridge of this song is probably the most clearly 'folk punk' bit of music I've put my name to. The combination of classic country or folk chords with a stylised hardcore breakdown could be described as 'folk punk', if anything could. I don't think the term has much to do with my back catalogue taken as a whole, but here it fits, and that's OK.

Back to 'The Road'. The song begins with my acoustic guitar, but also with a dual vocal – a new sound for me, and an obvious nod to the fact that it wasn't just me playing the songs on my own any more. For the lyrics, I threw everything I had from my years on tour into it. When I met Tim Barry on the first Revival Tour in 2008, after a few hours of getting to know each other, he'd chuckled and told me I was a 'lifer'. I took that as a compliment, one that I wanted to wear with pride and reflect in song. The lyrics also continue with my intended theme for the album as a whole – a defiant restatement of purpose and identity. I might have been 'old before my time, but now I keep the age away'. I started with the most basic and evocative image I could think of – a compass rose, something I'd seen tattooed on the majority of Revival people. From there, through a rejection of my static childhood (by way of a *Lord of the Rings* reference – 'Is it secret? Is it safe?'), to stories about grifters I met in Vienna (two mad English guys living in squats and making money gambling and pool-sharking), and finishing up with one of the better images I've come up with in my time – 'the horizon is my home'.

Two small notes on the lyrics, while we're here. Firstly, the song rather awkwardly cites hanging out with punks in 'old DC'. The word 'old' there is clearly crowbarred in to make the song scan, and, even at the time, I knew that 'Tennessee' would have fit much better. But I hadn't yet played a show in that state (I didn't until 2010), and I was a stickler for factual accuracy, so I went with the less poetic option. Also, in recent years, I've been enjoying changing the words, live, to 'and the nights, *two* thousand nights I've played . . .' Because I bloody well have!

*

That's the song. For the purposes of this book, however, the main thing I wanted to focus on was the arrangement. The version of this song on *Poetry of the Deed* is a good example of how I saw the band working, and it working out well.

As I've said, my vision for the band was a classic country-rock line-up. If you'll forgive me taking the wild risk of attempting some kind of sporting metaphor here,* it's supposed to work a little bit like a five-a-side football team line-up. The drums underpin everything sonically, right at the back like a goalkeeper, driving the song. The old adage is true, you only rock as hard as your drummer, but it's important to note the bass as well. The much-maligned bass guitar is actually one of the most crucial elements of any band because, like a defender, it bridges the gap between rhythm and melody, holding the whole team together. In the midfield, in front of those two, you have two elements out on the wings. To one side the electric guitar, to the other the keys. Either or both can swoop into the middle to play a central sonic role, but they then usually return to their peripheral starting points, twinkling and weaving through the edges of the music. In between these two, and maybe a step forward, is my acoustic guitar, playing rhythm chords that harmonically underpin the song. And finally, as the centre forward, we have the lead vocals, leading the attack of the whole piece.†

So it works in this song. Nigel worked up a wonderfully original beat. For the verses, it's a standard country-rock train-roll. When the choruses arrive, through a feat of physicality that I still have trouble getting my head around, he keeps that going, but somehow (a third hand?) brings in some open hi-hat work to

---

* I challenge anyone to know less about sport than me. Come at me!
† I know that makes six players, but (a) I'm singing and playing guitar, (b) fucking sports metaphors, and (c – related) this is my book.

fill out the sound. Then to the hardcore bridge. I'd initially envisaged him playing a more standard half-time punk rock beat, in the vein of Sick of It All. In the event, Nige took my suggestion and ran with it, creating something just as brutal and driving, but with a complexity and elegance of its own. And finally, he brings it back home with the last chorus, bringing all these elements together.

Tarrant's bassline works in a similar way. Starting with an orthodox country feel, he plays the roots and the fifths* underneath my strummed acoustic chords. This opens out in the chorus, and digs in for the bridge and the climax, pulling the melody and the rhythm together. Thus the bass, the drums and my guitar form the dominant architecture of the sound.

Over the top of this, Ben and Matt arc and swoop, occasionally coming in for the kill. In the first verse, Ben plays a delicate guitar line across the top of the chords. In the second, Matt takes his turn with a liquid Rhodes piano part. On the choruses, they meet, Ben backing my chords while Matt fills out the space with a Hammond organ line. When the breakdown lands, Ben hits the distortion and plays the inverted, more punk version of the basic chords, while Matt brings the surprising heaviness of a hammered piano to bear. The last chorus sees the whole team working together like a perfect team, everyone running head down for the finish line in perfect union, the final touch being the addition of a three-part vocal harmony. Thus it is that a song structured around eight simple chords rises from a raw acoustic start to a folk punk finish.

Poetry of the Deed was the first time the band played on record

* We call this the 'eins, fünf' – German for 'one, five' – mainly because, as we've noticed over the years, German audiences in particular go absolutely fucking crazy for any song that features this pattern on the bass.

as a band. We set up in the studio and played together, showing off the chops that we had started to learn on the road. Over the years, we've gelled much, much more, and expanded our range and abilities as a unit. Yet I think that this song in particular shows that, even at the beginning of our time as a group, we were a force to be reckoned with.

An addendum: for the video for this song, some idiot (me) decided it would be an idea to try to play twenty-four (solo) shows in twenty-four hours. I actually did do this – no cheating! It was a harrowing experience, not least because I made the basic error of starting in the evening, at 7 p.m., on the first day, rather than in the morning. I suppose it would have been nightmarish either way. The end product is, watching it back now, a lot of fun, and captures the vibe of the lyrics pretty effectively. It's a shame that

The last of 24 shows for the video for 'The Road',
at the Flowerpot, Camden

the band aren't a part of it actually, though the logistics of making twenty-four shows happen with full backline doesn't really bear thinking about. Every now and again, someone suggests that I should do it again, maybe for a tenth anniversary or something. The answer to which is an emphatic 'fuck no!' Even if I wasn't still suffering some form of PTSD from the first time around, I'm also (obviously) a decade older now, and I don't think my constitution could handle the attempt. Sorry, everyone!

ISABEL

So now the years are rolling by,
And it's not long since you and I could have been
Train drivers and astronauts.
And now we're stuck in furnished ruts,
But yet the thing that really cuts is that we can't
Remember how we got caught.
Filtered air, computer screens, muffled sighs and might-have-beens,
Count your blessings, then breathe, and count to ten.
And though it doesn't often show, we are scared because we know
Our forefathers were farmers and fishermen.

And so the world has changed, worse or better's hard to tell,
but my hope remains within the arms of Isabel.

So now our calloused hands once told a story honest as it's old
Of sowing seeds and setting sail.
But now our hands are soft and weak and working seven days a week
At these salvation schemes that are bound to fail.

And I'll admit that I am scared of what I don't understand.
But darling, if you're there, gentle voice and soothing hands,
To quiet my despair, to shore up all my plans, darling, if you're there . . .

And so the world has changed, and I must change as well.
The machines we've made will damn us into hell.

And the time will come when all must save themselves.
I will save my soul in the arms of Isabel.

* * *

In going through material to pick songs to write about in this book, I've spent a fair amount of time listening back to my own music. That's not something I usually do – the songs are living creations, I play a lot of them each night, and there's more than enough great music by other people in the world for me to get around to in my lifetime (and I'm not so self-absorbed as to spend my days sitting in a bunker re-listening to my own output; that's a bad look). But it's been fun, going through all the albums and demos. In the last couple of entries, I feel like I've been a little hard on the album *Poetry of the Deed*. Because of some of the problems with our methodology, as I've explained, I have some residual disappointments with certain aspects of the record. Yet when I sat down to listen to 'Isabel' again, I'm pleased to say I was very pleasantly surprised, and I write this now with a different picture of the song in my mind to the one I started with.

At the time that I was writing the album, I was, as is probably obvious, together with a girl called Isabel. We'd met in Los Angeles while I was touring *Love Ire & Song*, but she was from London, and we'd embarked on a serious, grown-up romantic relationship. In the end we were together, on and off, for four years. It didn't work out in the end, but I wasn't to know that at the time. Smitten as I was, I wanted to lay my feelings out in song.

Writing about her and our time together here is quite difficult to do, and that highlights a more general issue with the type of songwriting I'm known for. As I've mentioned, I have always written in a direct, autobiographical, almost confessional style. That's a reflection of my lyrical influences – Adam Duritz, Aidan

Moffat from Arab Strap, John K. Samson and so on. I've always adored that moment in a song (in art in general, in fact), when someone says something indisputably true, that can't be retracted; a revelation of their genuine inner self, a moment when the bone shows through the skin. That has meant, practically speaking, that I try to force myself to write as honestly as I can. There have been moments when a line I'm working on has made me wince a little, and I try to see that as a signifier that I'm onto something good, something meaningful.

All of that's fine, as long as I'm talking about only myself. It becomes more complicated when other people are involved. I have the right to be as open and confessional about my own life as I want to be when I write. It's an open question, though, how much I'm allowed to do that with other people. The question becomes more acute still when you're talking about a partner, someone with whom I'm sharing my life and all my inner secrets. Do I have to begin a date with a curt warning to a potential partner that anything that passes between us might end up in a song? At the other extreme, do I have to make sure that any relationships I have remain in an emotional realm that I'm comfortable discussing in public? Neither of those options makes much sense.

I was aware of these conflicts by this point in my career, so as I sat down to write a song about my girl, I came at it from a slightly oblique angle. Actually, I have something of a habit of writing love songs that end up being about the end of the world, or technological collapse, or something like that. There are many aspects of life in the modern world that make me feel insecure and nervous, and, like most people, I tend to take refuge from that in the intimacy of love and connection with another person. I used to joke that, before properly settling down, I hadn't written any love songs that didn't have a sting in the tail or an unhappy ending. That's not strictly true – this being a case in point – but it would probably be a stretch to describe 'Isabel' as a happy love song.

I wrote the words while I was away on tour. Interestingly (for me) quite a lot of the imagery I used prefigures the larger themes of my next album, *England Keep My Bones*. The big ideas I have tend to do that, spread from one period to the next, as I get my teeth into them and expand on them in my mind. The words mention 'train drivers and astronauts', and there's a general sense of the dislocation of modernity, as opposed to a more visceral, simple life of 'farmers and fishermen', an idea that also runs through the song 'Sailor's Boots'. However, in this instance, the song dances through all these themes before coming back, re-assuringly, to a basic romantic statement: 'I will save my soul within the arms of Isabel'. I really was very much in love. When I finished the song, I played it to her on a guitar while we were on holiday, and managed to evoke some real tears. It was a special and personal moment for us.

(Incidentally, a lot of the language and imagery of this song reappears in the song 'Wanderlust', which is about the ending of my time with Isabel, part of the reason that song is so damn sad.)

Musically, the song is simple and driving. The verse hangs around one chord, with a rising and falling melody. I initially picked it out around a G chord on the guitar, playing the melody on the top B and E strings. The vocal part harmonises with the guitar, a trick I love using, as it implies a larger orchestration with only a voice and one instrument. I spent some time trying to figure out what key to play it in. The capo is the songwriter's friend in this situation. By clamping your strings at different points on the neck, you can raise the key of a basic chord pattern to fit where you'd like to sing it (it also makes you sound like you know way more chords than you do!). The key a song is in is pretty important, and that in turn depends on your vocal register. You can play a song in such a way that you're right at the edges of your range, straining for the highs, or you can bring it right down and sing in a more relaxed way. The sound of your voice as you sing has a huge effect on the emotional delivery of the lyrics. For this tune, I settled on a capo on the fourth fret, placing the song in the key of B major, which is comfortable for me, but not lazy-sounding.

The overall arrangement is about as basic as I could make it. The song is propelled by a snare beat all the way through the first half of the song. It doesn't have much in the way of groove, but it's relentless. The variation comes, as before, from the use of different cymbals, and bringing in soaring guitars and keys in different registers as appropriate. I'm an unashamed fan of bands like Snow Patrol and Coldplay, who use this approach often. It reminds me, in fact, of stuff like Sunny Day Real Estate, second-wave emo bands that I adored as a teenager. There's a sweet-spot between brutality and delicacy in there somewhere that I was aiming to hit, and which seemed to bring the spirit of the lyrics to life in the best way.

The bridge of the song loosens up the drums into more of a rolling beat, bringing in the tambourine for some extra rhythmic propulsion. Then, for the final chorus, we drop another, more traditional hardcore half-time beatdown. There's a lot of the sound here that you could hear in the album *EndSerenading* by Mineral. Finally we land in the play-out, with Matt's chiming piano octaves restating the basic melody, and my first (and thus far, perhaps wisely, only) use of humming in a song.

Once we had recorded the song and released it, the label, Epitaph, was keen for it to be highlighted as a single. I was fine with this – the choice of singles from an album strikes me as a purely commercial decision, one that takes place after the artistic battle is over, so I'm OK for the people who handle the commercial side of things to take control there. I eventually found myself on a beach in California shooting a video for the song, which, let's be honest, was fucking terrible (and it wasn't to be the last one of those). In addition, after my first two records, and 'The Road', I think the general message and arrangement of the song was a little too soft and 'mainstream' for the audience I had at the time, so it didn't exactly set the world on fire.

I think this is part of the reason why this song started falling into my bad books. That, and the fact that, for reasons I cannot now recall, we decided to try our hand at some remixes of the song for the release. For anyone who's ever heard any of them (Matt, Nigel and I all did separate ones), I'm sorry, I don't know what came over us. They were not, in the usual usage of the word, good. At all. Thankfully they've been largely forgotten by history.* The other reason, of course, is that my relationship with Isabel didn't last − a topic I covered amply in song, and thus one I will get to in due course in this book.

In December 2009, we played a Christmas show at Union Chapel, in London. I barely made the show by the skin of my teeth, thanks to a transport logistics nightmare getting from Paris to Islington (which I wrote about in detail in my first book, *The Road Beneath My Feet*), so it was a little rough around the edges. Nevertheless, for the gig, we had worked out a different arrangement of a number of tunes, including this one. I really enjoyed the process, stripping things back again and trying to find the original heart of the song, and from then until now I have preferred that approach to the tune. I have to say now, though, that, on listening back to all the different versions to write this entry, the

* Until now . . . dammit!

original is the one that stands the test of time for me. The drive and the grit of the recording on *Poetry of the Deed* captures how the song feels in my head. Maybe we'll start playing it that way again sometime soon.

SONS OF LIBERTY

Once an honest man could go from sunrise to its set
Without encountering agents of his state or government.
But a sorry cloud of tyranny has fallen across the land,
Brought on by the hollow men who did not understand
That for centuries our forefathers have fought, and often died,
To keep themselves unto themselves, to fight the rising tide;
That if in the smallest battles we surrender to the state,
We enter in a darkness whence we never shall escape.

When they raise their hands up our lives to possess,
To know our souls, to drag us down, we'll resist.

Wat Tyler led the people in 1381
To meet the king at Smithfield to issue this demand:
That Winchester's should be the only law across the land,
The law of old King Alfred's time, of free and honest men.
Because the people then they understood what we have since forgot:
That the government will only work for their own benefit.
And I'd rather stand up naked against the elements alone
Than give the hollow men the right to enter in my home.

Stand up, sons of liberty, and fight for what you own,
Stand up, sons of liberty, and fight, fight for your homes.

So if ever a man should ask you for your business or your name,
Tell him to go and fuck himself, tell his friends to do the same.
Because a man who'd trade his liberty for a safe and dreamless sleep
Doesn't deserve the both of them, and neither shall he keep.

* * *

As I've outlined, in my early twenties I was thoroughly disillusioned with the politics of my youth. The basic starting premises still held for me – people are equal until they demonstrate otherwise through their own unforced actions, all conglomerations of power and authority should be treated with a large dollop of cynicism and mistrust, individuals are almost always the best judge of what's best for their own lives, and so on. I'd just become disheartened by the people and movements I'd encountered thus far on my intellectual travels. For the most part they seemed at best unworldly, and at worst completely self-serving. I wrote a bunch of songs on the topic, which struck a chord with some people, which was all well and good. But like the proverbial scratched cynic, deep down I was still a disappointed idealist, and I still held a youthful hunger for some sense of direction, meaning and hope.

Around the time we were touring *Love Ire & Song*, I stumbled across a nebulous philosophical approach to politics that made a lot of sense to me. Writers like Albert Nock, Karl Popper and Isiah Berlin (and before them, J. S. Mill, Adam Smith, and the American Founding Fathers – whence the title*) took the same basic principles but applied them to the world in a way that had

---

* The Sons of Liberty were a pre-revolutionary underground militia in the Thirteen Colonies that went on to become the USA after 1776, who fought against the authority of the British crown.

much more practical consideration, and thus effect. I disappeared down something of an intellectual rabbit hole for a few years, as newly converted enthusiasts tend to do. With the benefit of hindsight, I'd say my pendulum probably swung a little far in that direction for a time. These days I'm not much of a fan of any philosophical labelling of my approach to the world, whether 'libertarian' or 'classical liberal'. I'd prefer to say that I try, at all times, to lean in the direction of liberty and individual autonomy in considering any situation. But I don't have any blueprint I'm following, and I resolutely believe that the most important thing, in any given situation, is to listen and learn first, and try to be considerate of everyone's needs, motives and ideals.* I like to think of myself as a militant liberal.

Back in 2009, I was more gung-ho (and perhaps a bit less nuanced) about this approach to the world, and I wanted to capture it in my work. I was bored of writing pessimistic songs that sniped from the sidelines. I wanted to offer something more constructive to the debate. More to the point, I had an idea about language. Protest music has a long and noble lineage, and an accompanying set of images, tropes and phraseology. For the most part, protest songs lean to the hard left. I wanted to see if it was possible to use the same approaches and lexicon to write something that was more in a classical liberal vein, to try to express my newfound view of the world and society. Using someone else's paradigm and repurposing it for your own ends is, by definition,

---

* I'd hope it would go without saying that I have zero truck with any nationalist or fascist ideas – in fact, I'd probably say that my political motivation is to be as far away from any form of authoritarianism as possible at all times. But then I never cease to be surprised by the bad faith with which some people interpret my politics and differing opinions in general, so, for the record: fuck fascism, fuck Nazis.

a cheeky move (one that I would use again in the song 'Make America Great Again') and I suppose I was expecting some push-back over the resulting song; not, perhaps, as much as I got.

I've mentioned the Levellers a few times already. My sister got me into their music when I was young, and they are one of the few permanent entries in my record collection; I love them today as much as I ever did. Musically, their blending of punk rock musicianship with traditional English melodies and imagery is strikingly original, and remains very influential for me. Lyrically, their protest music struck a chord with me when I was young, and stays with me now. To get philosophical for a moment: my understanding of history, from my institutional and personal studies, is that humans have a terrible capacity for cruelty when power accumulates. Some people on the left of the political spectrum have a weird blind spot about this. I think using the state to help people is a good idea, but I still regard the state itself as a necessary evil at best, and certainly something that we should collectively watch like a hawk; self-declared good intentions are not good enough as a safeguard. Celebrating the power of the state and agitating for its expansion seems to me to be the very opposite of liberal egalitarianism. The Levellers, in my view, have always admirably stuck to the leftist traditions that tend towards an appropriate distrust of power, towards the anarchist end of the spectrum.

But it's the music I want to talk about the most here. The Levellers' records are an obvious signpost for the song 'Sons of Liberty'. The music is rooted around the note E, but it's not in a normal scale; instead it uses traditional Celtic modes, sometimes hitting the major third, sometimes the minor, dropping in a D (which, Matt Nasir tells me, is a flattened seventh). I'm not technically well versed enough to explain exactly what's going on with the key here, but the general feel is haunting and ancient. My friend Anna Jenkins, who I met when she played in Emily Barker's band, came into the studio to lay down a fiddle solo for the song. She's an expert player in this field, and her work effort-lessly highlighted the modal approach I was using.

The chorus plays with the harmonic ambiguity here. Beginning on a major second chord – F# – it then moves up to a G# minor, down to an E, before landing on a B major. Somewhere in the middle of this, the ear subtly switches up where it thinks the root of the music lies, so that when you land on the B it feels like a triumphant resolution, albeit one you weren't expecting.

Marrying these melodies with electric guitar and drums is a solid nod to the Levellers. The time signature of the song is, I think, 12/8. That's a count that allows a lot of room for synco-pation, suggestion and trickery. The first half of the song rolls along with a half-time feel, before opening up to something quicker for the instrumental bridge, and then settling down to a tribal feel for the play-out. Said climax also features something of a bass solo, something I was keen to include on this record, to give Tarrant's excellent playing a moment in the spotlight, and of course a gang-vocal singalong part.

Lyrically, as I've said, I tried to bring together my newfound sense of idealism, my rediscovery of a political voice, with the tropes of classic protest music – with a bit of history thrown in for good measure. I was reading a book about the Peasant's Revolt of 1381 (an event I have commemorated in my finger tattoos), which mentioned that Wat Tyler, on meeting King Richard II at Smithfield, demanded the return of the 'Law of Winchester'. That struck a strong chord with me, not least because I was beginning to slowly examine the ideas that would emerge as *England Keep My Bones*, of songs that openly name-checked the places that I knew (rather than, say, New Jersey or Florida). Obviously, the part-mythological legal code of King Alfred's time isn't actually any kind of practical political approach for the twenty-first century, but it's a striking picture.

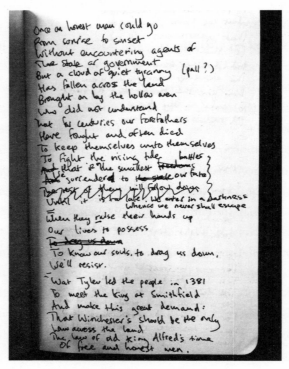

The first draft of 'Sons Of Liberty'

In line with that, I was also being provocative with my words, in keeping with the song traditions I was trying to ape. Clearly, I don't actually think that telling government officials to 'go and fuck themselves' is a useful (or considerate) thing to do. But it makes for a damn good lyrical coda for the song, borrowing from Benjamin Franklin for a biting finale to sing with the crowd.

Or not. When the album was released, quite a few people, particularly in the UK, rolled their eyes at the song. At best they thought it was something of a weird aberration in my writing;

at worst they thought it was a betrayal of the politics they had confidently assumed me to be signed up to, given the musical milieu in which I worked, and the people I called friends. The music world, both at home and in the USA, is a very left-leaning place. That's totally fine with me, but I had hoped, naïvely, that the song would be a contrary contribution to the debate therein, maybe bringing things back to the centre a little. In the event, it was taken by many as an attack (which, listening back to the tone of the lyrics now, is kind of fair enough). Ironically, for years people had been bugging me to write more political songs; most of those people weren't all that stoked when I actually did.

At the time, there were not so many people paying attention to me and what I had to say as there would be quite soon afterwards, so to a degree the song passed under the radar. When I got myself into some public political controversy a few years later, many people went back to this song and used it as a stick to beat me with. Interestingly, I've read a number of journalists, in reference to this piece, refer to me witheringly as a 'libertarian Billy Bragg'. That's not actually that far off the mark of where my head was at when I was writing the song. Billy has become a friend (since the song was written, incidentally), and he's one of the best songwriters and people I know. But in this case I was very much trying to use his brilliant stylistic approach to say something slightly different.

It's not a song I play all that often these days. Part of that is because I have felt pretty burned at times over the years when it comes to my politics in my music. I think that's only natural, given the ferocity of the criticism I've occasionally faced. Often I'd prefer to think about, talk about and play music, which has always been several orders of magnitude more important for me. But I also think, in retrospect, that this song is a little too harsh in places, a little too brittle and self-important. I'm also not super-comfortable with the predominant masculinity of the words – 'sons', 'free and honest men' and so on. It seems a little archaic to me, to put it politely. At the same time, I don't want to roll over, intellectually. I believe what I believe (and, in essence, that boils down to the fact that I don't have the right to tell anyone else what to do with their lives; if that's something you find problematic, I'd gently suggest an examination of your own feelings about authority), and I'll stand by it.

THE BALLAD OF STEVE

Let me tell a little story about a flight attendant
Who now stands in court as a lone defendant.
After twenty long years in a job that tough,
He decided one day he'd had enough.

Steve had to leave.

As the plane touched down in Philadelphia,
One old lady didn't do what Steve had told her.
She got up to get her bags while the plane was still moving,
Steve marched down the aisle all disapproving.

Steve was polite, but he knew he was right.

Steve always did the best that he could.
He knew that when he finally left, he had to make it good.
So Steve had an awesome exit planned:
Steve is the fucking man.

Steve was a bro, Steve had to go.

The old woman didn't listen to what Steve had said,
She pulled down her baggage and it hit him in the head.
So he went back to the front and he got up on the mic,
And he spoke to all the passengers and caller her on her shite.

Steve spoke the truth with a cuss word or two.

Steve pulled up the lever and down fell the chute,
And then he went to the drinks trolley and he grabbed a beer or two,
And just before he jumped off the plane, he turned he turned and yelled:
'I'm out of here you fuckers, I'll see you all in hell.'

* * *

I met Jon Snodgrass, as I've mentioned, on the Revival Tour. He's a wonderful, loveable man from Colorado, who started out in music guitar teching for The Descendents, before making his own music in bands like Armchair Martian and Drag the River (with Chad Price). We got on very well on the road together, and as we parted ways at the end of the tour, we'd exchanged phone numbers. Jon, in fact, had said to me, as I entered my digits, 'Be careful with giving me your number – I'm the kind of guy who's going to use it.'

And use it he did. At the time, my older sister lived in Longmont, Colorado, and I'd often finish a run in the USA with a family visit. Jon lives not far away in Fort Collins, so in time he'd often join these gatherings, an honorary Turner. As time went by, sipping whiskey on the veranda in the hot summer of the Rockies, or huddled inside during the harsh but clear winters, the conversation meandered towards the writing of songs.

Jon is a naturally collaborative musician. Personally, as I've said, I'm in no way opposed to the idea. Million Dead's writing process was purely democratic (often to a fault; we nearly broke up over a drum fill once). Since going my own way in 2005, however, I hadn't ever really sat down to make up songs with anyone else. Partly, the opportunity hadn't arisen, and partly I was fired up about forging my own creative path. But hanging out with Jon, those two objections, practical and philosophical, started to seem redundant. Somewhere along the line, Jon proposed a wild idea for an album.

Actually, the story began earlier, on the road with Chuck Ragan and the gang. We played a show in Little Rock, Arkansas, in November 2009, at a venue called Juanita's Cantina. As the luck of the road sometimes shakes out, we had a pretty dismal turnout that night. In fact, Jim Ward was able to pour a shot of whiskey for the entire touring crew *and* the audience from a single bottle of Jameson. There were maybe ten paying customers. Nevertheless, inspired as we all were by the dicta of Henry Rollins and Black Flag, we played our hearts out, and actually had a really fun show.

A few days later, while killing time before taking the stage in Orlando, Florida, Jon and I had, casually at first, put together a song about the incident. The writing process lasted half an hour, if that, as we threw words and chords to each other in the parking lot. In no time at all, we had a fun little song, called 'Big Rock in Little Rock'. We played it at the last show of the run, raised a laugh in the audience, and went our separate ways.

Jon's suggestion, a while later, was that we reprise this method of writing to make an entire record together. We would sidestep the potential complexities of collaboration by setting ourselves strict time limits on the process. In fact, in the end, we decided to try to write an entire album of songs in one day. A date was set, a spare night at my sister's place, and Jon drove down with his guitar and a handle of whiskey. After a delicious home-cooked meal, we sat outside in the garden and started trying to think up some songs.

I can't really stress enough how different this methodology was from my usual approach to songwriting. Habitually, I slave over ideas, drafts, different versions and so on for many months.

Writing 'Buddies' with Jon Snodgrass in Colorado

This time, the plan was to write ten songs in one session, and then drive up to Jon's place the following day and lay the material we had down as an album, to be released as it was, with no opportunity for tweaking any of it later. The sheer audacity of this actually gave me shivers. It put me into a totally different mindset, and, surprisingly, actually stoked the fires of my creative imagination to a huge degree. Being forced to work within artificial limitations can actually, in the event, be a form of release.

The quality of the record that we made – *Buddies* – is, naturally, pretty variable. Some of the songs are really quite good, in my humble opinion. And some of them are borderline worthless, not least the calamity that is the last track, 'Mo'Squitoz', which features a primitive drum machine, Jon on bass, and me attempting to rap. What can I say; we were quite deep into the whiskey by the time that idea rolled around. Probably my pick of the bunch is the song 'The Ballad of Steve'.

Finding inspiration for a song, a basic starting point, is one of the hardest parts of the entire process. You need something to say and a way to say it that feels authentic and original. I spend endless time fumbling in the dark of my imagination trying to catch the sparks that could become songs. In this situation, we had to do that right then and there, *ten times over*, and there was no time to waste. So naturally we cast around for ideas. In the news that day was a crazy story, one you might vaguely remember, that was just about mad enough to serve as the basis for a song.

Steve Slater was a flight attendant with JetBlue airlines. On 9 August 2010 (the day before Jon and I met in Longmont), after a long and storied career, he'd finally cracked. As the plane taxied in to the gate after landing, a passenger had stood up to get her bag. Steve had remonstrated with her, the bag had hit him in the head, and he decided he'd had enough of the whole thing. He announced on the public address system that he was quitting, grabbed a couple of beers off the drinks trolley, pulled the lever that opened the evacuation slide, and exited the plane in serious style.

Jon and I read this with a mixture of incredulity, hilarity and admiration. What a way to go! And, of course, it quickly started shaping itself into a song. We settled on some basic country chords (not too far distant from those of 'The Road') and began trying to fit all the facts of the incident into the allotted rhythmical structures. Jon was tickled by the line 'Steve had to leave!' so that became one of the central pillars of the burgeoning construction. Time was against us, so, as with all the songs we wrote that night, the arrangement and layout of the song is very simple, the lyrical niceties a bit rough around the edges. But I like to think that the version we captured has charm, and serves as a fitting tribute to our hero.

We recorded the song the following day in Jon's home studio, and the record was released, unpolished, later in the year. We later found out some extra details about the story, worth mentioning here. Firstly, legend has it that Steve drove home from the airport, and, by the time the police arrived at his door to arrest him, he was *already in bed* with his boyfriend. I love the image of him getting home, crackling and alive with his act of protest and self-realisation, and immediately losing himself in the throes of passion. You go, Steve.

Slightly less wonderfully, there was a fair amount of dispute about his original version of events, and it was later suggested that Steve was suffering from mental health issues, and may have had issues with alcohol. It was never our intention to belittle either of these matters, of course. In later years, since the song has been released, I'm told he's heard it, been amused by it, and has even attended one of my shows in San Francisco, though we didn't meet.

Regardless of the truth of the matter, we ended up with a fun song, and it's still one that I'll crack out at my solo shows from time to time. When Jon and I cross paths, as we sometimes do, we always talk about doing the whole thing again. As a writer, it was a completely different experience for me (as well as being one that was easy on my schedule!), and it opened up the possibility, in the long term, of me working more with other people on songs. We did in fact do one more song – 'Happy New Year' – a while later, but we have yet to actually make *Buddies Two – Buddies Take Manhattan* (as Jon has suggested it should be called). Maybe one day.

EULOGY

Not everyone grows up to be an astronaut.
Not everyone was born to be a king.
Not everyone can be Freddie Mercury,
But everyone can raise a glass and sing.

Well I haven't always been a perfect person,
And I haven't done what mum and dad had dreamed,
But on the day I die I'll say
'At least I fucking tried.'
And that's the only eulogy I need.

* * *

On *Poetry of the Deed*, I'd tried, with mixed success, to use the methodology of a solo album to make a record with a full band. The lesson was firmly learned, and when thoughts and schedules began turning towards my next visit to a studio, I was determined to do things differently – in a word, better.

A major change taking place at this time was the steady professionalisation of my career. The early days of touring like a vagabond, flying by the seat of my trousers and playing anywhere and everywhere, were coming to an end. The pace hadn't slackened at all – quite the opposite in fact – but the logistics were more regulated now. I know that doesn't sound romantic, but the streamlined operation meant that I could get more done, travel to more places, and indeed take the band with me. In 2010, I'd taken the boys to the USA for the first time, for a gruelling couple of months opening for Flogging Molly all across the country. The rigours of that tour, chasing the headliners' tour bus in an Econoline van, sleeping on the floor most nights, only one crew member (Casey was driving, tour managing and doing sound, while I was selling my own merch), and, not least, trying to win over several thousand unfamiliar and uninterested Americans every night, had disciplined us as a unit. As a collective entity, my band and I were forged in the fires of the American road.

Another facet of our increased schedule outside the UK had a striking impact on my songwriting and lyrical subject matter at this time. Whether solo or backed up by Nigel, Ben, Matt and Tarrant, most nights I was in a very small national minority on stage, an Englishman singing to a room full of people from somewhere else. I'd always had a strong self-consciously English element to my songs, but the experience of explaining where I was from and what some of my reference points were, night after night, made me start thinking about the subject in more detail.

That dovetailed neatly with another strand of my musical exploration. I had used the word 'folk' around my solo music from the start, but it had always been as much an ideological statement as a musicological one. I didn't play traditional songs, didn't have a particularly wide or deep knowledge of the genre. What I was trying to do was make a statement that I considered the music I was making to be for everyone, to be part of a broader tradition, to be demotic in content and intent. Nevertheless, over time I'd copped a fair amount of criticism from folk traditionalists for using the term, and in a way, I agreed with them. In order to redress that imbalance, I had started reading about and listening to traditional music from the British Isles. The most interesting part of that journey of discovery, for me, was English folk. Scots and Irish songs are more culturally familiar. Outside of a few Fairport Convention records, I'd never really heard any traditional English songs.

It is, annoyingly, still important for me to insert a caveat here. I don't think anyone's nationality contains any moral content. No one is better or worse because of the accident of the location of their birth. Hell, I wasn't even born in England – I came into this world in Bahrain, of all places. I don't have some confected nostalgia for an imaginary prelapsarian English idyll, and I don't identify myself as some kind of faux farmhand. English music captured my attention and imagination because, for better or worse, it's where I grew up. In point of fact, folk music, as a popular tradition, more often than not captures the anarchic, anti-authoritarian spirit of the English people through history, in stark contrast to the bombast and chauvinism of more 'official', court-based music.

So it was that a vague idea of an album of songs about England was starting to come together, somewhere in the back corner of my mind. Actually, I do my very best not to write in a pre-directed fashion. That seems artificial to me; I'd rather let the songs arrive in the manner of their own choosing, and then pick out the unifying threads after the event – that's what the choice of songs and sequencing of an album is for. Nevertheless, if I have an overarching intellectual preoccupation for a time, a brain itch, then it tends to come out in song, and usually in more than one.

July 2010 was a hectic month. Festival season was in full swing, and my schedule had me regularly jetting back and forth across the Atlantic. The most intense bout of international travel came at the end of the month. I was booked to play at the Calgary Folk Festival in Western Canada. A few days later, I was to appear at the Lowertown Festival in St Paul, Minnesota – across the border, but not that far away in global terms.

Unfortunately, my journey from one to the other was not destined to be quite so simple. My manager, Charlie Caplowe, had been contacted by *Kerrang!* magazine and told that they were planning on giving me an award that year. Very flattering, we can all agree, but the award ceremony, at which my attendance was required, was taking place in between my shows in Calgary and St Paul – in London, England. As per usual, my gung-ho attitude towards travel overrode any practical considerations, and so it was that I flew back to the UK for about twenty-four hours to pick up the Spirit of Independence Award.

Oh this little thing? It's just a *Kerrang!* award

The day after the ceremony, hungover and exhausted (and still carrying the massive K-shaped award, which I had been supposed to leave with Charlie, but which I'd staggered off with at the end of the night, and now had to explain to the unimpressed security agents at Heathrow), I flew back to Minnesota, via Chicago. By the time I checked into my hotel that night, I was beyond wiped out. I've done a few of these quick transatlantic hops in my time, and in a way, the fact that you end up in the same time-zone you started in makes things worse, not better. I had also done the whole trip on my own. I felt good about getting an award – my mum was pleased – but I was also having an introspective moment of wondering how much of this kind of schedule I could withstand. I wandered down to the airport hotel bar and got pretty drunk alone, before crashing out in my lonely room.

The following morning was perhaps more than a touch rough around the edges. I peeled myself out of bed and threw myself into the hotel shower. While washing away the grime of tiredness and alcohol, I started humming myself a little tune. I've often found the shower to be a place where good ideas arrive (stop with those dirty thoughts!). Something about the solitude, the sense of getting clean, empties my mind and lets new thoughts arrive. Within a few minutes, I had a short but self-contained little melody and the beginnings of some words as well. It was another case of music and lyrics arriving in tandem, which, as I've said, always gets me excited; it's the mark of something special.

I read a book recently – well after writing this song – by Philip Ball, called *The Music Instinct*. It's an absolutely fascinating tour through the way music works and how it interacts with our conscious and unconscious minds. One point that really grabbed me was the idea of there being a grammar to melody. Some patterns of notes just seem to make sense more than others, to have the feel of a well-written sentence, to have a satisfying resolution after taking you somewhere interesting. I'm nowhere near expert enough to practically apply these ideas to my own music (or anyone else's), but I can see what he means, and the little melody I had in that shower fits this bill, to my ears. Something about it feels complete, even though it's short.

Speaking of brevity, somehow I knew from the beginning that

this would be a very short song. Usually, I tend towards the traditional three minutes and thirty seconds mark, but there's a place for shorter (and indeed longer) songs. One of my benchmarks has always been the fact that 'Fix Me', my favourite Black Flag song, is fifty-eight seconds long; anything beyond that is open to the charge of dawdling. Writing a song as a specific introduction piece felt like it might be a little forced and fall foul of my rule about not pre-determining my writing. All the same, at that moment in time, with that melodic structure, I felt inspired to try to write a brief statement of purpose. Before the hot water ran out, I had the whole thing, complete with a nod to Freddie Mercury.

Aside from the song being a short manifesto, the other governing idea I'd had was that its two halves would be radically different, in terms of sound and arrangement, and would represent the two musical worlds I was drawing from. Once the band crashed in, I also had very clear ideas on the specific parts that would be played. After the chaotic sessions working out *Poetry of the Deed* in a rehearsal room, I wanted to claim back control of the arrangements of my songs. I had a clear, three-dimensional picture in my mind of where each instrument would sit, and what it would bring to the table. I wanted the song to begin as a clear, simple folk piece, but once the band landed, I wanted it to be heavy and loud. In the course of less than a minute of music, I would restate my first principles, and then define the ambitions I had for my sound as boldly as possible.

This was achieved (and then some) in the Church Studios in Crouch End, north London, with Tristan Ivemy at the helm. Tristan had recorded some early demos and mixed *Love Ire & Song*, but this was the first time he actually worked as my fully fledged producer. He did a fantastic job of helping me lay out in simple but bold strokes my sonic vision, and *England Keep My Bones* remains probably my favourite of the records I've made in sonic terms. Towards the end of the album sessions, as the shape and tone of the record became clearer, I had an idea to add one last piece of preamble to this introductory tune. One of the most evocatively English sounds I know is that of a Northern brass band. I asked Matt if he could use his proper musical education to write a horn arrangement of the basic melody. Actually, my specific instruction to him was to 'make it sound like a Hovis advert'.* And so it was that the final ingredient was added, and my fourth album was to open with a song called 'Eulogy'.

Having an introductory song as the opener of what was, for a long time, my most successful record, became something of a burden for a while, in terms of setlist choices, in a mirror image of what had happened with 'The Ballad of Me and My Friends'. For the initial album tours, it was a perfect opener. But after a while it just became so obvious, and I found it difficult to envisage a different spot for it in the set. So after the first year or so of touring *England Keep My Bones*, more often than not it would fall off the setlist altogether.

The song was given a new lease of life, from a live perspective, by a German guy called Peter Lütkenhaus, in 2013. The upcoming show in Cologne was sold out; Peter had promised his girlfriend a ticket for Valentine's Day, but had failed to grab any in time. In a last-ditch effort to get into the show, he emailed me with a full German translation of the song, asking for guest list tickets in return. He even included a video of him singing the song himself, at the piano, so that I could hear the pronunciation and scansion.

* For my overseas readers: a brand of bread that famously, in the 1980s, had a successful run of TV adverts featuring maudlin brass band music and sepia-tinted footage of urchins pushing bikes down cobbled streets.

I was absolutely thrilled by his work. I've always tried to say a few sentences in the local language wherever we play. It just seems like good manners, an indication that you're aware that you're the visitor. Actually singing a whole song of my own in German was a fantastic way of making friends in that country, so it became a staple of our sets there. Not long afterwards, someone else emailed me to say that, contrary to what I'd previously believed, Swiss German was significantly different enough to require a slightly different translation – which my correspondent provided. A precedent had been set. At the time of writing this, I have sung my eight-line song in twenty-four different languages, including four different types of German; Basque, Catalan and Spanish; Welsh, Luxembourgish and Cornish; and the hardest to pronounce of all (by a country mile), Czech. I even did the French translation myself. And to this day, when we're in a country where English is not the local language, I'll make an effort to add 'Eulogy', in the local lingo, to the setlist.

I STILL BELIEVE

Hear ye, hear ye, friends and Romans, countrymen.
Hear ye, hear ye, punks and skins and journeymen.
Hear ye, hear ye, my sisters and my brethren.
The time is coming near.

Come ye, come ye, to soulless corporate circus tops.
Come ye, come ye, to toilet circuit touring stops.
Come ye, come ye, to bedrooms, bars and bunker squats.
The sound is ringing clear.

Now who'd have thought that after all,
Something as simple as rock 'n' roll would save us all.
Now who'd have thought that after all, it was rock 'n' roll.

Hear ye, hear ye, now anybody could take this stage.
Hear ye, hear ye, and make miracles for minimum wage.
Hear ye, hear ye, these folk songs for the modern age
Will hold us in their arms.

Right here, right now, Elvis brings his children home.
Right here, right now, you never have to feel alone.
Right here, right now, teenage kicks and gramophones,
We hold them in our hearts.

And I still believe in the saints,
Yeah, in Jerry Lee and in Johnny and all the greats.
And I still believe in the sound
That has the power to raise a temple and tear it down.
And I still believe in the need
For guitars and drums and desperate poetry.
And I still believe that everyone
Can find a song for every time they've lost, and every time they've won.
So just remember folks, we're not just saving lives, we're saving souls,
And we're having fun.

Now who'd have thought that after all,
Something so simple, something so small . . .
Who'd have thought that after all it's rock 'n' roll?

* * *

The biggest audience that I've ever played for was when I was asked, by Danny Boyle, to perform at the Opening Ceremony of the London Olympic Games in 2012. The band and I, backed up by a collection of friends like Ben Marwood, Emily Barker and Jim Lockey, performed on a fake hill at one end of the new Olympic stadium in Stratford, full to capacity with around 80,000 spectators. We played three songs, the third of which was broadcast live to a domestic TV audience estimated at 27 million people (as I was helpfully informed just before I walked onstage, doing wonders for my nerves). The song we performed was 'I Still Believe'.

It was a great honour to be asked to play at the Opening Ceremony – a once-in-a-lifetime event. It certainly didn't do my career any damage (aside from annoying a handful of humourless, seething, more-underground-than-thou punks). That said, we didn't exactly sell 27 million records overnight either, and I suspect that the reaction of the vast majority of people watching the television that night was something along the lines of a shrug and a question – 'Who the fuck is that guy?' I like to think I soundtracked the making of many millions of cups of tea.

The choice of songs to play at the ceremony was Danny Boyle's. He did actually say I could pick whatever tunes I wanted, but, from our first planning meeting, his vision for the entire performance was so carefully thought out and fully formed that I felt it was safer (and more respectful) to follow his artistic vision. Actually, if he was going to insist on picking one of my songs to close the first half of the ceremony, it didn't surprise me much that it was this particular one. As a songwriter, you hope to hit big every time you sit down to write – but of course, you don't; sometimes you hit gold, and sometimes you end up with handfuls of dirt. Even without the Olympic performance to its credit, 'I Still Believe' has always, since I first played it, been one of the bigger songs I've written. And I'm proud to have written a song that has connected with so many people. There are some writers who become almost jealous of a big hit on behalf of their other songs, and that seems misdirected to me. I still plan my setlists around this song as the climax, to this day, and most likely always will. That's fine with me.

The song has a strange and roundabout backstory, which begins, in all places, in the People's Republic of China. In 2010, amidst my other international gallivanting, I undertook a tour of China that was, arguably, illegal, in that I didn't have any of the paperwork or visas required to perform in the country. Nathaniel and Archie, American and Scottish expats respectively, set up two weeks of shows for me, and provided me with a wonderfully eccentric and capable tour manager in the person of Ciga, a fashion blogger. She and I travelled from Shenzhen, near the border with Hong Kong (over which I simply walked, with a guitar case), up through Wuhan, and on to Shanghai and Beijing.

The experience of being in China in such an unsheltered and hand-to-mouth scenario was an incredible and unforgettable adventure that will stay with me for ever. I did my best to keep my eyes and ears open, to try every different type of food, to ask questions, and to learn. I've written about the trip in more detail elsewhere. The important point here is that the trip also brought forth a new song.

Living in the comfortable Western world as I do (and as I suspect most people reading this do too), the art form colloquially known as rock'n'roll is culturally ubiquitous. From morning till night, we hear short, energetic songs, driven by guitars and drums and usually simple lyrics, blaring out of our televisions, car radios, speakers, headphones, even storefronts and coffee shops. It's easy, in the midst of this cacophony, to forget how totally radical and revelatory this music was when it first emerged in the 1950s. Rock'n'roll isn't (necessarily) the inherently revolutionary force it once was for us, but then you could make a historical argument that that's because, in part, the music *won*. The culture wars of the 1960s ended up with rock'n'roll triumphant. Ronald Reagan used a Springsteen song for his campaign, and no matter how misguided the politics of that may have been, artistically, that's quite something. You could argue that rock music was cowed and gelded in the process, or alternatively, as a music fan, you could be happy that the art you love has become more widely accepted and appreciated, but my point here is that it's all around us, it's no longer something shocking and exciting for us.

How lucky we are. This is something I realised on my tour through China. This is not a history book, so I'm not going to try and expound a watertight theory on the changes in Chinese society since the Deng reforms of the late 1970s, but, broadly speaking, the Communist government in Beijing has, in recent years, tolerated a fair degree of cultural and economic liberalisation, while keeping a tight rein on political power. Where that will lead in the long term is anyone's guess; what matters in this telling is that, for the Chinese people I met and played for in 2010, rock'n'roll was a radical and exciting new sound. And in watching people's reaction to this fresh art form, I was given a new appreciation of it myself.

In each venue we played, a small crowd of young people gathered. They were clearly people on the cutting edge of culture – these were small, punk rock shows, in bars and bunkers, advertised through word of mouth or badly photocopied flyers. They were very obviously ravenous for innovative sounds and new ideas, and the central, primal power of music was visibly changing their lives in real time. The atmosphere at some of the shows made

A crowd of punks in Shanghai

me think of what it must have been like to be at CBGBs in the mid 1970s, or at the Cavern Club in the early 1960s – not because of the music I was playing, but because of the audience and their enthusiasm, with all the zeal of the recently converted.

The biggest shows of the tour were the last two, Shanghai and Beijing, the big cities with the most tuned-in crowds. I was fascinated by the other bands on the bill with me – Chinese rock and punk bands, powered by a fresh vitality that I hadn't seen in London in years – if ever. It was like they had only just figured out that *this* chord, followed by *that* chord, played fast with drums and bass underneath and yelling over the top, was the greatest feeling in the world. They were dressed in absolutely mad clothes: wild DIY fashions hacked out of something old and stale into something perfectly original and individual. It was authentic, inspiring and utterly raw.

And most of all, for me, it was humbling. Rock'n'roll music has been the passion of my adult life, my hobby, my obsession and my career. And yet I still take it for granted more often than not. China showed me up as being a careless lover, and I wanted to rectify that, in a rock'n'roll song.

Every songwriter wants to write classic, timeless songs. Unfortunately, for most of us, there's a tricky paradox at play. If you aim directly for something with universal appeal, you will almost certainly miss your target, and end up sounding cheesy and forced. It's like one of those Magic Eye pictures that irritated me through most of my adolescence; you have to not quite look at it directly, but spot it from the corner of your eye.* I'm not the one to say whether or not 'I Still Believe' is a 'classic' or not, but it's certainly one of the more enduring songs I've written. I think,

* No, I never fucking saw the sailboat.

in the event, I was so enthused by my time in China that I just poured the song out of me in the most natural way.

Lyrically, the song begins with a town crier: 'hear ye!' That was very much in the spirit of the English songs I was writing for this album, even if, in terms of subject matter, this song doesn't really fit that theme. Still, I enjoyed the historical clash within that imagery, and it felt like a strong and important opening call to arms.* From there, why not borrow some Shakespeare, and extend Mark Antony's prospective audience, in the idiom of Joe Strummer? And then, of course, lay out the places where we might all meet. Incidentally, once I started playing arena shows, various people snidely read back the lyric about 'corporate circus tops' to me, as if that was some kind of 'Gotcha!' moment about me selling out. Rather obviously, that doesn't make any sense; clearly, it's a list of the type of places I was playing shows *at the time the song was written.* The circus top I had in mind was the second stage at Reading Festival, for the record.

And so we reach a chorus, and a simple, direct statement of ideological intent. In fact, an earlier draft of the song had a different line at the end of the chorus. Rather awkwardly, instead of singing 'Who'd have thought that, after all, it was rock'n'roll?', I had a line about how rock'n'roll would 'help us all to glimpse the soul'. The idea of music being a medium through which one could 'glimpse the soul' (of . . . something? Life? Myself?) was a brief lyrical fixation of mine at the time. I'm glad that I revised that into one of the better chorus lyrics I've written! Never underestimate the power of redrafting.

---

* Quite a few people over the years have said that they initially thought the next lyric was 'Kanye! Kanye!', as if the song was some bizarre call-out to everyone's favourite delusional rapper. It's not, alas, though that's kind of a fun idea.

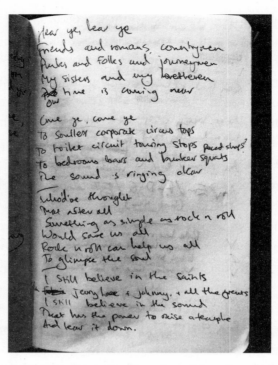

The first draft, complete with the awkward last line of the chorus

One of the criticisms that has been levelled at this song, and thus by extension at me and my art in general, is that it's overly earnest. Some people like their pop music to be laced with irony, and find sincerity to be either uncomfortable or just ridiculous. That's fine, I suppose, though it's never made much sense to me. I don't really see the point in putting all this effort into writing and playing songs if I don't actually mean the things I say (and by extension, I find it hard to engage with music that implies that it might all be one big joke). Beyond that, I'm aware that in this song I am engaging head-on with an idiom that easily verges into the territory of cliché, and that's a potentially risky move (one, incidentally, that Springsteen is adept at pulling off). In being so direct and wilfully simplistic, you find yourself walking a tightrope between sincerity and schmaltz. Opinions can differ about how successfully I negotiated that minefield – in fact, the lyric about 'minimum wage' has long been slightly uncomfortable for me, precisely because I feel it falls on the wrong side of this line – but overall, I like to think the song works because I really *did* mean what I was saying. There's more humour in the chorus lyric than I'm often given credit for – it's supposed to be slightly over-the-top, using borderline religious imagery about popular art. But the song then finishes in a sincere place, with the extended final chorus (something that was also lacking from the demo version – keep working over your songs till they're right, people!). Something as simple, small and silly as guitars, drums and desperate poetry really has saved my life, over and over again.

Musically, the song is of a piece with the arrangement of 'Eulogy' – bringing together all the influences I had been working with to date, but presenting them in a more streamlined, better-thought-out package. The driving acoustic guitar, reminiscent of Chuck Ragan and my Revival Tour days, underpinned by a driving rock beat (inspired, in part, by the work of Adam Phillips of The Architects), filled out by guitars and pianos inspired as much by The Clash as the E Street Band. Again, I had a very clear idea of how the arrangement would be structured. In order to make sure we got this one right, I actually rehearsed the parts with each member of the band separately. Starting with a drum workout with Nigel, in our rehearsal space outside Oxford, I began bolting the song together. And with each musician, I got more and more excited as the whole picture of the song started to come into view. Nigel's part was instantly exhilarating; Matt's high octaves brought the song to new heights; Tarrant's bass part was classic 'eins, fünf', pinning the whole structure together; Ben's guitar was wild and muscular. The moment we all finally came into the room together to play the song as one was truly magical.

The chord sequence and melody of the song are not complex or strikingly original ones. It stays within the parameters of the four most basic chords for the verses and choruses – C major, A minor, F and G major. The bridge of the song changes the mood and brings in some slightly more adventurous chords, not least the chromatic ascent into the harmonica solo. But I know this isn't a song that reinvents the wheel. The power lies in its simplicity and the directness of the message. The idea for a call-and-response middle-eight came from a song by the band Fake Problems, touring buddies of mine from Florida, called 'How Far Our Bodies Go', which opens with a similar part. I'd heard them play it on tour, night after night, and in time had started thinking about how to use that approach in my own style. It fit perfectly in with the imagery of the town crier from the start of the song, and it was a bold and big enough section to carry the weight of the rest of the piece forward.

In the studio with Tristan, we kept things reasonably simple. I played the guitar on the introduction so hard that you can hear my plectrum smacking against the wood on each downstroke on the finished recording. We toyed with various approaches for the backing vocals in the call-and-response section. In the end, I played the song (solo) at that year's Reading and Leeds festivals, teaching the crowd the singalong part beforehand, and we recorded the roar of the crowd for the album. I had planned to get a proper harmonica player in for the solo, doubting my talents, but in the end, Tristan encouraged me to give it a go. The one on the record was the first take – I got lucky, or else something was in the air that day.

We ended up releasing the song as the lead track of an EP (called, fittingly enough, *Rock & Roll*) before the album proper, in late 2010. Instantly it picked up steam, getting more radio play than I was used to at that time, not least in the USA, where it was even adopted as a theme tune and rallying cry by the Boston station WFNX as they fought a legal battle to continue broadcasting on air. It became a central part of the live show as we toured stateside, opening for Social Distortion, complete with a built-in lesson for the crowd so they could sing the backing vocals each night, even though they had no idea who we were. We shot a great video, directed by long-time collaborator Ben Morse, that included me getting the title tattooed on my arm by my tattooist friend Matt Hunt. By the time *England Keep My Bones* was released, it was obviously the first among a strong set of equals. And then of course there was the Olympics.

As a songwriter, I'm not quite in the position of being a one-hit wonder. Partly, that's because it would be a stretch to call any of my work a 'hit' in the conventional, chart-based sense of the word. But it's also because I've had a few songs that have carried equal water for my career, alongside this one. My setlists are not quite so one-sided and unbalanced as some bands I have known and seen play, and I'm grateful for that. Nevertheless, this will likely always be one of my biggest songs, and I couldn't be prouder of it, ultimately because, if I am to be remembered for any one song or sentiment, I'm happy that it's one that celebrates the art of rock'n'roll as a whole. To be but a small part of that tradition is more than enough legacy for me.

I AM DISAPPEARED

I keep having dreams
Of pioneers and pirate ships and Bob Dylan,
Of people wrapped up tight in the things that will kill them,
Of being trapped in a lift plunging straight to the bottom,
Of open seas and ways of life we've forgotten.
I keep having dreams.

Amy worked in a bar in Exeter.
I went back to her house and I slept beside her.
She woke up screaming in the middle of the night,
Terrified of her own insides.
Dreams of pirate ships and Patty Hearst
Breaking through a life over-rehearsed.
She can't remember which came first:
The house, the home, or the terrible thirst.
She keeps having dreams.

And on the worst days,
When it feels like life weighs ten thousand tonnes,
She's got her cowboy boots and car keys on the bedstand
So she can always run.
She can get up, shower, and in half an hour she'll be gone.

I keep having dreams of things I need to do,
Of waking up but not following through.

But it feels like I haven't slept at all,
When I wake to her silence and she's facing the wall.
Posters of Dylan and of Hemingway,
An antique compass for a sailor's escape.
She says 'you just can't live this way',
And I close my eyes and I never say:
I'm still having dreams.

And on the worst days,
When it feels like life weighs ten thousand tonnes,
I sleep with my passport,
One eye on the back door,
So I can always run.
I can get up, shower, and in half an hour I'll be gone.

And come morning,
I am disappeared,
Just an imprint on the bedsheets.
I'm by the roadside with my thumb out.
A car pulls up, and Bob's driving.
So I climb in;
We don't say a word
As we pull off into the sunrise.
And these rivers of tarmac are like arteries across the country.
We are blood cells alive in the bloodstream
Of the beating heart of the country.
We are electric pulses
In the pathways of the sleeping soul of the country.

*   *   *

I am often asked what some of my songs mean by the people who listen to them, and I've always felt it's a slightly redundant question. In my opinion, once a song (or any other piece of art) leaves the hands of its creator, it ceases to be their exclusive property. The act of creation is also the act of releasing something into the world. How it then fares, who it interacts with, how it is interpreted, is beyond the control of the artist, and that's as it should be. In fact, more often than not, I find the differing interpretations people put on my songs to be one of the most interesting parts of what I do. There's a guy in Germany I met once who has a grand conspiratorial theory that all of my songs form one over-arching narrative. It's not true, but I told him that it was, because I was intrigued to see where he would go with it.

The different angles and glosses that can be put on a piece of work don't only change and shift over time for listeners. Some of my songs evolve in my own mind – not only in the sense that they grow organically as I play them live night after night, but also in that what I think some songs 'mean' now is not the same as when I wrote them (like with 'Love Ire & Song', as mentioned). In fact, I think it's probably helpful to dispense with the idea of objective 'meaning' for songs at all. My favourite of my songs – and 'I Am Disappeared' is one of them – are ones that I struggle to sum up succinctly. Indeed, if I could say in simple prose what it is the song is trying to express, there might perhaps be no need for the song itself. After all, as Martin Mull put it, 'Writing about music is like dancing about architecture.'

I'm aware that the last paragraph strays dangerously close to invalidating the entire purpose of this book, but bear with me. As I've said, songwriting is an art and a craft. We can talk about, examine and rehearse the craft part of it. The ephemeral heart of art, the inspiration part (as opposed to the perspiration), remains somehow ineluctable, beyond the scope of language, in a way, and perhaps that's how it should be. I find that there's something joyous in knowing that some part of art can't be laid out on the dissection table. We can examine the circulation, breathing and digestion of a song, but we can't put a pin through its soul.

At some point in 2010 I had a weird dream. I had recently, on the Revival Tour, played a show in Dallas, Texas, for the first time in my life.* For whatever lurking subconscious reason, in my dream shortly afterwards I was standing on the street outside the club, trying to hitchhike. A car slowed down and pulled up next to me, and I hopefully opened the door. Sitting in the driver's seat was, of all people, Bob Dylan – the Bob from the cover shot of *Desire*, complete with cowboy hat. He sat silently across from me, smoking a cigarette. He waited for me to get in and then pulled off onto the highway and headed for the horizon. At no point did he ask where I was going, and at no point did I try to give him a destination. In fact, in the moment, it was quite disappointing, somewhat frustrating, that he wouldn't say a word to me. The overall impression the dream left on me was less romantic than it sounds here.

I woke up, and, as some dreams do, the pictures stuck with me for a few days. I started toying with various words, trying out a song that began with this image. After a few false starts, I shifted away from strictly trying to write about the dream, and just used that for a first line, a jumping-off point. I wanted to keep the vague sense of unease that had pervaded my sleep, but not be quite so literal about it. I had long felt that both the life I lead and the songs that I write are defined, in part, by a central tension in my character, between wanderlust and homesickness. I'd spend month upon month on the road, yearning to go home, and then

* The Door, 14 November 2009, show number 744, to be precise.

once I got there, I'd be climbing up the walls, desperate to escape within a week. This unresolved conflict served as the motor for a lot of my art at this time in my career, and never more so than for this song.

Once I'd managed to harness my initial word picture to this inner sense of dislocation, the lyrics and the symbolism of this song came together quickly, naturally. I couldn't really meaningfully pull apart why it is I mentioned falling lifts, antique compasses, Patty Hearst, car keys or Hemingway posters (I did have a Dylan poster at the time).* The sleepwalker feeling had kicked in again, as it does at the best of times, and before long I had a draft of a set of words that went as far as the end of the second chorus of the finished version. I was pleased as Punch with the poetry I had down on paper, and decided that, however this song was to sit, musically, it had to be special.

It's probably worth a brief detour here to talk about the 'Amy' character mentioned in this song. I'd used the name in the song 'Reasons Not to Be an Idiot' a few records previously. That had been a reference to someone I know (not, to be clear, called Amy) who had been slightly winding me up at the time with her addiction to melodrama. My relationship with that person expanded over time, in a slightly doomed way, and became passingly romantic. She did spend some time in Exeter, and she did work in a bar from time to time, but I'm not sure she did both at the same time. After a while her character in song, such as it is, became composite to a degree, and elements of other people I know started bleeding in to the picture. So it's probably not quite true to say that 'Amy' is one real individual, but it's also not quite

---

* Also, a rarely spotted reference – the line about life weighing 10,000 tons is a slight nod to the opening line of the Weakerthans song 'Everything Must Go!'

accurate to say she's not, either. Hopefully that clears all that up? In seriousness, I suppose here she stands for something or someone unrequited, unsettled, and perhaps as a bad choice of partner (or crutch) for me, if I was feeling the same way.*

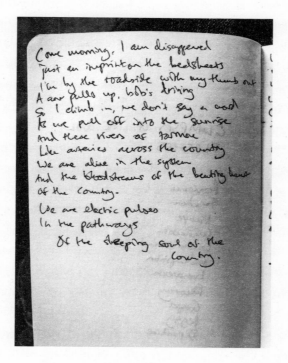

The first attempt at the new end-piece for 'I Am Disappeared'

Anyway, back to the music. I had been toying with a guitar figure that was a variation around the middle and top end of my favourite chord, C major. Every guitar player has a favourite chord, and that's mine. What I was enjoying was that, if you picked your way through the highest four strings of the chord,

---

* She was to surface for a final and unhappy time in the song 'Telltale Signs'. I'm done with writing about her now.

it was implied that you were playing a C, but you could in fact be playing an A minor 7 chord. Dropping in the open A string underneath was like a reveal, showing that a pattern that had sounded major key was in fact minor, brooding and sad rather than optimistic. Reasonably soon I started working this melody with a syncopated rhythmic pattern. It's that pattern I'd used before, stressing beats one, four and seven in a bar of eight, on songs like 'I Knew Prufrock Before He Got Famous' and 'Our Lady of the Campfire' (the latter song arguably stands as a less successful trial run for this one, in retrospect). Usually, I'd either play the rhythm with all downstrokes in my right hand, or with an alternating up-and-down pattern that emphasised the stresses as required. Lately, though, I'd worked out a more complicated strumming pattern that really drove the feel of the part home by making all the stressed beats into downstrokes, which then requires some deft alternating work between strums. It took a while to nail it, but once I did, it became second nature. All those years of practising thrash guitar parts as a kid, with their manic right-hand complexity, were paying off. Thanks, James Hetfield.

So, before long I had the first couple of verses worked out. Based around the staggered rhythm, beginning with the major feel, and then dropping the A bass note to take the song into minor territory. Very early on, while I was messing around with this guitar part, Nigel suggested offsetting the guitar pattern with a straight, four-on-the-floor kick drum from the start of the song. Not only was that a pleasing contrast that took this piece away from copying previous ideas of mine, but it also brought in a weirdly electronic, dance influence to the song, in line with stuff like The Postal Service, a band I have long adored. To emphasise that angle on the song, I had Ben using an EBow on his guitar to create a synth-like drone, and could even hear a rolling timpani sample across the start of each phrase (an idea I'm reasonably sure I borrowed from a track by The Streets).

The song was now, as they say, cooking with gas. I had a slight dilemma though. Traditionally, a song will lift into its chorus. But by the time I'd got through these first two verses, the energy level of the tune was already quite high. I was in danger of leaving myself no room to progress. I remember playing that first couple of verses around and around on a guitar to myself backstage at a club called Tavastia in Helsinki, when finally the obvious idea struck – to take the choruses *down* instead of up, accompanied only by Matt's floating lead piano melody. That left space for the arrangement to evolve in the second verse, with Ben's brilliant aching guitar line and Nigel's steadily evolving beat, before finally peaking with the more traditional rock impact of the second chorus, complete with washed-out cymbals and roaring power chords.

At this point, I hit something of an impasse. The verses and choruses felt so strong to me, that I was unable to come up with a standard bridge that would, in usual song structuring, take us back into a reprised final chorus. That standard approach felt redundant, too normal and boring for the material I was working with. So my first attempt to finish the song involved a simple play-out after the second chorus, using the same rhythm but new chords and melody, with a repeated (and slightly lame) lyric of 'as long as I can fall asleep'. There's even a video of me playing the song with this ending at a show in a club somewhere in Los Angeles on the internet. It was something of a damp squib, and I knew it. So I set about trying to find a finale worthy of the first half of the song.

Given that I felt that a customary composition was not the right approach, the way was open to throw in something completely different, to dispense with the idea of resolution. As

I've already admitted, I'm often quite conventional in my writing, but from time to time I throw caution to the wind. The other thought that occurred was that I had left the initial vision of the song, being in a car with Bob, far behind; in fact, it had barely featured in the lyrics at all, despite being the starting point. So I decided to try a gear shift for the last section of the song. A new melody, a new rhythmic feel,* even a new (slightly faster) tempo. Before long, I had a section that had a similar feeling of build, of a car speeding up as it pulled out of a city, as the first half. So in a funny way it is a reprise of the beginning of the song, but only in terms of narrative arc.

The coup de grâce of the song was the final image. It came in something of a stream-of-consciousness writing moment. The idea of me, as a traveller, passing through the tarmac arteries of England as I went from town to town, spreading my songs throughout the organism, felt like the perfect conclusion of this hymn to feeling trapped. And perhaps not just me – perhaps with Ben, Nigel, Matt and Tarrant as well. I had long wanted the boys to have a band name of their own, so that people would know who they were, that I was playing with the same people each night and on each record. I actually tried not to influence their choice of name, but I was extremely happy when someone suggested The Sleeping Souls, from this song. It was exactly the right moniker for them.

As the Souls and I expanded the circle of our international wanderings, and became more successful, our methodologies similarly developed. Around this time, we were able to actually properly demo the new material we'd been working on for the first time. In retrospect it seems crazy to me that we never did that before,

---

* Vaguely based on the feel of the Radiohead song 'Weird Fishes'.

but it makes some sense. On the first two albums it had been mainly me constructing the arrangements in the studio. On *Poetry of the Deed* we had rushed through the process of arrangement in one short burst. This time around we had the time and the money to actually demo the songs properly, like real, grown-up bands do. One day on tour we passed through El Paso, Texas, where my Revival Tour friend Jim Ward, of At the Drive-In and Sparta, has a recording studio. We loaded in on our precious day off and hammered out what material we had already worked out.

Listening back to the demo of 'I Am Disappeared'* now is fascinating for me (God, I'm so interesting, sexy and cool; endless fun at parties). The basic structure of the song is in place, and the central building blocks of the arrangement are likewise present and correct. But there are a host of small changes that were made between that session and being in Crouch End with Tristan, all for the better. The drum part in the second verse is better thought-out, the backing vocal arrangement at the end was added later, and so on. To have the ability to be able to sketch out a song you're working on, walk away from it for a time, and come back with fresh ears, is a privilege, of course. But it can also be hugely important for refining and perfecting your material. Herein lies the difference, arguably, between my third and fourth records. I'm extremely grateful, and relieved, that we had the chance to do that for this album. 'I Am Disappeared' would not have been the same song without that.

As *England Keep My Bones* was released, we used this song as the initial 'leak track' for the promotional campaign. We put the song up on the internet before any of the other material was available (with the exception of 'I Still Believe'). It seemed to land

* Titled, at the time, 'Bob Dylan'. The actual title came right at the end, and I have always loved its slightly archaic grammar.

with people instantly, and has long been one of the 'fan favourites' in my catalogue. Over time, it's also the song I've experimented with the most in a live setting. There have been slow, finger-picked solo versions, a cappella introductions, added rock outros and the like. I suspect that's a (positive) reflection of the fact that on some level, like the song itself says, I remain unsettled about this piece of work. And as I said before, I think that's a sign of its essential strength.

ONE FOOT BEFORE
THE OTHER

On the very day I die, the very last of my desires
Is that you take my broken body and commit it to the fire,
And then when the fire is finished, scrape the ashes in a tin,
Take them down to London's drinking reservoirs and throw them in,
And then specks infinitesimal of my mortal remains
Will slide down 7 million throats and into 7 million veins,
And I will creep through their capillaries to the marrow of their bones,
And they will wake to bright new mornings and then wordlessly they'll know

That I remain;
I am remembered.

So these 7 million innocents, they will have me in their blood,
And when they die they'll burn their bodies or be buried in the mud,
And I will spread through streams and rivers like a virus through a host,
From the hamlets to the cities, from the rivers to the coast,
And from there into the channel across the great Atlantic Ocean,
And ever onwards to the new world through the water's gentle motion,
Until parts of me are part of every land mass, every sea,
In the rain upon your crops and in the very air you breathe.

I remain;
I am remembered.

And though the things I love will be washed away in the rain,
I remain.

I'm not convinced of the existence of these things that don't exist,
By Jewish boys with big ideas and scratches on their wrists,
By a loving or a vengeful God or one who condescends
To wash his hands down in the mire among the misery of men,
Or by ever turning circles hanging timeless in the sky,
Like a dream catcher distracting from the fact you're going to die.
But I place one foot before the other, confident because
I know that everything we are right now is everything that was,
That Wat Tyler, Woody Guthrie, Dostoevsky and Davy Jones
Have all dissolved into the ether and have crept into my bones,
And all the cells in all the lines upon the backs of both my hands
Were once carved into the details of two feet upon the sand.

So we remain
We are remembered
And though the things we love will be washed away in the rain,
We remain.

* * *

England Keep My Bones was my fourth record as a solo artist. The distance between me and my musical past was steadily increasing. In the early days of making music on my own, I had been at pains to put clear water between myself and Million Dead and the scene we'd come from. Partly this was a kind of psychological self-defence; I needed to create something new and artistically distinct, to define myself as an individual. I didn't want to spend my life having 'ex-Million Dead' written under my name on show flyers. Also, I'd made a reasonably extreme stylistic left-hand turn in the transition to releasing music under my own name. I wanted to make that step a credible one, to engage properly with the new genres I was exploring. There have been more than a few solo ventures from heavier bands which have ended up producing the exact same style of songs, just with less drums, and I didn't want to fall into that trap.

All of this meant that I had often taken stylistic decisions in my writing that, whether consciously or not, had steered me away from anything too close to the music of my old band. I had veered away from doing anything too heavy, too riff-driven. But now I'd reached a point where I was working on my fourth record alone, whereas Million Dead had only ever made two. We'd been a band for four years, in total, but now I'd been a solo artist for five. Slowly, I allowed myself to drop my guard. I didn't need to spend any more time defining myself defensively, in terms of what I wasn't. I made a decision to allow any and all musical impulses into my work, with equal weight. It was my name on the masthead, so I could make whatever sounds I wanted to.

So it was that I found myself cautiously exploring the idea of a song that would be considerably heavier than anything on the preceding three records. This venture wasn't just some abstract conceptual project. It was prompted by the arrival of two ideas that suggested moving in that direction, one musical and one lyrical.

The first idea had come to me when I was raiding the back of the cupboard of musical ideas to see what might be lying around. At one point, towards the end of the band, Million Dead had worked up a song that we never recorded. The words I eventually salvaged and put towards a different set of chords, which emerged as the song 'Carthago Est Delenda' from our second album, *Harmony No Harmony*. The music that was then left on the scrapheap included a guitar riff of mine that I'd never quite forgotten. It was a high, plaintive piece, using a sliding diad chord shape on the A and B strings, with a ringing open G in between, shifting down from a root G minor chord to a C minor. Often, when allowing my fingers to vacantly wander across the fretboard, they'd land in those same positions. While we'd had a collective ethos with regard to writing in my old band, this was a riff that I had contributed on my own and which had never been properly used, so I didn't have any qualms about repurposing it now.

The second point of origin for the song was a bizarre set of words I had in one of my lyric notebooks. In the summer of 2009 I'd spent a few weeks staying at my friend Joe's apartment in Williamsburg, New York, while we recorded the vocals for the album *Poetry of the Deed* in Alex Newport's nearby studio in Greenpoint. The walk from the studio back home took about forty minutes. It was a burning hot New York summer, so more often than not, at the end of a long working day, I'd take my time strolling back through the city to my bed. One night, on an evening whose heat was especially oppressive, even ominous, I'd begun idly kicking a few words around in my head at the start of my walk. By the time I got back to where I was staying, I had dreamed up an entire poem. I kept going back to the start and reciting it to myself again every few minutes, to make sure I hadn't forgotten anything, as I didn't have a pen or paper on me. That kind of pure inspiration comes to me only rarely, so when I got back into the flat I ran to my bag to get my notebook and furiously scribbled down everything I could.

The poem that I looked back over the next morning felt very different to me. The voice that sounds out felt like a side of my character that I hadn't allowed to the forefront since my days in Million Dead. The language and the feel is archaic, almost biblical. The tone, in contrast to the confessional style I habitually used in my solo work, felt prophetic, bombastic.* There were traces of Nick Cave, Leonard Cohen, perhaps even the King James Bible. I was still as captivated by it in the cold light of day as I had been on the hurry home, but for the time being I wasn't entirely sure what to do with it.

In time these two ideas started to gravitate towards each other, drawn together as much by their shared misfit quality as anything else. Musically, I built up from the initial idea by using more doom-laden harmonic minor tones, unusual in my canon, such as the flattened seventh in the C minor chord in the verse (that means adding a discordant note of A, to the layman like me). Lyrically I allowed the words to go yet further off-reservation, bringing in some higher-brow literary references – from the Apocrypha, Shelley, and *Blade Runner* – alongside farming metaphors and an esoteric list of historical and fictional figures, that started out as a kind of fantasy dinner party guest list, and ended up as a roll-call of personalities I'd merge with in the fanciful afterlife of the song. Before long the two streams had become one raging creative torrent.

The subject matter of the piece was grandiose and ambitious, but also bled out into other ideas I was working with across the putative album. This song nodded towards the imagery of another from that album, 'Rivers', landmasses defined by their internal and external waterways, but took a much darker angle on that idea. Similarly, the song attempts to describe an atheistic worldview; I'd address that subject matter much more directly on 'Glory Hallelujah', but here it forms part of a more oblique answer to one of the eternal philosophical questions. If there is no afterlife, no God, then

* I had briefly dipped my toe into these poetic waters on 'Journey of the Magi' – another example of me prefiguring a big idea on one record with a relevant experiment on its predecessor.

what's the point? The answer offered here was inspired by an idea I'd had years before, when, as a teenager recently arrived in London, I'd filled my unemployed days wandering around the fringes and wastelands of the metropolis. In the north-east of the city, the area I've long called home, there is a long strip of drinking water reservoirs, stretching up from Clapton to Enfield. They have a timeless, barren feel to them, a weird pause in the urban landscape, somehow devoid of peace or comfort. As a frustrated kid, I'd fantasised about making my mark on London by sneaking my ashes into their water pipes. Now, in the song, the idea became a touch less bitter, and drew more on the rhetoric of Carl Sagan, recognising the inherent interconnectedness of a world in which particles and energy are eternally passed on.

It's been noted by many that on this album I list several different ways in which I'd like my remains to be disposed of in the event of my death – dropped into reservoirs, floating in the sea around the British Isles and so on. It's safe to say I had something of a fixation with the idea of mortality at the time. Not so much in the sense of being scared of death per se, more just that I found the fact of our inescapable ending both fascinating and extremely motivating. If we're going to die, well, get the fuck on with it, do something worthwhile with the limited time we've been granted! But to settle the argument, for the prospective executors of my will: I think the reservoir plan, in this song, is easily the coolest. Let's hope it's not for a while yet.

I took the component parts of the song to The Sleeping Souls, as was now becoming standard practice, and we began hammering out the details. We recorded a demo in El Paso, which enabled me to tweak some parts, not least the vocal melody in the verses. In the demo version it's slightly directionless, and reaches its peak of energy and plateaus far too early. In the finished version I was able to rewrite it so that the ascent is steady throughout the duration. The bridge part, which had originally been played on guitar, ended up metastasising into a dark and distorted keyboard line. This was an early example of an approach I'd use much more in the future: decoupling the central drive of the music from my acoustic guitar part. A regular right-hand strumming pattern doesn't always have to lead the ensemble. Nigel's drums were a masterclass in controlled chaos, driving yet unpredictable. Ben's guitar work played to his strengths, unleashing an uncomfortable and threatening lead across the song. Finally, we added some bells and whistles – a scratch across the exposed strings of a piano at the start of the bridge, a bass dive-bomb sample in the drop into the denouement of the song.

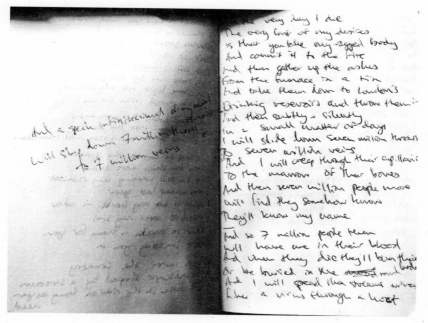

My notebook after the long walk home from Greenpoint

The lyrics, I'm pleased to say, didn't change much at all from the original late-night drafts. The only notable addition was a small but significant change in the final chorus. For most of the song, the defiant refrain is the idea that 'I remain, I am remembered'. But once we've been through the valley of the shadow of the bridge of the song, we land somewhere subtly but importantly different. Despite the pervading sense of darkness through the song, overall I regard it as an optimistic piece in its way. In the final analysis, 'we remain'. Collectively, the world will continue, and some residue of our existence will be contained within it.

GLORY HALLELUJAH

Brothers and sisters, have you heard the news?
The storm has lifted and there's nothing to lose,
So swap your confirmation for your dancing shoes,
Because there never was no God.
Step out of the darkness and onto the streets,
Forget about the fast, let's have a carnival feast,
Raise up your lowered head to hear the liberation beat,
Because there never was no God.

There is no God,
So clap your hands together,
There is no God,
No heaven and no hell.
There is no God,
We're all in this together,
There is no God,
So ring that victory bell.

No cowering in the dark before some overbearing priest,
No waiting until we die until we restitute the meek,
No blaming all our failings on imaginary beasts,
Because there never was no God.
No fighting over land your distant fathers told you of,
No spilling blood for those who have never spread a drop of blood,

No finger pointing justified by phantoms up above,
Because there never was no God.

And I know you're scared of dying man and I am too,
But just pretending it's not happening isn't going to see us through,
And if we accept that there's an end game and we haven't got much time,
Then in the here and now we can try and do things right.
We'd be our own Salvation Army, and together we'd believe
In all the wondrous things that mere mortals can achieve.

Because I've known beauty in the stillness of cathedrals in the day,
I've sung 'Glory Hallelujah! Won't you wash my sins away?'
But now we're singing my refrain and this is what I say,
I say there never was no God.

* * *

As well as being one of the most important inspirations in the formative years of my solo career, Jay has long been a friend, a touring partner, and an occasional sounding board. Being a solo artist can occasionally be a lonely furrow to plough. One of the benefits of the camaraderie of an egalitarian band set-up is that there are inbuilt walls to bounce ideas off. If you're out there on your own as a writer, you have to find people whose opinions you trust to serve that function. The obvious candidates for that for me are, of course, The Sleeping Souls, but that's not quite as simple as it might seem, as I'm usually working through arrangements with them as well, which is a different angle on the material. I have a small list of people who get to hear unfinished demos and half-formed ideas, people who I know will give it to me straight. Jay is one of those people.

Jay has come with me on many tours over the years as an

opening act; he does a great job of warming up the crowd, and we all love having him around, to the extent that more often than not he bunks on my tour bus. Somewhere on the road, sometime in (at a guess) 2009, I was up late in the back lounge one evening, playing Jay through some snippets of music and words that I had lying around and had yet to turn into complete songs.

One of the passages I played him that night was a deliberately provocative chorus, as yet in search of a song to go with it. The chords and the melody were self-consciously modelled on the tropes of American gospel and country music – specifically a Townes Van Zandt song called 'Two Girls' – but twisting the lyrics around into a brazen atheist anthem. I lay back on the sofa and drunkenly picked my way through the guitar part, softly murmuring, 'There is no God, so clap your hands together . . .'

The atmosphere in the room suddenly changed as Jay reacted to the music. In truth, while I liked what I had so far, I hadn't really worked on it with any sense of purpose since coming up with it. It seemed perhaps a little overly sardonic to me, a touch obvious maybe. Jay, on the other hand, was completely fired up by what he heard. We talked it over for quite a while, and alcohol has blurred the details of my memory, but I distinctly remember him saying, 'You have to finish this song – not to do so would be cowardice.' With those words ringing in my ears, I set about making the snippet into a song.

In truth, part of the reason this little idea had stayed on the unfinished pile for so long had to do with my grandfather. My mother's father was a man of God – a priest, and even, towards the end of his life, a bishop in the Church of England. He was a dominant figure in my family growing up. My mother is predictably religious as well, and I was raised going to church often, both at home and at school. My grandfather, Richard Fox

Cartwright, was a kind, wise and decent man, but he also carried himself with gravitas and heavily implied moral weight. The idea of writing an explicitly atheist song was one that I had been reluctant to complete, at least in part because I respected his life's work (and didn't want to get into an argument with him, or, God forbid, my mother, while he was still alive). In the end, he passed away peacefully, aged ninety-six, in 2009. I didn't think about it in such concrete or calculating terms, but thereafter the way was clearer for me to write this song.

On the subject of atheism . . . I was raised in the traditions of the Church of England, as you might expect, given my family background. In my early teens, I combined the natural curiosity and defiance of adolescence with a taste in metal and punk music. My initial rejection of religion was a bratty one, inspired by Bad Religion, Slayer and, if I'm honest, Marilyn Manson. Over the next few years, I wavered a little on the subject. My obsession with T. S. Eliot, who extravagantly embraced High Church Anglicanism midway through his life, made me re-examine my ideas about God. I found out that some of the bands I loved (such as Mineral) were Christians. It wasn't a simple process, arriving at a conclusion on such a grand subject. In the end, I reached a place where I'm happy and secure in calling myself an atheist. It strikes me that the burden of proof is firmly on anyone who posits anything beyond the world we see and experience – and that natural world is plenty super enough, properly understood.

While part of what brought me to this conclusion was the books of the new atheist writers, I've never been fully comfortable aligning myself with people like Richard Dawkins. There's a smug cruelty to their arguments in places that seems vindictive at times, and I find that as distasteful as I do the furious rejectionism of bands like Deicide. After all, any thinking person engaging with

Western culture must necessarily immerse themselves in the Bible and the traditions of Christianity – most art would be unintelligible without that. And there are strong arguments to be made that our liberal social values are entirely based on the precepts of the gospels, no matter how allegorical we might now consider them to be. More than anything, I find the angry, irritable, pessimistic tone of most public atheism to be pretty grating. The only song I could think of which addressed these issues in a more measured way was 'Heads Roll Off' by Frightened Rabbit, a band I was in the middle of falling in love with at the time.*

So when I came to write a song on the subject, my choice of style – a pastiche of American gospel music – wasn't just a case of sarcastic parody. I love gospel, I love the unalloyed sense of joy in the face of adversity that underpins it, and I wanted to employ that tone in my own discussion of religion and atheism. I find the idea of a godless universe to be liberating,† and I wanted to highlight that, while also keeping the message open and accepting of other people's ideas. I knew, from the start, that it would be a narrow tightrope to walk, rhetorically. But, as Jay had said, I had a duty to finish the song and say my piece on the subject as best I could.

There's a band I should have mentioned in discussing this period of my songwriting and haven't, yet. So let's get MewithoutYou into the discussion. Every artist goes through cycles of fecundity and writer's block. More often than not, the thing that pulls me through a moment of low inspiration is just stumbling across a

---

* A song that has become infinitely more poignant since Scott's tragic suicide in 2018. I miss that man every day.

† The line in the song about a 'liberation beat' is a nod to my favourite hardcore band, Refused, fact fans.

new writer, a new band, a new voice, something that blows the sand out of my eyes (ears?) and allows me to see (hear?), once again, the endless horizons of possibility in music. At a moment in 2010 or so, when I had been feeling drained and spent as a writer, I came across an album called *It's All Crazy! It's All False! It's All a Dream! It's Alright*, by a band called MewithoutYou.

I'd been vaguely aware of their work for a while, as a lyrically literate post-hardcore band, but for whatever reason, the songs I'd heard hadn't grabbed me, and I'd never really delved deep into their back catalogue. *It's All Crazy . . .* is their fourth record, and was a significant stylistic departure for the band. It's an album of folk rock mysticism, allegorical songs about animals, hymns and parables about life, meaning and God. Both the music and the lyrics completely blew me away. There was an inventive simplicity to the arrangements, while the words were poetically ambitious in a way I've rarely heard before or since within the confines of popular music. I was (and am) so revitalised by the album that I ended up tattooing the backs of my hands with a fox and a crow, in tribute to the second tune, 'The Fox, the Crow and the Cookie'. It remains one of my all-time favourites.

The album is explicitly religious, drawing on the ideas of a Sufi mystic called Bawa Muhaiyaddeen. It might sound odd to say that a religious album inspired an atheist song, but again, I was trying to repurpose the language and forms of belief to talk about my own disbelief. The whole record made a deep impact on my songwriting on *England Keep My Bones*, but in particular I was inspired by the last song, 'Allah, Allah, Allah'. There was a joyous, hymnal quality to the song, and I also liked the fact that the record finished on such an energetic, euphoric note. My previous records had tended to end on a downer. This time around, I wanted to finish with a different feel. So 'Glory Hallelujah' came together as an end-piece. In the studio, Matt even suggested reprising the melody of 'Eulogy' on the piano over the fade out, to give the record a sense of completion.

One of the other points of interest about the recorded version of the song is the centrality of Matt's parts, first on a church organ and then on honky-tonk piano. This was a further step down the road of trying to break away from my tendency to drive every arrangement with my acoustic guitar part (as well as being an idea that sounded good for the song, of course). On the recording, my guitar is actually panned out to the right for most of the song, altering the spatial layout of the band from that sports team idea into something more interesting.

And then there's the gospel choir arrangement. In keeping with the stylistic conceit of the song, I wanted to employ the classic sound of an ensemble of voices in a broad harmony part. Actually putting that together in a studio is easier said than done, as I discovered. The limitations of budgetary constraints meant that I wasn't able to simply hire an actual gospel choir; I had to try to put one together using friends who I knew could sing, and then work out the breakdown of the different parts myself. On the day itself, I stood in the main room of the aptly named Church Studios on a podium in front of a line of singers, and did my best to explain and conduct the choral arrangement. It was a huge challenge for my untutored musical abilities, but we got through it OK, and I'm pleased with the end result.*

There was a moment when I questioned the merits of including the choral part. That was because I was worried about any part of the song coming across as sarcastic or superior. Obviously, a religious person hearing the song would naturally disagree with the lyrics, but I didn't want that person to feel that they were

* Though having now worked with actual gospel singers, on 'Brave Face', I can appreciate how amazing the real thing is.

being sneered at. I wanted it to be my own positive contribution to the debate, and for it to retain its sense of optimism. I wondered whether a gospel part would undercut that. I'm glad that I went ahead with it – it sounds great and it's an integral part of the song – but, despite the many hours I spent revising the words to this song, there are still some moments in the finished version that occasionally prick my conscience. The line about 'some over-bearing priest' falls into that category (an early draft used the word 'illiterate', which was too much, as well as being historically unlikely). The ringing of a 'victory bell' at the end of the chorus seems a bit vindictive, in retrospect. And there was a draft of the song that included a background shout of 'Judas Priest in all his glory!' On its own I still think that's pretty funny, but I'm glad we cut it from the finished take.

One line that I didn't question was the idea that 'we [could] be our own Salvation Army'. I love the image – so much so that I actually floated the phrase 'Salvation Army' as a title for the entire album. I later found out that, sadly, there was a high chance of the organisation complaining about this and blocking me from using it, so the idea was dropped – which felt a bit un-Christian to me, somehow (but fair enough, I suppose, given the thrust of the lyrics).*

I knew, before it was released, that the song was provocative, and would probably evoke some critical reactions from some quarters. There is a place for provocation in art, I think, and I was fore-warned and ready for whatever would be coming my way. Even

* The actual album title, a quote from the lesser-known Shakespeare play *King John*, was suggested at the eleventh hour by my friend Ben Morse. I'd been through about a hundred other suggestions in the meantime, of varying quality.

so, the afterlife (sic) of this song over the years has thrown up some interesting situations and conversations.

The first memorable encounter I had was at a signing session in a record store somewhere in the USA shortly after the album was released. A couple reached the front of the queue and lifted their child, maybe four years old, onto the counter. The boy was initially bashful, but, after some coaxing from his folks, cheerily volunteered a chorus of the song: 'There is no God!' I laughed, a touch awkwardly, and thought to myself, holy shit, I'd better be right about this one, otherwise I'm in serious trouble.

A few years later, in Norfolk, Virginia, the song earned me an important rite of passage for any musician who grew up listening to bands like Black Sabbath and Iron Maiden. After soundcheck that day, I was relaxing with a book, when I received a text from Nigel, who'd left the venue to find some food. It simply said: 'Come outside, immediately, you won't regret it.' I duly obeyed his command, and was overjoyed to encounter two men staging a (very small) religious picket against my show. The louder of the two was holding a big sign with a picture of Jesus and some Bible verses, and was chanting a litany of allegations about me: 'Frank Turner is Antichrist! He's a false prophet! Do not trust him!' My personal favourite was an aside – 'Souls don't sleep, souls burn in hell!' The other guy was handing out evangelical pamphlets. I had my picture taken with them both (they had no idea who I was) and beamed with pride.

Beyond those two, I've had many other conversations with people over the years about the song. For the most part they've been good-humoured, or at least intelligent. Contrary to what a lot of my friends had thought, America, including the South, has generally been fine with the song. I've had much more grief back home (though, of course, that may reflect the different natures of my audiences on either side of the pond). Some people have politely asked me not to play it, or pointed out that it might be seen to go against the welcoming, collectivist ethos I try to inculcate at my shows. On the other hand, some religious people have taken the point I was trying to make and have found ways to enjoy it. My proudest moment for the song was at my first arena headline show at Wembley in 2012. Billy Bragg told me afterwards that he'd been filled with joy and admiration to see me leading a room of 12,000 people singing 'There is no God' together in song. I thanked him for the sentiment (and felt immensely flattered), but if I had to pick a line from the song to linger on in that context, I'd choose 'We're all in this together'. Regardless whether I'm right or wrong about religion, that seems like a sentiment worth singing about.

With my new protesting friends in Norfolk, Virginia, USA

BALTHAZAR, IMPRESARIO

My name is Balthazar, Impresario,
And you'll find me at the bottom of the page.
I have artist's hands, though I'm a working man,
But my craft has been forgotten by the age,
So tonight will be my last night on the stage.

This is my family's trade, my father built this place
At the turning of the twentieth century.
I have been working here for some fifty years,
But the young these days are glued to TV screens,
And the old girl is dying on her feet.

My friends from theatre school all thought I was a fool
For leaving Shakespeare for the music hall,
And now my son's left home and set out on his own,
And the critics think we're quaint but set to fall.
But they've only seen the show from the stalls.

Once more to the boards,
One more curtain call.
Give the crowd everything they're asking for and more.
Always make them laugh,
Try to make them cry,
Always take the stage like it's the last night of your life.

And all the things I've seen behind these tattered scenes,
And all the upturned faces with the lamplight in their eyes,
And each imperfect turn flickers as it burns,
Only lasts a moment, but for me they'll never die.

We are respected,
But we're not remembered.
We are the ghosts of Vaudeville,
Unnumbered.
We are the fathers of the halls,
But we will never be famous.
We aren't just artists, we are something more:
We're entertainers.

I smooth my thinning hair in a gilded mirror
To try to hide the tell-signs of my age.
My name is Balthazar, Impresario,
And tonight will be my last night on the stage.

*   *   *

There are various stock interview questions which, if you're someone who does a lot of interviews, you're certain to encounter from time to time. One such is this: 'Do you have any regrets?' And the stereotypical punk rock answer expected is to say something along the lines of 'Hell no! No apologies, no looking back!' That's always struck me as especially asinine. Any thinking, engaged adult, who has attempted to do anything of note with their life, is going to have put their foot wrong from time to time. I know I have; there's a long litany I could recite of moments where I could have made a better call. Before this paragraph becomes overly remorseful or psychoanalytical, I should hasten to specify what I'm talking about: 'Balthazar, Impresario' should not have been a B-side.

For every record I've ever made I've had more songs than I've needed for the normal running length of an album. And call me a traditionalist if you will, but I do still believe in the album as an artistic format – a collection of songs that runs to around forty to fifty minutes of music, and which has an internal coherence, a thread running through it. For example, while I emphatically don't usually write concept albums, in the case of *England Keep My Bones*, I was able to pick a suite of songs from the material available that had a contiguous feel. The end result was an album that is, in essence, about national identity (and mortality). I didn't set out to write a record like that – I try to let songs come in the manner and timing of their own choosing – but the end result feels satisfyingly complete, to my ears.

All the same, I don't always get this call completely right. There are a few track-listing choices in my past that I'd probably do differently now, none more so than the case in point here. I cannot now, for the life of me, remember why it made sense to me to leave this song off the album. It was one of the earlier songs I wrote in this period, I genuinely feel it's one of the stronger songs I ever wrote, and, thematically, it fits right in to the mood I was seeking for the album as a whole. In fact, one of the earliest contenders for an album title was *Ghosts of Vaudeville*, a line from this song, which would of course have necessitated it being on the actual album. Looking back it seems like a bizarre lapse of judgement on my part. The song is out there, I suppose, and people can happily listen to it in this modern world of streaming and playlisting. All the same, I want to write about it here, thus hopefully setting the record a little straighter.

*

As a kid, dreaming about being in a band, my heroes included Iron Maiden, Nirvana, and latterly Black Flag. I wanted to be one of that rare and weird breed I read about in (maga)zines – a touring musician. Genuinely, the glitz and glamour of being a 'rock star' never much troubled my imagination. I just wanted to be someone who lived for music, for the road, who wasn't tethered to any 'normal' existence, but who was always on the move, always playing.

By this point in my life, I had arguably attained that goal. In so doing, I'd expanded my understanding and knowledge of the history of my trade, learning about how rock'n'roll touring had developed over the years, the links to the worlds of blues and jazz, folk and ragtime. I had also, as mentioned, begun investigating folk music in the proper sense of the word, learning traditional songs. In investigating all of this, my own sense of identity shifted subtly. Increasingly, I found little to connect with in the image of the pampered, aloof 'star', referring to themselves incessantly as 'artist(e)s'. The aristocratic remove from the audience stuck in my craw, raised as I was on the radical iconoclasm of punk rock, which taught me, as it were, that there was no such thing as a 'rock star'. The thing I grew to respect was dedication to the craft, of playing music well, night after night, around the world, being part of an international infrastructure that facilitated this kind of art existing on an underground level. In a way, I guess I can own up to wanting to be part of something that felt honestly blue collar (something entirely lacking from the social background I was raised in).

The word 'entertainer' is one that is often viewed with disdain from the lofty heights of stardom. I've seen plenty of bands over the years insist that they're above such a workaday description; they're something more noble, more upper class than that, thanks very much. By contrast, the older I get, the more the word 'entertainer' seems like the best description of me, not only in terms of what I do now, but in terms of my ambition. From a sociological point of view, it is exactly what I do. At the end of a working week, people with more down-to-earth, productive jobs need a moment to have the weight of the world lifted from their shoulders for a few hours. That's the role I play, and it's one I'm proud of. To describe myself as an entertainer, then, is not only accurate (I spend the vast majority of my working life actually on a stage trying to elicit a response from a crowd) but also appropriately humble. I'm not a nurse or a teacher or anything vital like that. I serve a social purpose in entertaining people, and I'm satisfied with that.

The other advantage of using the term to describe myself is that it immediately places me in a broader historical tradition, one that includes not only rock and folk musicians, but also jazz, blues, vaudeville, music hall, the circus, travelling players, medicine shows and more, back into the mists of time. We are all of us entertainers, and I want nothing more than to be considered as a respectable part of that roll of honour. To see entertainment in its proper social place is not to belittle it; in the moment of creation, on the stage, I believe passionately in throwing everything into my performance, of playing each show like it's the last night of my life. And, like the countless ghosts that have preceded me on the stage, and those who will come after, if I have done that, I can sleep easy.

The art form known as music hall, in particular, was haunting my thinking about all this at the time. Music hall was popular entertainment in Britain, especially London, from the mid nineteenth century through to the mid twentieth. It was a mixture of music, drama and comedy that was idiosyncratically English. It also largely predated recording technology, and is generally thought to have been difficult to translate into other formats, and so the form is largely forgotten today. Names of stars like Marie

Lloyd and Little Titch, once huge celebrities in their day, raise barely a shrug. Given the fact that these performers dedicated their lives to the stage, there seems to me to be a fundamental injustice, or at least sadness, to our modern amnesia. John Osbourne, in 1957, wrote: 'The music hall is dying, and with it, a significant part of England . . . this was truly a folk art.' I wanted to find a way to commemorate their passion, their art, ultimately their sacrifice (most of them died penniless and ignored) in a song.

Now obviously I am not a music hall performer, and the phenomenon was dead and buried generations before I was born. So if I were to write a song about this piece of history, I would have to find an approach beyond my usual autobiographical style. Before I wrote this song, I had almost entirely written in the confessional first-person singular. I just found it easier to channel the emotion that I feel is needed to carry a song if I drew directly from my own experience. That's not to say I have any problem with the idea of a character-based song – Springsteen is a master of the form, particularly on the album *Nebraska* – it's just something I hadn't really tried, and didn't think I'd be much good at.

Over time, I started to put together my fictional narrator. Music hall was a genre largely controlled by a series of great theatre owner-operators, known as impresarios – creatively engaged people (mostly men) who would find and foster talent, programme shows and build audiences. These behind-the-scenes moguls were the organisational heart of music hall – known as 'the fathers of the halls' – and I couldn't help imagine the wealth of knowledge they would have taken to the grave at the end of a long life treading the edges of the boards. I didn't really have any one person in mind, but I read up about people like Charles Morton and Oswald Stoll. The name Balthazar was pure creation on my part, but it felt suitably theatrical.

The final source that I drew in for this song was a speech by Joseph Grimaldi. Grimaldi was the great clown, the king of Regency-era pantomime, and arguably one of the first celebrities in the modern sense of the word. After a lifetime on stage (starting aged three and retiring at forty-eight), he'd given a farewell soliloquy at his final performance, which included these lines: 'Ladies and gentlemen, I appear before you for the last time . . . my desire and anxiety to merit your favour has excited me to more exertion than my constitution would bear, and, like vaulting ambition, I have overleaped myself.' The first time I read it, it brought tears to my eyes, as it does still.

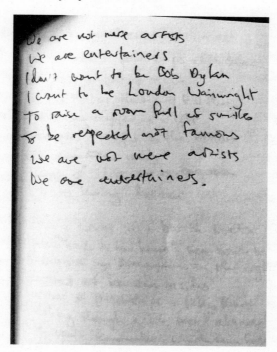

The original draft of the bridge of 'Balthazar, Impresario'

So with all this material amassed, I sat down to write the song. The music began as what I would call a 'soundcheck riff' – a motif that my fingers stumbled across of their own accord one day, and which I was in the habit of running around when testing the sound levels of my guitar before a show.* It's a reasonably standard folk pattern, though unusually for me it's in the key and shapes of D major. The guitar part includes the vocal melody, picked out as incidental notes within the root chords. The chorus opens with an unusual chord — a Dsus4, or a D major with a renegade G note in the middle of it, leaving an uncertain, unresolved feel in the ear — before descending into more normal melodic territory. After a time I had the basics of the chords and the melody laid out, and they naturally meshed with the lyrical images I was drawing from my sources.

I reached a point of playing a first, solo draft of the song around in soundchecks and dressing rooms. Unusually, Matt overheard me playing the song and joined in with a second acoustic part — I tend to back my guitar parts with other instruments, but his use of a capo to force himself into alternative chord voicings gave his part added sweetness. One day we were running the idea around and Nigel joined in on Matt's mandolin. The arrangement was padded out on the album with some strings, but in essence it remains an acoustic folk song, appropriate to its subject matter. Listening back to the recorded version for this book, I was struck again by how proud I am of the song, and by how mystified I am by my failure to include it on the album proper. It fell by the wayside somehow, much like many of the characters it sought to commemorate — which feels oddly, ironically appropriate.

* Another one of these was the main riff to the song 'If Ever I Stray'.

RECOVERY

Blacking in and out in a strange flat in East London,
Somebody I don't really know just gave me something
To help settle me down and to stop me from always thinking about you.
And you know your life is heading in a questionable direction
When you're up for days with strangers and you can't remember anything
Except the way you sounded when you told me you didn't know what I should do.

It's a long road up to recovery from here, a long way back to the light.
A long road up to recovery from here, a long way to making it right.

I've been waking in the morning just like every other day,
And just like every boring blues song I get swallowed by the pain,
And so I fumble for your figure in the darkness just to make it go away.
But you're not lying there any longer, and I know that that's my fault,
So I've been pounding on the floor and I've been crawling up the walls,
And I've been dipping in my darkness for serotonin boosters, cider and some kind
Of smelling salts.

On the first night we met you said 'well darling, let's make a deal:
If anybody ever asks us, let's tell them that we met in jail.'
And that's the story that I'm sticking to like a stony-faced accomplice,
But tonight I need to hear some truth if I'm ever getting through this.
You once sent me a letter that said 'if you're lost at sea,
Close your eyes and catch the tide my dear and only think of me.'

Well darling now I'm sinking, I'm as lost as lost can be,
And I was hoping you could drag me up from down here towards my recovery.

If you could just give me a sign, just a subtle little glimmer,
Some suggestion that you'd have me if I could only make me better,
Then I would stand a little stronger as I walk a little taller all the time.
Because I know you are a cynic but I think I can convince you,
Because broken people can get better if they really want to,
Or at least that's what I have to tell myself if I am hoping to survive.

Darling, sweet lover, won't you help me to recover.
Darling, sweet lover, one day this will all be over.

* * *

My career continued with its slow but inexorable rise. *England Keep My Bones* had taken me from playing medium-sized theatres around the UK to playing all over the world, and playing huge rooms back home – in 2012, I headlined at Wembley Arena in front of 12,000 people. That was also the year I was asked to play at the Olympic Opening Ceremony. I had outgrown the underground music scene that fostered me (and some of its denizens were none too pleased about that, predictably), but I felt like I'd done it on my own terms.

After a couple of years on the road, my thoughts naturally began to turn towards what I would do for my next record. In the interim, I had completed my international recording contract with Epitaph records, and my manager Charlie Caplowe (who runs Xtra Mile Recordings) and I decided to take the ambitious step of licensing my records on to a major label – Polydor in the UK, Universal internationally – for distribution. It was an enterprising move, designed to broaden the horizons of my potential audience, and it also meant that the budgets available to me for making records were significantly higher. I wanted to move my career and the art that I was making up a gear.

England had been an ambitious record in itself, dealing as it does with bombastic themes such as national identity and mortality. In the midst of my upward leap, my creative brain was whirring in a distinctly counterintuitive way. It struck me that it would be interesting, perhaps even provocative, to accompany this bold step with a record that was much smaller and more intimate in its subject matter, one that looked inwards rather than outwards. This decision was aided by the fact that my personal life at this time was taking something of a nose-dive. In an entirely predictable fashion, the new strains and temptations that accompanied ever-greater success had corroded my long-term relationship with Isabel beyond the point of no return. I should stop using the passive voice here – I fucked it up, I was selfish and dishonest, and, standing amongst the smouldering wreckage, I only had myself to blame.

There are many classic records that can be classified as 'break-up albums' – in fact, *August and Everything After* by Counting Crows, the record that had taught me so much about music and songwriting as a kid, is probably the definitive example. Almost without exception, they are written by the injured party and are characterised by plaintive laments and furious recriminations. It occurred to me that it would be interesting to write a break-up album from the point of view of the perpetrator; it felt like a gap in the court records, as it were, as well as the market. And I had plenty of material to work with on the subject. In fact, around this time I was manically creative, writing songs like they were going out of fashion. By the time I got to the studio to make *Tape Deck Heart*, I had more than twenty songs in consideration, more than I've ever had, before or since.

*

The song at the centre of this new blizzard of ideas was 'Recovery'. Right from the start, I knew it would be a key track on the record, so I worked hard to get it right. It contains all the themes I was working with – broken relationships, self-loathing, and a romantic hope. The break-up I'd gone through had not been a clean or simple one. We'd parted and reconciled a number of times (the song 'Redemption' on the previous album prefigures all this, written as it was about an earlier stumble). Even as I was writing and recording *Tape Deck Heart*, I had some residual hope that things could be worked out between us.

During our chaotic descent towards our finish line, I'd found myself one night at a party in east London – an area I don't usually frequent, and one that is stereotypically more of a haunt for hipsters than my more familiar stamping grounds to the north. In fact, I ended up at the house of a reasonably well-known model, whose birthday it was. At the time, there was a new drug doing the rounds – 'meow meow', or mephedrone, a kind of cheap cocaine substitute. In my confusion and misery, I'd ended up taking quite a bit, and found myself seeing in the dawn wired and incoherent. Like the broken-hearted idiot I was, I decided that this would be a fantastic moment to call up my ex and try to have a conversation about how we could fix things. I could barely formulate a sentence at the time, so needless to say it didn't go very well. As a meagre consolation, I found myself jotting down the beginnings of some words a few days later, once I'd overcome the truly miserable comedown (one that featured me crying my eyes out at the end of *Robin Hood: Prince of Thieves*, when Sean Connery arrives as King Richard, but that's another story).

That level of debauchery was reasonably common in my life at the time. I've had my ups and (more frequent) downs with drugs in my life. At the time of writing, I'm pleased to say they're behind me, though of course it's something I have to be constantly vigilant about. The word 'recovery' had been floating around the edges of my mind for a while (I often get hung up on certain words). This is partly because of my desire to get clean, partly a reference to the simple act of getting over the benders that were so common for me back then. It was also the title of an excellent album by Loudon Wainwright III (one of my all-time favourite writers, whose old D'Angelico archtop guitar I happen to own now, my pride and joy) in which he'd revisited some of his classic songs from the 1970s. I'd been instantly struck by its suggestive power and versatility as a word.

The other component tributary for this song came from a new but immediately close friend. I'd met Erin Smolinski in New York on tour, in a bar after a show of mine to which she'd been dragged by a date. We got on like a house on fire; in fact, that very night, she jokingly said to me, over a drink, that if anyone was ever to ask her where we'd met, she'd tell them it was in prison. I made a mental note. Not long after that, I was spending an uncomfortable day on Bamburgh Beach in the northeast of England, shooting the promotional video for the song 'If Ever I Stray'. The clip features me walking into the sea, and let me tell you, the water in that part of the world is not warm, even in summer time. I'd been texting Erin to moan about my predicament, and she'd replied with a photo of some graffiti she'd sprayed on a wall for me, somewhere in Brooklyn, which read: 'Fox:* When you are cold and out to sea, close your eyes and think of me me me.' Erin is, as you might have guessed, a wonderful poet. So it is that in fact the lyrics in this song are actually referring to two separate people – my ex and Erin – though of course, with the help of some creative licence, the implication is more singular.

* Her obscure nickname for me, which would take too long to explain properly here.

Erin's inspirational graffiti, somewhere in Brooklyn

I began the song, as I often do, with a hastily written first verse, penned in the aftermath of that terrible party. I liked the fact that it was lyrically dense. In my Million Dead days I'd had something of a reputation for my machine-gun delivery, syllables packed into the lines with such precision that to misplace even one would cause the song to crash and burn. Mick Shiner, the man who published my first four records through his company, Pure Groove, even compared me to one of his other artists, Mike Skinner of The Streets. Whether or not that was valid, I enjoyed jamming as many words as possible into my songs. In my solo career, this was a habit I'd largely left behind, keen as I was to focus on the simplicity of country and folk songwriting. But now I had begun with something as quick-witted as anything I'd written in my (post) hardcore days, so I decided to run with it.

Sometimes, when I have a strong start for a song and no clear idea of where it should go next, I employ the following technique.

I just play what I have, with as much confidence as I can muster, and then let my mouth and my fingers lead the way into the next section – whatever that might be – as if it already existed. It's total improvisation, but it's based on the simple idea of letting my instincts tell me what comes next. On some levels, songwriting is as simple as just trying to make something that sounds good and feels right. In this instance, I hit the jackpot. I played the opening verse, and my hands naturally wandered down to the E major chord, my voice up to the high A note, and the chorus of (arguably) my most popular song just sort of fell out of me.

There's a little more to it than that, of course. I can trace the musical genesis of this song quite precisely, in fact. On the Revival Tour, I'd crossed paths with a singer called Possessed by Paul James – Konrad Wert, to his friends, among whom I quickly numbered myself. He has a beautiful song called 'Fathers and Sons' which, in the spirit of the tour, we had ended up playing together as a duet. The chord structure of the song is wonderfully simple, ascending up the first four notes of a major scale. Something about that device appealed to me, and fit in with the general idea of recovery. I began my own song with a similar approach, a climb from A major up to D major. It's not identical, but I believe in acknowledging my influences, so there it is – thanks, Konrad. And in fact the chorus that I'd stumbled upon actually complemented the verse by reaching higher, at the start, to the V chord, E major, thus giving a sense of arrival when that section (and the band) dropped.

This topographical design continues through the song. The chorus lifts, as described, while the bridge peaks with the VI chord – a relevant F# minor – taking us into different harmonic territory. At the end of that section, leading into the piano solo, the chords chromatically descend with increasing speed, conjuring a sense of careering out of control. The solo itself reprises the basic upward motion of the song, but accentuates it – Ben's guitar line keeps climbing up from the D chord, ever upwards to the top of the scale, so that the impact of the final chorus is ever greater. On the final play-out ('Darling, sweet lover . . .'), Tarrant's bassline performs a similar trick, rising from the low E to an F#, a G#, and finally a high D. The overall atmosphere of the song (hopefully) accompanies the lyrics perfectly, characterised by a sense of reaching, stretching, yearning for some kind of resolution, which is almost delivered in the final, a cappella lyric – 'One day this will all be over.'

The material I wrote for *Tape Deck Heart* was, in keeping with the general trajectory of my career, yet more thoroughly worked over, demo'd, pulled apart and put back together again before we got into the studio. In looking through my archives to write about this song, I found nine separate versions of it, varying from solo sketches to full band arrangements, all recorded before we ever left for California to meet Rich Costey.

Rich is a big name producer. He's worked with a veritable *Who's Who* of modern rock bands, producing many classic records that have sold by the bucketload. Before deciding to work with a major label, he was completely out of my price range. One of the key advantages of signing a licence with Polydor was that my budget for recording, and thus my range of possible producers, was greatly expanded. After having a lot of different phone conversations with various people, I settled on Rich as my choice to make my fifth studio album.*

It can be quite hard to explain to people who aren't in the

* Rich clinched the deal by enthusiastically agreeing with me that albums should be a maximum of forty-five minutes long, so that they fit on one side of a ninety-minute cassette tape. The album title was lurking in there somewhere.

business of recording music exactly what the role of a producer in the studio is. Of course there's a wide spectrum of approaches that they can take to the project at hand, but it's possible to make some general comments from my own experience with Rich. He was not just an engineer – in fact he had a couple of very talented assistants who were in charge of moving microphones around and plugging in leads. Neither did he contribute to the song-writing, as the songs were all conceptually fully formed by the time we arrived at El Dorado Studios in Burbank, CA. And he didn't play any instruments or sing any vocals.

Perhaps the best way to describe the producer's role is through another sporting metaphor (brace yourself, I'm out of my comfort zone again). He or she is like a football coach, a boxing trainer, or, my preferred image, like Mr Miyagi in *Karate Kid*, to my Daniel. The producer oversees the creative project as a whole, and constantly works to make sure that you, as an artist, are pushing yourself to the limits of your abilities, exploring every option, never slacking off or letting the quality of your decisions and performances fall below the highest possible standard. They keep an eye on the overall coherence of the record, and check that everything is conforming to the vision that you set out together in discussions at the start of the session.

I can pinpoint Rich's contribution to this particular song by listening back to all the sketches that I made with The Sleeping Souls before getting into the studio proper. Once we were in the room with Rich, we'd run through the version we had already worked out and then sit around to discuss the arrangement and structure. I can vividly remember Matt, Ben and I sat in a circle, with a piano, an electric guitar and an acoustic respectively, Rich stood in the middle of the circle, playing the chords to the chorus round and round, each time changing the individual parts we were playing, shifting inversions, octaves and feel. The finished recording of the song has more of a 'swung' feel to it; Nigel's drum part is a little simpler, but overlaid with a tambourine part. The tail end of the chorus has a descending bass part which came about when Rich demanded some addition to that section; after trying a lot of different options, that's what Tarrant came up with on the day. On the whole the song is a little slower, which gives the lyrics a bit more room to breathe – a compromise reached after I'd refused to cut out any of my carefully calibrated syllables. There are more backing vocals on the final version, especially on the choruses. In short, Rich brought the song up to a new level of sonic ambition, complexity and coherence, while still making sure that the soul of the piece shone through.

As I'd imagine you already know if you're reading this, *Tape Deck Heart*, led by the song 'Recovery', went on to be a huge success for me. The song actually reached the number 1 spot on the AAA radio charts in the USA, and my friends back home regularly complained that they couldn't listen to the radio for any length of time during the day without hearing it at least once. On tour in the States after the album was released, the new label had me on a punishing schedule of radio sessions around the shows, and I've definitely played 'Recovery' more times than any other song I've written. It's not a number we need to practise much.

After every record I've ever made, I go through a phase of internalised backlash. Within a few months of leaving the studio, all I can hear is the shortcomings of the album, what I wish I could have done differently, or what's missing from the overall picture. In a way, this is a healthy process, representing as it does my creative brain searching for new ways to evolve and move forward. It usually takes me a couple of years, or another inter-vening album, before I can listen back to a body of work with some degree of detachment.

The enormous success of *Tape Deck Heart* intensified this process of self-examination. It was also bolstered by a small but vocal burst of criticism from some people who felt left behind by the record (and more realistically by the exposure that came with it). It's certainly true that this was my most heavily produced record to date, and was something of a sonic departure in places from my previous work. To a large extent, I'd argue that that's the entire fucking point – artists have a duty to change and develop their sound. All the same, I went through a long period of time in which I was slightly down on the sound of this record, wondering if, in working the songs over so thoroughly with Rich, I had in some way been guilty of the compromises that the punk rock internet was accusing me of.

Listening back now, with the passage of time and a couple more albums under my belt, I'm pleased to say that I can leave that reticence about *Tape Deck Heart* behind me. It's a clean and full-sounding rock record, but not in a way that is outside my own music taste and vision. It happily achieves what I set out to do with the album – to take my existing sound into a bigger, bolder place, but also to hide within it a more raw and introspective lyrical approach. I don't think there's been another rock song with that many words in it at the top of the charts in recent years, or that deals with such an excoriatingly difficult subject matter. The song has served me as well as or better than any other, in career terms, and includes some of my favourite turns of phrase that I've ever put down on tape. So I'll stop sounding defensive, and enjoy the song. She did me proud.

THE WAY I TEND TO BE

Some mornings I pray for evening,
For the day to be done.
Some summer days I hide away
And wait for rain to come.
It turns out hell will not be found
Within the fires below,
But in making do and muddling through
When you've nowhere else to go.

But then I remember you,
And the way you shine like truth in all you do.
And if you remembered me,
You could save me from the way I tend to be.

Some days I wake up dazed my dear,
And I don't know where I am.
I've been running now so long I'm scared
I've forgotten how to stand.
I stand alone in airport bars
And gather thoughts to think:
That if all I had was one long road
It could drive a man to drink.

Because I've said I love you so many times that the words kind of die in my mouth.
And I meant it each time with each beautiful woman but somehow it never works out.

You stood apart in my calloused heart, and you taught me and here's what
I learned:
That love is about all the changes you make and not just three small words.

And then I catch myself
Catching your scent on someone else
In a crowded space
And it takes me somewhere I cannot quite place.

*   *   *

'Recovery' was a big hit for me, and I'd had a feeling it would be from the start. The other massive song from this moment in my career had a much less certain genesis and a very long gestation period. It's one with which I have a complicated emotional relationship, and which has continued to evolve musically more than anything else I've written. Nevertheless, 'The Way I Tend to Be' is, for better or worse, a very important song for me, so let's talk about it.

As mentioned before, the dying relationship that provided my central theme at this time had been faltering for some while. The short-term break-up that gave me the song 'Redemption' had occurred in 2010, and in that fraught period, I had written another song on the subject as well. Somewhere between New Zealand and Hong Kong, in the airless hub of some Australian airport, I had had a moment of pure introspective misery, brought on by the feeling that Isabel was moving on from me, forgetting about me (alas, it took her a few more years to actually do the smart thing and cut her ties; I'm pleased to say we're friends now). Various ideas began coalescing in my head, spurred on by a bizarre moment in the departures lounge, when I sat next to a stranger wearing, of all things, her distinct brand of perfume.* By the time I arrived in mainland China a week or so later, I had a set of words. I felt like I'd written them in a daze, and, going back through my notebooks and demos, they never really did change much from the first, borderline stream-of-consciousness draft.

Hanging out with a fragrant koala in Brisbane, 2010

In a hotel in Shenzen, I married these words with a guitar figure I'd been toying with for a while. My formative years as a

---

* I have told a story on stage many times over the years about the actual olfactory culprit being a koala bear, in an animal sanctuary in Brisbane, Australia. It is true that my ex used eucalyptus-scented shampoo, and that koalas tend to smell of the only food they can eat, but the story is basically apocryphal, a fun bit of stage banter. Sorry to ruin it for people.

guitarist had been playing alone to accompany a room full of singers. In that context, one of my prerogatives was making as much noise with one instrument as I could, and, if possible, suggesting a denser arrangement. Over time I'd learned that simply hammering an acoustic as hard as I could wasn't quite the trick. In fact, using chord voicings that leave as many strings ringing open as possible makes any given song sound much fuller and more resonant, as the open strings allow the full body of the instrument to sing. That discovery gave me, over time, a taste for slightly odd chord shapes which use open strings for unexpected augmentations. The simplest version of that might be leaving an open G string ringing in the middle of an F chord, but you can get more adventurous with your fingers further up the neck. A lot of Million Dead riffs use unexpected and slightly jarring open strings in this way, and it's there in that original, rock version of 'Jet Lag'.

In this particular instance, I was enjoying experimenting with shifting the finger shape of a C chord up and down the neck. C major is, as I've said, my favourite chord – every guitarist has one, just get them to pick up a guitar and play the first chord that comes to mind, and there you go – but I wanted to see where I could take it. By using my pinkie to hold down the high E string, I found a shape that left only the G string ringing, all the others being covered by my fingers. And by sliding that up and down the neck, I found my way to a weird, spindly but melodic riff, one that moved around a lot but was held together by that central G note drone. The key changed to G major as well, which gave the final landing on the natural position for the chord (C major) a satisfying feel.

Having established that part of the musical equation, I kept going with the same approach of playing with open strings, and got the chorus together. The first chord is a C chord played with both the G and high E strings ringing open.* By moving that shape around, I wrote a part that built on the drone of the introduction and filled out the sound further. Throwing the lyrics into the mix, I found my top-line melody, a structure for a verse and a bridge, and finished the song. And then I shelved it.

For reasons that I will make an honest attempt to get into here, I had strong reservations about the song from the beginning. I knew that, architecturally, it was a finished item; I didn't think that there were problems to be ironed out. There was just something so very direct and simple about it that felt almost too raw, too naked. And at the same time, its sense of melody, when allied to that simplicity, left me feeling like it was very – for want of a less loaded term – *pop*. And while I've tried hard to get over that particular punk rock prejudice, somehow this song felt like it might have crossed a line.†

The proof of how serious I was in my discomfort was the fact that not only did I not seriously consider the song for the album I was then working on, *England Keep My Bones*, I even toyed with the idea of trying to sell it to a pop artist. I'm attracted by the idea of writing songs for other people – minimal effort, maximum return, someone else does all the promo work! – but have never

* It's a chord shape that also features in the song 'In Hope' by BoySetsFire – one of my absolute, all-time favourite songs.
† While we're here, a quick word on the subject of James Blunt. The line about 'catching your scent on someone else' was written, as mentioned, about a very real incident. Nevertheless, after I'd finished the song, it struck me that there was a passing resemblance between that final breakdown in my song and Blunt's execrable (but very successful) 'You're Beautiful'. It's completely unintentional, and I'm satisfied that there's enough clear artistic water between the two ideas for me to remain credible, but nonetheless, I suspect this may have contributed to my hesitations about this song.

really been able to make it work, as the songs I actually get around to finishing tend to have enough personal weight for me to want to record them myself. I'm not saying this song had no emotional weight – far, far from it – but I just didn't quite know what to do with it. I didn't feel like I could make it fit into my existing oeuvre. So I knocked out a quick demo of it in a hotel room and put it aside.

Fast forward a couple of years, to 2012, and the preparation period for *Tape Deck Heart*. The liaison between a large record label and an artist is the infamous A&R guy.* Before working with Polydor, that's not a role that needed filling, as the label consisted of a handful of people at Xtra Mile, all good and trusted friends. Now that there was a much bigger machine (and bigger sums of money) involved, I'd started working with a big, gruff Irishman called Richard O'Donovan in this role. He's the one with whom I signed the deal, and he was the creative and logistical point man for me. His job, in essence, was to push me creatively to make the best (and let's be honest, most commercially poised) record that I could. Of course, as an independently minded soul, I had my own opinions about songs and producers, so we have had some professional friction. At various times that has become a serious issue – we'll get to that – but at this period of time, he was much more a help than a hindrance, pushing me to dig deeper into my creative hinterland.

In practice, one of the things this meant was that he kept asking me to produce more new songs, to reach right back into the darkest recesses of my bottom drawer to find whatever I might have had lying around. I found myself demoing new ideas

---

* 'Artist and Repertoire', since you ask. No, me neither. And yes, 'guy', habitually. Personally, I have not encountered a woman working this job in my time in the industry, which actually says quite a lot about how fucked it is.

in Toronto in May 2012, and, at his instigation, really laid out everything I could think of – including that old pop misfit idea, 'The Way I Tend to Be'. I still felt odd about the song – it was sincere, unforced and whole, but somehow uncomfortable all the same. Nevertheless, I put down a version and sent it over. Richard went nuts. I can still remember him telling me on the phone, 'This will be a huge song for you.' He wasn't wrong.

So it was, finally, that the song was lined up for an album, after one of the longer gestation periods in my history as a writer. However, there was no light at the end of the tunnel just yet. The arranging of the song was a drawn out and fraught process, one that certainly didn't end with the release of the album, and one that arguably continues to this day.

I took the solo version of the song I'd written to the rehearsal room for me and the Souls to work over. The band's initial musical instincts were governed by the facets of the song that I found disquieting, the softness of the feel and the subject matter. We kicked the parts around for this more than any other piece in that period, but the common theme of each take is a lightness of touch that accentuates its gentle qualities in a way that, to be honest, ended up sounding overly saccharine. I mean no disrespect to anyone's musicianship; they were following my lead. All the same, listening back to the reggae-lite drum parts and soupy Rhodes piano lines now kind of makes my teeth hurt. In fact, it did at the time, but I was busy trying to work with my A&R rather than against him, and to trust his powerfully positive instincts about the song, so I went with it.

So the version that Rich Costey heard when we arrived in California was *very* pop indeed. I suppose I felt like I was already out of my comfort zone, so I might as well try seeing where it went. To his enormous credit, Rich was able to see the potential of the song through the car-crash of the arrangement we presented him with, and (without being overly rude about it, thankfully) he set about reconstructing the music from the ground up.

The making of *Tape Deck Heart* at El Dorado in Burbank was not a universally pleasant experience. Rich worked us hard, pushed us all as musicians, and from time to time pulled rank as a majorly successful producer of records. That wasn't always a comfortable thing to be on the receiving end of, even if, most of the time, his ideas were sound. I think the person who suffered the most in this way at that session was Nigel – Rich was a completely unforgiving taskmaster when it came to drum and percussion parts. In this instance, though, it was Nigel himself who, in the end, and after a lot of going around the houses, turned the whole song around by suggesting a rock-solid foundation that would pin the piece down, and work against the gentle nature of the material rather than with it.* That approach can be summed up with two timeless words: 'John Bonham'.

Once we had Nigel powering the tune like a Led Zeppelin piece, the rest started to fall into place. We moved the key of the song up a massive two whole steps (from G to B, using a capo on the fourth fret of my acoustic, leaving the top chord of the chorus only just playable), which completely changed the feel and brought an extra level of new energy to the track, as well as allowing my vocals to shine through much more clearly. Tarrant's bassline became a tighter, more rhythmic affair, and Matt was tempted away from the Rhodes to the mandolin. Using a different inversion of the opening riff on that instrument, with its different

---

* Something that Nigel actually remembers as being very much against his instincts, a last-ditch attempt to salvage the arrangement of the song. Sometimes the best ideas are the last and least likely ones.

tuning, brought a completely new set of ringing open paired strings to the party, which turned that introduction to the song from being something thin and uncertain to a majestic, unique explosion of harmony.

These two structural changes – the feel of the drums and the key – utterly revolutionised how I felt about the whole song. Suddenly I could hear the potential that Richard and Rich could. And yet in this process of arrangement, the song itself had not changed. The lyrics, melody and structure remained the same, and now I could look at the unadorned, plaintive nature of the piece as a strength rather than a weakness. In the mix, Rich exaggerated that contrast, between the hard rock sonics and the mournful words, and in the process made a piece that could match 'Recovery', both artistically and commercially.

The song was released on *Tape Deck Heart* in 2013. Initially, the album rode a wave of success on the first single, but it was given a new lease of life by the success of this song, its second. The juggernaut took a while to get going, but once it had picked up speed, there was no stopping it. The album version of this song still gets played on radio stations, in convenience stores and at weddings around the world, and very proud of that I am too.*

Unfortunately, my niggling discomfort with the song wasn't over yet; in fact, it had ample time to fester and grow, given the number of times I had to play the song, both live, at radio sessions, on TV (including a German soap opera!) and so on. It was further

---

* And all this despite the fucking *worst* video of all time. It would take a significant chunk of another book to explain just quite how much I hate that video with the stupid fucking sandwich board that *makes no sense at all* and the hole in the ground and the shitty news report and AUUURGGH. My bad.

amplified by the obvious fact that the song eventually became the closest thing to a pop hit I have ever had (yet!). Rather than selling the song to a pop artist, had I accidentally become one myself?

Over the years, I have continued to tinker with the arrangement of the song. Initially this was simply a case of finding a way for Matt and I to play it as a two-piece, for radio sessions when we couldn't take the whole band and backline. After I damaged my back in 2013, and toured without being able to play guitar standing up for six months or so,* Matt and I put together a version where he played piano and I sang. I enjoyed that approach, but it still felt dangerously gooey to me. Those two approaches came together for the duo recording on *The Third Three Years*. Again, close, but no cigar.

Finally, when I was putting together the *Songbook* record in late 2017, with its selection of alternative takes on some of my old songs, I sat in a room in west London with producer Charlie Hugall and tried to explain everything I've just written down. Charlie's suggestion, a brilliant one, was to take it back to the moment when I first finished it, in a lonely hotel room in China. So many of the musical ideas I toy around with never make it anywhere near a finished song, so for me to have crossed that threshold, he argued, there had to be something special lurking in there. So I took off the capo, returning to the original sombre key of G, dropped my pick and played with my fingers, trying to put myself back into the moment of creation. And, believe it or not, it worked. I think that the song's added history, accrued in the interim, plus a healthy extra dollop of maturity for me, both as a performer and a writer, allowed me to finally reconnect with the soul of the music. I might even venture to say that, with

* I know, I know, I'm an idiot; I was young! Well. I was thirty-one.

Songbook, I've finally laid down a version of this song that I am happy with. But give me another couple of years to think about it, and I'm sure I'll change my mind.

FOUR SIMPLE WORDS

Because we're all so very twenty first century,
You're probably listening to me on some kind of portable stereo.
Maybe you're sitting on the back of the bus,
Or it's running up your sleeve, and you're across from your boss,
Or you're sitting in your bedroom on your own with the lights down low.
I'd like to teach you four simple words, so that next time you come to a show,
You could sing those words back at me like they're the only ones that you know:

I want to dance, I want to dance,
I want lust and love and a smattering of romance.
But I'm no good at dancing, yet I have to do something.
Tonight I'm going to play it straight, I'm going to take my chance, I want to dance.

Hi ho hi ho hi ho, we're heading out to the punk rock show.
Colleagues and friends condescend with a smile,
But this is my culture man, this is my home.
The dark huddled masses gather at the gate,
The doors are at 7, the show starts at 8.
A few precious hours in a space of our own,
And when the band comes on, the only thing I really know:

Is anyone else sick of the music
Churned out by lacklustre scenesters from Shoreditch?
Oh it's all sex drugs and sins, like they're extras from Skins,
But it's OK because they don't really mean it.

I want bands who had to work for their keep,
Drove a thousand miles and played a show on no sleep,
Sleeping on the floor in a stranger's place,
Hungry just to do it all again the next day.

Put your hands on your hips, bring your knees in tight.
Yeah we do this shit together man, no fists, no fights.
We're not trying to shape the world so people think like us,
We just want our own space to dance, no favours no fuss.
On blood sweat and vinyl we have built ourselves a house,
So if the roof is on fire then we're going to put it out.
Forget about the bitching and remember that you're blessed,
Because punk is for the kids who never fit in with the rest.

Somebody told me that music with guitars
Was going out of fashion, and I had to laugh.
This shit wasn't fashionable when I fell in love,
So if the hipsters move on why should I give a fuck?

I want to dance, I want to dance,
I want you and me both to join hands down at the front.
So the next time I see you, remember these words so
We'll sing like the barricades are down, and we'll dance like no one's around,
Singing four simple words.

* * *

In writing in these pages about the new levels of success I reached at this point in my career, I have enjoyed being a little snide from time to time about the predictable criticisms I received from some quarters of the punk rock scene. Let's be honest, it's easy, and it's fun. And this is my book, so I get to settle my scores, damn you all. The problem, of course, with being overly defensive, especially in an unprovoked way, is that after a while it starts to tell the world more about your own insecurities, shortcomings and psychoses than it does about the enemies you're busy trouncing in print.

So, to lay it out clearly: Million Dead were part of some kind of scene: arguably, the brief flowering of British underground rock music (with a dash of post-hardcore) that followed in the wake of Hundred Reasons in the early 2000s.* I think we considered ourselves to be a punk band at the time – Ben Dawson and I had grown up going to underground hardcore shows in London, and at the start we played on a lot of those bills. Either way, by the time I went solo in 2005, I was keen to put some clear water between myself and whatever that scene was, in large part to help define my own identity as an artist, and to prove that my unlikely musical change in direction was a serious one, not just a passing novelty.

As my solo career progressed I received a sort of grudging honorary membership of the punk club in my home country, especially as my early albums became popular on the grassroots scene. Abroad, things were clearer cut; from 2009 onwards, I released records outside the UK through Epitaph records, and largely toured with bands like The Offspring and Flogging Molly. My punk credentials there were assured.

After my career started peeking around the corner of the mainstream, my relationship with the people who constitute the punk scene started to change (though never, for the record, my relationship with the ethics, as I understand them). Wired deep into the conceptual DNA of punk is a suspicion of success. This

* I still have no idea what to call that decade, and I'm not having 'noughties'. For shame.

has excellent motivational underpinnings – the history of the genre is littered with people who traded ideals for easy riches, who bastardised the art form for financial gain.* Unfortunately it's a pretty indiscriminate impulse, and the same history is full of great bands who were cruelly shunned and beaten down by the scene that birthed them for the simple reason that they successfully made art that communicated beyond the narrow confines of the scene.† I'm not claiming the martyr's crown – that probably belongs to Jawbreaker – but there were some pretty laughable 'attacks' on me at this period in time. After I played the Olympics (at Danny Boyle's request, without payment, if I need to rehearse those arguments again), the singer in an obscure London punk band even wrote an 'open letter' to me (my email address is on my site, always has been), telling me I'd 'sold out the scene' (I'd not actually met this guy before). How I laughed.

All this brings into focus my least favourite part of the concept and practice of punk: the clique. Punk can become a popularity contest, a fashion show, a weirdly internalised reproduction of all the shitty social behaviours that had me running away from 'mainstream' social culture as fast as I could. And here's the point: punk, for me, first and foremost, was a refuge. I was raised in a social milieu that I hated, that made me feel rejected and humiliated, and that I found politically unacceptable. In the throes of that adolescent maelstrom, I remember finding this shining idea, which later became an actual group of real people, dedicated to acceptance. As Propagandhi sang: 'Maybe you're a lot like me / identified for fourteen years, without a choice / and terrified, on the morning you woke up to realise / that when you jump ship, you can either swim for shore or drown / don't let the fuckers

* Hello, Billy Idol.
† Hello, Against Me!

drag you down.'* Never before (and probably not since) had a song spoken to me so directly. So when, in my adult life, punk gives in to its exclusionary worst instincts, it makes me sad and angry in equal measure.

That's a really long preamble for writing about this song, and it still feels a little overly self-justificatory. Ah fuck it, this is my book, and indeed my song. My point, better and more briefly put, is that I was starting to think about writing a song that would both answer the sniping of my detractors and reassert what it was that I found inspirational and redemptive in the ideals of punk rock; I wanted to reassert my claim to the use of that term. So, obviously, I wrote a Queen-style, multi-part mock opera on the subject.

It all began in the summer of 2011, when I was on tour in Europe with Social Distortion. One evening in Amsterdam, I was hanging out with their bass player, Brent Harding, after the show, sipping whiskey and setting the world to rights. We'd already discussed the lost art of the talking blues (in fact we resolved to write a talking blues about the fact no one writes them any more, which would be called 'The Talking Blues Talking Blues' – I never did get around to that). Somewhere in the curled smoke of the conversation, I started idly musing on the idea of a vaudevillian punk song, a song that would serve as an introduction piece for a show, welcoming the audience and setting the scene for the evening's festivities. It was a fun flight of fancy; and then it was time for bed. All the same, I made a mental note.

In a foreshadowing of the methodology that I would go on to extensively employ on my next album, this was a song that came

* In the song 'I Was a Pre-Teen McCarthyist' from their album *Less Talk, More Rock*, a real life-changer for me.

together piecemeal in soundchecks on tour. I took that initial idea and ran with it, throwing together some ideas for a verse and a chorus. I wanted the meat of the song to be solidly punk rock, based on straight drums and simple power chords, drawing on the sound of bands like Social D and early Clash. In a way, I suspect I was also using this song to counterbalance some of the softer musical ideas that were coming through in songs like 'The Way I Tend to Be' – I wanted the gestating album to have light and shade, and to have enough ballast to keep at least part of one of my feet in the punk world from a musical point of view. In fact, the song was easily heavier and more traditionally 'punk' than anything on my preceding albums. It felt good to take the Souls through the paces of playing fast, direct and heavy.

But the song wasn't as simple as all that, of course. For a start, there's the drawn out, theatrical introduction, as I'd dreamt up with Brent – in the first draft a cappella, then with acoustic guitar, and finally with piano. But I also ended up experimenting with a waltz breakdown, at Ben's suggestion. The song fell into three clearly defined movements. We rehearsed harder, and eventually started playing it live, as yet unreleased – the first time was in Graz, Austria, in December 2011 at a venue called PPC. The crowd went ballistic from the moment the drums kicked in. I felt like I was on to a good thing, a crowd-pleaser for sure. The song continued to grow, feeding off the audience reactions – we added singalong backing vocals, call-and-response sections and more. It got faster and leaner in the middle, more drawn out and playful at either end. In some senses, the song was almost written to be a live piece. There's a functionality to the way it's written, and some people have criticised it on those grounds, but I'll own up to it and say I don't see it as a problem really. I spend much more time playing songs live than writing or recording them anyway, and I don't regard performance as being somehow a lesser form of artistic expression, as discussed for the song 'Balthazar, Impresario' above. I like to think that this song brings some of the drama and humour of music hall into my work. It's a song with a fair amount of its tongue in its cheek, replete with 'smatterings' and 'centu-aries'.

By the time we came to record the album, this was probably the most fully formed of the songs on the table, because we'd been playing it out live. It took a while to figure out how to record the song, technically, but once we started laying down the structure, Rich Costey didn't have much to add, other than that he loved the idea. It came together as well as it could have done, and it remains my (probable) favourite from the album. That's partly because it sounds and feels great, but it's also because I believe the song achieves what it sets out to do.

I genuinely can't dance for shit. Part of my feeling weird around the mainstream pop culture my friends were into when I was a teenager was the fact that I couldn't make my gangly limbs do anything meaningful, let alone attractive, in time with the insipid repetitive shit that got played at parties and in the few pubs that would let me and my friends in. By contrast, while I fully accept that the mosh pit is not a particularly graceful or coordinated exposition of human physicality, it had the great advantage of being, for me, an easy and direct way of losing myself and my body to the music that spoke to me. To this day I won't go near a regular dance floor, much to my partner's annoyance, particularly because, as she has justifiably pointed out, I do actually dance in public a lot – but only when I'm making music and communing with my audience.

But that's the point; on stage is where I feel comfortable, where I can really let go and allow myself to get lost, even in front of an audience. All my friends tell me they've never seen me so happy as when I'm playing a show. And, in a way, that's what punk was supposed to be, for me – a space where you could just let it all out, throw yourself around the room and into your friends, the kids who never fit in with the rest, and let the music envelop and overwhelm you, and say the things you could never quite find the words for in your awkward isolation. That kind of dancing is an expression of individuality and joy that is specifically removed from considerations of cool and acceptability and judgement. And that's what punk still can be, if you let it. So, there it finally is, the 'Four Simple Words' – I want to dance.

As a final aside here, I'm aware that, as a thirty-six-year-old man, I've just written a couple of thousand words about the various possible meanings of punk. As my good and wise friend Ian Winwood has told me time and time again, I'm way too old to give a fuck about that kind of adolescent didacticism now. I also feel very strongly that way too much time, effort and ink has been spilt trying to define this utterly esoteric and not very important corner of youth culture already. So forgive my indulgence in this tiny piece of argumentation; I should almost certainly just let the whole thing go. Oh well; it's only punk rock, but I like it.

ANYMORE

The single saddest thing that I ever heard you say
Was on the day I told you I had to go away.
You said 'Darling baby please, if you really mean to leave,
Can't I just hold you for a little while longer?'

And the single hardest thing I ever had to do
Was take your arms from round me and walk away from you.
And I know I shouldn't have kissed you as I left,
Darling I should have been stronger.

Not with a bang but with a whimper.
It wasn't hard, it was kind of simple.
Three short steps from your bed to your door,
Darling I can't look you in the eyes now and tell you I'm sure
If I love you anymore.

I did my very best, I've given you these years
Of love and understanding, telephone calls and tears.
But now the little things you do that used to make me love you
Now just cramp my heart a little and let it slip.

And we've met this sorry end from a picture perfect start,
The romance and the running down to disconnected hearts
Of two people sad and free, who know they used to be
More than just a pair of sinking ships.

I'm not drinking any more, but then I'm not drinking any less.
I can't do this anymore, oh you know I did my best.
Oh my darling,
I don't love you anymore.

* * *

Writing about the song 'Anymore' is not going to take much time, from a musical point of view. In the midst of the storm of ideas that I had for *Tape Deck Heart*, I wanted to have at least one song that went back to first principles, to the basic idea of my solo career – one person with one instrument, singing the truth. The chord sequence is as basic as could be, the structure even more so. It's in C major and uses, for the most part, basic open chords.

Tracking guitar for 'Anymore', California, 2012

It's sung at the very bottom of my vocal register, by design, so that I had to sing it softly. I don't have too many demo versions of this song in my archives; it arrived fully formed. In the studio, I got Rich to put away all the fancy technology and simply set up two microphones, and played the song live. We mixed it right there and then and made a deal to leave it exactly as it came out that day. I have a paradigm in my head of a certain type of song – the song that's sung into a dictaphone, or a hotel room answering machine, in the middle of the night, completely unadorned. That's what 'Anymore' is supposed to sound and feel like.

All the same, I want to write about it here. *Tape Deck Heart* is not, in the final analysis, a concept album, but it has clear over-arching themes, and a central subject matter: a break-up. At least once on the record, I wanted to really dig down deep and find the heart of the sentiment of taking the decision to leave someone, and to channel that in the most raw and direct way that I could. The scene I set in the song is a real description of the moment I told her I didn't want to be with her any longer (though I did not, of course, actually say the words 'I don't love you' – I'm not a monster). The feelings I lay out are the absolute truth. In the process of writing in this way, I ended up with a song that is, to be blunt, unkind. And that gives me pause.

The real-world impact of writing a song like this was driven home for me by an unfortunate series of events. As I see it, the song is a necessary component of a larger statement of honesty. The album as a whole paints a picture of the end of a relationship, and this is part of that – but only a part. In the finished whole, it is counterbalanced by songs like 'Recovery', 'The Way I Tend to Be', and most of all 'Plain Sailing Weather' – a song that pretty much openly says I wanted us to get back together again. So the message here is context-dependent. Alas, that wasn't how it was initially received by the woman I was writing about. Somewhere on the road around this time, I played this song at a show. Someone videoed the performance and uploaded it to YouTube. Someone else – a defensive friend of Isabel's, who wasn't a fan of mine at the time anyway (which was kind of fair enough), stumbled across the video and sent it to her. She was, predictably, devastated by it, and I found myself on the receiving end of an entirely justified tirade of hurt and anger.

In fact, I was relieved that I had in fact edited out the harshest line of the song. The second verse originally contained a line about wanting to 'wring your skinny neck'. I just wrote that in a sort of automatic state, trying as I was to let the truth flow out of me. On reading it back it felt true to the darkest parts of my thought process, but in the end I felt I couldn't actually say that out loud, and I'm glad I cut that from the finished piece, even if it is a brutal and visceral piece of imagery. In the end, that's a small mercy; Isabel was still completely heartbroken by the song, despite my protestations that it was more complicated, that she should listen to the whole album and hear the sentiment in its proper place.

Even before that happened, I was a little queasy about the song. It's lyrically the harshest number in my catalogue, and it's difficult to find a time and a place where it feels appropriate to play at a show. I have written plenty (perhaps the majority) of songs about sad or uncomfortable situations, but this song has a streak to it that is just plain mean. After I saw the damage it did to someone that I emphatically still cared about, I was even more reticent to play it in front of an audience. These days it's extremely rare for me to pull it out of the bag, and I certainly wouldn't play it within a 500-mile radius of where she lives now, just to be on the safe side.

One final note about this song. The line at the end – 'I'm not drinking any more, but then I'm not drinking any less' – is a quote borrowed from my friend John C. Stubblefield, of the band Lucero. The very first time we met, backstage at a Social Distortion show in Salt Lake City, the first show of a tour together, he'd burst into our shared dressing room, delivered the killer line, and then taken a huge swig from a bottle of Jameson whiskey. I laughed, and then of course made a note. I've always loved the stereotypically Southern turn of phrase, and a lot of the country songs I adore are illuminations of these aphorisms. I wrote that one down and kept it in a notebook in the hope of writing something playful like a George Jones song (like 'If Drinkin Don't Kill Me (Her Memory Will)'). In the end, it found its home somewhere infinitely sadder. I think a sense of humour is an important and versatile weapon for a songwriter, but I guess I just didn't have it in me here.

BROKEN PIANO

As I walked out one morning fair,
I found myself drawn thoughtlessly
Back to the place we used to live,
And you still do, now without me.

Around the back, away from the road,
Behind the bins, beneath your window,
I found the hulk, the rusting bulk
Of a shattered old piano.
Someone had torn out some of the keys
With cruel care, not thoughtlessly,
In such a way that one could only play
Minor melodies.

So I sat down in my sadness, beneath your window,
And I played sad songs on the minor keys of a broken piano;
A sinner amongst saved men on the banks of the muddy Thames.

As I have wandered through this city,
Like a child lost in the London fog,
From Highgate Hill, down to the river,
Then washed downstream past the Isle of Dogs,

I've had time enough to think upon
The question of what kind of songs

That you would choose to listen to
Now that I am gone.
And as I drift beneath that bridge,
Just down the road from where you live,
I've often thought I might have caught
Your voice upon the wind.

But as I stroked those broken keys
You did not join in harmony.

* * *

In the excellent Tim Burton film, *Ed Wood*, there's a wonderful moment at the end when Johnny Depp, playing the hapless director, says to himself, as he watches his masterpiece unfold on the big screen for the first time, 'This is the one, this is the one I'll be remembered for.' I often get asked to make a list of my favourite songs that I've written, and the shortlist includes some obvious ones, songs that have resonated most with my audience and brought me the most success, like 'I Still Believe' and 'Photosynthesis'. But every time I make one of those lists, I tend to include a song that really isn't one of my better-known compositions: 'Broken Piano'. It's probably the most progressive, ambitious bit of writing that I've completed and released, and I like to think that it's one that will stand the test of time, that people will remember after I'm gone.

The song began in an unusual way. My ex, Isabel, the subject of the whole album, lived in a flat in Putney, south London. I never had my name on the lease, but for a good long while I left a few bags of my clothes there, and it served as my home when I wasn't on the move. When things began to finally, irreparably fall apart for us, I spent many a forlorn afternoon there, packing my things, thinking over what had happened and the mess I'd made of something beautiful, surveying the wreckage.

She had a microwave oven in her kitchen which was old and didn't work particularly well. I used to cook myself cheap student food there to tide me over during the day while she was at work. The microwave made a lot of noise as it heated up. Specifically, it used to hum loudly. After a while I noticed that the hum it made was a blend of the notes A and F# – in other words, a perfect A6 dyad chord. A sixth interval is an interesting, ambiguous one. It sounds unfinished, expectant. It has a particular power in its simplicity, in that you can drop a number of different notes into the middle of it and thus build other chords. For example, if you were to add (say, by humming, as you waited for your Pot Noodle to heat up) the note D to the middle of it, it becomes an inversion of a D major chord – A, D, F#. If you shift that D up to an E, the fifth note of the A major scale, it shifts back to being an A6 again. If you hum an F#, or even a C#, the harmonic implication takes you to the relative minor, F# minor. It's an open, versatile sound, and on those lonely afternoons I had a lot of time to spend humming different notes along with the broken machine.

I'm known, broadly, for writing songs that are usually classified as being folk, punk, country, or I suppose indie rock. That's all well and good, but it's not the full extent of my taste in music. In my early twenties, I went through a phase of trying to listen to all the most far-out sounds that I could. I started listening to a lot of grindcore and sludge, and that gave me a taste for weird and extreme music. In time I went through a lot of free jazz, electronic music, and in particular lots and lots of post-rock. Post-rock is a weird, amorphous term, that covers a lot of very different music, but it's held together by a sense of postmodernism, a desire to stretch the boundaries of the form of rock music to breaking point and far beyond. I was listening to a lot of stuff like early Sigur Rós, Glenn Branca, the catalogue of Canadian labels Constellation and Kranky records (including Godspeed You! Black Emperor, Set Fire to Flames and more), Mick Turner, The Necks, and of course later period Radiohead albums.

It's a rich vein of inspiration for me, but not one that I have actually delved into that much in terms of the music I release on my regular albums. In part that's because I was a little unsure of how to go about making those kinds of sounds. At one point, my childhood friend Chris Blake and I spent a lot of time making ambient soundscape tapes, hanging microphones out of our bedroom windows and running the sounds of the outside world through weird effect units, scrambling daytime TV samples and so on. It was a lot of fun but it didn't add up to anything especially coherent. Later, as this book has outlined, I got lost in the idea of songwriting, and, while I kept listening to a lot of experimental music, I didn't ever think to try making much of it myself.

In the midst of the tumultuous break-up, sitting next to the faulty microwave, it occurred to me that this was an artificial limitation that I was placing on my creativity, and slowly I started evolving the idea of a song that would use the disembodied ambient sound of a malfunctioning machine as its central theme. I knew that, as far as my fanbase was concerned, it was an approach that was likely to come out of leftfield – fans of Social Distortion and the Dropkick Murphys are not necessarily people who also have an interest in soundscapes – but it's my record, and I was creatively fired up by the thought of taking this approach, so, in the depths of my misery, I started working on the nascent idea.

The other main component of the song came from about as far away as it could possibly do, in musical terms. There's an old English folk song called 'The Banks of Sweet Primroses' that, in some versions, opens with the lyric 'As I walked out one morning fair'. On my experimental microwave afternoons, I had on occasion tried singing various songs in the key of A to see how they'd fit with the A6 drone. There was something attractively counter-intuitive to me about singing an ancient song along with a damaged artefact of the twentieth century. That opening line fit perfectly, so I used it as the jumping-off point for the lyrics.

The final conceptual catalyst for the song was a free approach to timing. Singing along with a microwave gave me melodic context, but there was no rhythm to the drone, so I could sing freely, letting the timing of the lines stretch and distort as much as I liked. Pretty soon I'd settled on the idea that the verses to the song would have no time signature, though they would have their own internal form. Writing words without the formal

A bench by the Thames in South London, where
I wrote much of 'Broken Piano'

constraint of rhythm was a liberating experience for me; it felt closer to writing free verse, and I was able to stretch my literary capabilities. The general vibe of musical freedom also took me towards singing some of the lines in a falsetto voice, something I had always shied away from previously, nervous of how my voice sounded when it was so high and thin. In this context, it just added to the surreal atmosphere.

The lyrics themselves are based, of course, around the image of a broken piano. My ex's flat was near the River Thames, and when I wasn't haunting her kitchen, I'd often go and sit on a particular bench to contemplate the world, wallow in my sadness and, occasionally, write. There were some bins nearby but, I must confess, there wasn't actually a piano, broken or otherwise. That specific picture came to me in a photograph I saw somewhere of an old piano abandoned in a house in Chernobyl, left to moulder in the radioactive aftermath of the disaster. It haunted me, and somehow made me think of the microwave, another broken machine.

The picture of the broken piano that got my brain whirring . . .

Now, of course, anyone with any scant knowledge of musical theory and the piano will quickly tell you that it probably isn't really possible to pull out a selection of keys from the instrument in such a way as to leave the player only able to play in a minor key. That's a flight of fancy, a literary conceit. Nevertheless, I was hung up on the idea of malfunctioning technology, and I was captured by the image of an instrument that, in its decay, constrained the kinds of musical statements you could make with it. It fitted my mood at the time, I felt like what was happening in my personal life had broken some part of my creative function, leaving me only able to say sad things.

So the song began to grow into something coherent. The verses stayed loose but told the story, the melody wandering around as much as the timing did. The chorus brought in the beginnings of some rhythm, while also bringing in some bass notes which suggested the chords, in the way I'd worked out in that kitchen – D, F# minor, A, and E. Here, the story started to come together in the words as well. The early drafts of the song were lacking in something here, I needed a statement that would bring together not only the strands of this particular song, but the album as a whole. Somehow, somewhere, I got it: 'A sinner amongst saved men, on the banks of the muddy Thames'.* It's one of my proudest achievements as a writer, one of the best couplets I've put down, and I actually insisted on it being featured prominently in the artwork for the album.

As the song grew, I realised it needed to reach a climax of some sort. That hadn't always been where I was planning on taking the piece – a lot of post-rock tracks don't give in to that traditionalist instinct for form. But I wanted the song to land

* The last part of that was something of a nod to the title of a Nirvana live album, *From the Banks of the Muddy Wishkah.*

somehow, while retaining its sense of otherness. After a while I came up with the idea of using a tribal drum pattern, simple and stark but massive, looped over the end of the song. I didn't want it to feel like a normal drum part, more like something primeval and weird, but also huge. The approach was, in a literal sense, post-rock — taking the ingredients of a rock song, drums and crashing electric guitars, but recontextualising them to the point where they would feel unexpected and new.

It all came together in the studio in California. We recorded a long A6 drone and started building the song around it. It was a refreshingly illogical way of building a piece of music for me, and a lot of fun. The vocals were the second thing to be put down, which is very unusual, but the rest of the arrangement flows around the words, so it made sense. On the second verse, the Souls and I had a whale of a time digging into experimental soundscape territory, messing around with tape loops, feedback, and odd percussion. At one point I had slivers of silver foil tucked between the strings of an open-tuned acoustic guitar, run through a distortion pedal and an amp, which I was tapping with felt beaters — and I wasn't even high. We spent a lot of time getting the sound of the drums right for the finale, me leaning over Rich Costey's shoulder shouting, 'Bigger! Bigger!' In the end we had the five of us set up in the live room with a floor tom and a snare each, playing through the jolting rhythms like some mad marching band. We added layer upon layer of backing vocals to the last chorus, filling out the sound until it was a huge choir, a veritable explosion of harmonies.

I can remember listening back to a rough mix of what we had, at the point where we had finally decided to stop adding extra bells and whistles. Sitting in the control room of the studio, the speakers blasting, the song washed over me like a religious experience. And just like Ed Wood, I might even have whispered to myself, 'This is the one!'

*

'Broken Piano' had to be the last track on the album, there was nowhere else it could go. Once the record was released, it provoked some interesting reactions, as I'd suspected it would. Some people (a minority) got it straight away. Some people didn't ever really come around to it, a common fate for final songs on a playlist. Interestingly, a lot of people seemed to be unable to understand the melodic ideas in the verses. The high falsetto note is a major seventh, a G#, which is supposed to sound weird and slightly off-key, jarring with the root A note; but a lot of people just thought I wasn't very good at singing in that register and had missed my mark. Sigh.

I felt like the penny dropped for a lot of people when they saw us play it live. Surprisingly, we found it quite easy to recreate the atmosphere of the song outside the confines of the studio, and for a long while we took to finishing the main part of the set with this song. I'd reach the feedback-drenched end of the music and take a moment to stand at the microphone and survey the audience. It was a satisfying way to finish the show, not least because the crowds we were playing to by this point were the biggest they'd ever been.

In 2014, I did my first ever arena headline run in the UK. I'd done the Wembley show, but this tour was seven of those in a row around the country. Taking my show up to that level required some adjustment – not of the songs, but of their presentation. To that end, we had various extras on the stage, from specially built risers to a string section. My production manager at the time, Graham Kay, suggested to me that this might be the point in my career where I could experiment with pyrotechnics. I was initially very sceptical, but he persuaded me to think it over, and I came up with a plan. At the end of 'Broken Piano', as the final section drops, 'on the banks of the muddy *Thames*', we'd have some sparkler explosions go off across the front of the stage. A design was drawn up, a pyro guy was added to the crew, and we were set to go.

Cut to the first date of the tour, the Motorpoint Arena in Cardiff. My conceptual doubts about pyrotechnics returned, with a vengeance. It felt needless and showy to me, the kind of thing you might expect from a KISS show, but not from me. In sound-check, as they rigged the explosives, I started panicking and saying I wanted to cut them from the show. Graham was dismayed – it had taken a lot of time and effort to organise, and was also costing me a fair amount of money. I suggested that we could just let them off unexpectedly during Jay Beans On Toast's opening solo slot, without forewarning him, as a prank, but was firmly informed that that would be completely illegal. In the end, band and crew prevailed on me to give them a try that night, as planned. If I didn't like how it felt, we could drop them from the rest of the shows.

Come the moment of truth on the night, I had actually completely forgotten about the pyro, lost as I was in the moment (which, to be honest, is usually a mixture of artistic rapture and *trying not to fuck up the song*). As I sang the last line, I gazed out over the crowd, and only just managed to contain my shock as the front of the stage exploded into a galaxy of stars. There was an audible gasp from the crowd, and . . . it was just fucking glorious. It felt perfect, for the song, the night, the whole occa-sion. Standing there in the smoke and the noise, as one of my proudest musical achievements rang out over several thousand people, I felt like I'd achieved something with my life. This is the one, indeed.

GET BETTER

I got me a shovel,
And I'm digging a ditch,
And I'm going to fight for this four square feet of land
Like a mean old son of a bitch.
I got me a future,
I'm not stuck on the past.
I've got no new tricks, yeah I'm up on bricks,
But me, I'm a machine and I was built to last.

I'm trying to get better because I haven't been my best.
She took a plain black marker, started writing on my chest.
She drew a line across the middle of my broken heart and said
'Come on now let's fix this mess'.
We can get better because we're not dead yet.

They threw me a whirlwind,
And I spat back the sea.
I took a battering but I've got thicker skin,
And the best people I know are looking out for me.
So I'm taking the high road,
My engine's running high and fine.
May I always see the road rising up to meet me and my enemies
Defeated in the mirror behind.

It's just a knot in the small of your back:
You could work it out with your fingers.
It's just a tune that got stuck in your head:
You could work it out with your fingers.
It's just some numbers tangled up in your sums:
You could work it out with your fingers.
It's just a simple braille missive from the person you miss,
A reminder you could always be a little bit better than this.

So try and get better and don't ever accept less.
Take a plain black marker and write this on your chest:
Draw a line underneath all of this unhappiness,
Come on now let's fix this mess.
We can get better, because we're not dead yet.

*   *   *

Releasing and touring an internationally successful record through a major label is a discombobulating experience. The tour schedule for *Tape Deck Heart* was, to my surprise, longer and more intense than any I'd experienced before, and had the added excitement of a major back injury, sustained at Tennessee's Bonnaroo Festival 2013, which resulted in surgery and half a year of not playing guitar standing up. The success of the album had also taken me further into the mainstream of musical consciousness than I'd ever been before, or indeed since. Some of the ramifications of that were distasteful to me. I found myself being interviewed by 'celebrity' journalists backstage at festivals in the 'artist gifting' area a few too many times for comfort. I don't want to protest too much – being commercially successful is bloody lovely, for the most part. But there were a few creeping discomforts at the back of my mind.

At the same time, I had begun to emerge from under a self-imposed cloud in my personal life. The dust had settled on my previous broken relationship, and I was starting to enjoy my own company and rebuild my confidence. I was busy on the road touring a dark and introspective album, but in doing so, I was winning the race, playing bigger venues, all over the radio, selling records. It was an odd contrast. I started to feel like the next statement I made would be something more assertive and defiant.

These thoughts naturally fed into my creative process, which, as ever, was ticking over quietly in the background. In its way, *Tape Deck Heart* had been an experimental recording, within the paradigm of my own music. Experimentation is all well and good, but the forays into glossier production had left me hankering for a return to something earthier. I was also increasingly conscious of how unusual my career was starting to become. Very few artists, these days, find themselves in the position of making a sixth studio record while still on the upslope of their career. As the seemingly endless tour rolled on, I became obsessed with the idea of a restatement of purpose, a return to first principles. I wanted to remind myself and my audience who I was, where I came from, and why I deserved their attention.

The practical upshot of this newfound sense of purpose was technical. My crew had suggested and then succeeded in building a completely self-contained touring sound rig.* We brought with us every piece of equipment on the stage from show to show, down to the microphones, the stands, the cables, everything. Each day, no matter where we were, we were plugged in to the exact same audio system. The sound ran through our own digital monitor desk, positioned on stage left, and from there into our

* Enormous props to Graham Kay, Johnny Stephenson and Dougie Murphy here.

in-ear monitor ear-pieces, each one of us with a personalised mix, hearing exactly what we needed to hear. All of this meant that, once the crew had set up the backline, we didn't need to have a normal soundcheck, where you laboriously run through each instrument, tweaking the volume. In theory (and it did usually work!), once we were set up, we could just plug in and play, and everything would immediately sound perfect in our ears.

The great benefit of running our touring audio set-up this way was that it gave us, as a band, a couple of hours just to play *every single day* on the road. One of the things I'd noticed over the years is that songs change a lot in the live environment. This is natural, nothing to complain about per se. But it can be quite frustrating to work on a song in the studio, and then a month after the recording is released, in the context of playing it night on night in front of an audience, you finally work out the now-obvious kinks in the music or the lyrics* – but by then it's too late, the track has been released and accepted by the audience. My plan at this time was to try to circumvent that perennial problem by playing the new material in as much as possible, as a band, before getting anywhere near a studio. So it was that during 2013 and 2014, the Souls and I – and it's important to stress their contribution, to all the records they played on, but particularly this one – worked on the songs that became *Positive Songs for Negative People* for two hours every single show day for nearly two years.

As has often been the case, the first song I finished for the next album was a light in the darkness, leading the way. 'Get Better'

---

* Examples: 'Polaroid Picture' is too slow on the record; 'The Way I Tend to Be' needs a piano part in the final chorus, which Matt now does live. And so on.

was a song that came easily. I began with first principles: the key of G major, open chords, 4/4 time. With the deliberate exception of a major second in the bridge (A major, over a C#), the song uses only the four most basic chords, G, E minor, C and D. Lyrically, I had attempted to picture myself in my new, defiant resilient state, and had come up with the idea of standing my ground, shovel in hand, digging a moat around myself against whatever tides might come my way. In fact, the song's working title was 'Shovel Song'.*

While I was trying to keep my eye firmly on the prize of simplicity, the lyrics are a survey of where I was at that point in my life. I was determined to be an artist who was not 'stuck on the past', moving forward and saying new things, despite the fact that I had recently been (emotionally) 'up on bricks', and whether or not I had any 'new tricks'. I wanted to draw a line across (or perhaps under) all the heartbreak. I'd also recently experienced my first real taste of the downside of being more in the public eye, in the shape of a media character-assassination storm conjured up on Twitter and by the *Guardian* newspaper about politics. It wasn't any fun, at all, but, while keen to clarify some badly phrased, dumb, drunk statements, I had stood my ground, I had 'spat back the sea'. And in the midst of that nightmare, I'd been hugely touched by the support and friendship of The Sleeping Souls – truly the 'best people I know looking out for me'.

One of my favourite lyrics in the song, if not on the whole album, was actually given to me by, of all people, John Lydon,

* I also realised, after the song was finished and the album was being pressed, that I'd subconsciously borrowed the actual title from a song by Dan Le Sac Vs Scroobius Pip (who, among many other things, opened up the Wembley show in 2012). I messaged Scroobius and begged his blessing, or at least forgiveness, and he was nothing but charming about it. Thanks, Scroob.

a.k.a. Johnny Rotten, of the Sex Pistols and Public Image Limited.*
I happened to meet him backstage at a festival we were both
playing in Italy. I've heard of some people having bad experiences
with John, but in the brief moment we hung out he was perfectly
affable. I asked him to sign something for me, which he gladly
did. He wrote: 'To Frank: may the road rise to meet you, may
your enemies be defeated behind you.' I thought it was the coolest
thing I'd ever read, and immediately resolved to work that into
a song. Hence the second verse of 'Get Better'.

The bridge employs a metaphor about fingers. Working things
out with your hands has always struck me as the epitome of
keeping this simple. It's an idea I also used in an old Million
Dead song, 'Murder and Create', in the lines, 'The absolute zero
/ is arithmetic / on fingers and toes'. I wanted to say something
about keeping calm and remembering to go back to basics. I also
spent a lot of time in this period having my spinal disc injury
worked on by sports massage therapists, with their magic digits.
When your back hurts, or when you have a tune half written, or
when you have something to say but can't quite find the words
to say it, take a breath and count it out slowly.

Finally, the song has a lyrical turnaround for the final chorus,
a trick I fell in love with listening to Counting Crows songs.
And there at the end is the most basic statement of defiance I
could think of. There is always the possibility of improvement,
whether personally, artistically, or in any other domain, as long
as you're still alive and kicking. I've often been accused of being
an incorrigible optimist, and talking about this song, I suppose
it's a fair point.

* It really annoys me when people don't mention PiL when talking about
  Lydon; they are easily the Pistols' equal, possibly their superior.

So the basics of the song were in place. Now, as ever, for the lengthy process of working out the arrangement. The difference this time was that this was a practical rather than theoretical process. The monitor rig meant that the Souls and I could play through each iteration of the song we came up with and tweak it day by day. Our fancy audio desk even had the capacity to record what we were doing, so we could take away the day's work and mull it over in the quiet of the tour bus. And from time to time, always with a polite request for people not to record it,* we'd play the new songs as part of the set, to see how the crowd felt about it. I think it's possible to over-value audience reaction – if that was your only yardstick, you'd only write mosh parts and singalongs – but the attention of a few thousand strangers can certainly focus your creative mind on the strengths and weaknesses of the piece you're presenting to them.

Weirdly enough, my first approach to this song was based on my obsession, then and now, with the album *One Night Stand: Live at the Harlem Square Club* by Sam Cooke. It's a live soul workout, an absolute tour de force, but it's so raw and direct in its delivery that it sounds very punk to my ears. The drums are almost distorted, the songs are sharp and to the point and roll into each other every two minutes or so. It's an amazing album; you should check it out if you don't know it. It was a guiding star for *Positive Songs*, but in the end (thankfully) that was more about feel than specific sounds or styles. Still, at the beginning, 'Get Better' had a driving soul beat, like the song 'Chain Gang'. Over time that was edged out by a simpler approach, snares on the beat, and in fact the original drum part only survives in the

* Which always, with one exception, worked. Bands, you don't need to put up aggressive signs around the venue about photos and filming, you just have to treat your audience like adults and ask them nicely.

very last bar of the song now. Listening back through the myriad demos I have of the song (each labelled with the name of the town we were soundchecking in – Hamburg, Columbia MO, Leeds), I can hear the arrangement evolve. I was adamant that we'd explore every musical avenue that occurred, but also that we'd let the songs win the argument every time.

Aside from the drum beat, the other element that changed a lot over time was my own guitar part. On the original solo demo I'd naturally played the biggest, boldest open chords I could, to give a sense of the size of the song I was aiming for. Once the rest of the band were playing, I went through various different approaches – keeping the same chords, playing inversions, not playing at all. I had a frustrating time trying to figure out how to make it work, until Nigel finally suggested that I try playing electric on the song instead of acoustic. I never really had any specific animus against the idea of playing electric (so you can save your cries of 'Judas'), it just hadn't really occurred to me before, and I didn't have a rig or a guitar to use. That latter problem was quickly fixed by the crew, I tried it out on my new white hollow-bodied Gibson ES series Les Paul electric (be still my beating heart), and the question was answered. The song rocketed up in intensity.

I made a few more tweaks, as ever aimed at streamlining and strengthening the song. Originally, the song had a brief instrumental introduction before the lyrics began, but, at Matt's suggestion, I cut that out – get to the point! At one moment I decided to try scrapping everything we'd worked up and starting again, and was pleased to discover that we naturally found our way back to pretty much the same parts, proving that we were in the right place all along. Eventually, I was satisfied; the song was now ready to be recorded. Surely that'd be an easy thing to organise!

My relations with Richard O'Donovan, my A&R, suffered an unexpected dip at this point in my career. I can talk about all this now with the benefit of hindsight and a little humour, and rifts have been happily patched up, but it wasn't always an easy ride at the time. Much of the trouble I went through around this period is covered in my friend Ben Morse's documentary film about me, also titled *Get Better*. But to briefly summarise: I wanted the album to sound raw and capture the spirit of the live show that the Souls and I had perfected over the years. In practice, that meant I wanted to rehearse the songs to within an inch of their lives in a performing context, as we were doing, and then record them as quickly as possible, a band playing live in a room. Unfortunately, none of the producers suggested to me by the label seemed to grasp or accept this methodology, and we reached an impasse in late 2014 that saw me stuck at home in London with nothing much to do other than seethe about the fact the album had stalled. I spent a fair bit of time reacting to this by getting completely fucked up and letting my drug problems run out of hand; it was a dark time in my life, and I'm not overly proud of it.

In the end a solution was reached, in the person of Butch Walker. I knew of Butch as a singer-songwriter whose material and approach wasn't a million miles away from my own. I was surprised to learn he also produced records, so I managed to get in touch with him via some mutual friends. What I hadn't realised was that a lot of his production work was in the pop major leagues, with people like Pink and Taylor Swift. The label, when hearing me bring up his name, assumed that he would be out of my price range, but we'd already established a rapport, and a deal was easily struck. So it was that the band and I flew to Nashville in December 2014 to make a new album.

The session was a dream. We cut the whole album in nine days.

With each song, we'd run through what we had once or twice for Butch, he might make the occasional suggestion for a small tweak here and there, and then we'd start running takes. Almost every time, we used the third take of four. Once we had a run we were all happy with, we'd re-cut my acoustic guitar (if that's what I was playing), add some electric guitar doubles, re-cut the vocals and backing vocals, and finish the entire song. The first tune we worked on, and our introduction to this working method, was 'Get Better'. We didn't even realise that Butch was recording full takes at first, we were just running the song, but it was so natural and played

In the studio with Butch Walker and The Sleeping Souls,
Nashville, 2014

in that we had it down in no time. I was sober and off the cigarettes at the time, and I was singing really well. In fact, for every song on the record, we used a complete vocal take, no tuning or editing in sight. I'm proud of that.

When we finished the song, I remember hearing it back and

being filled with a sense of relief. It was everything I'd hoped it would be. It felt like an instant classic, as far as my own songs go, and in the event it was received that way by the audience. You know you've done good when a song can stand to be a set opener or closer in a live show, when you see the words inked on strangers' skin, when you can step back from the microphone and let the crowd sing the last chorus for you.* And, serendipitously (if a little weirdly), the message of aggressive optimism that I'd written into the song came back around and helped me out of the rut I'd fallen into before we got to Nashville. It was strange but reassuring, to be on the receiving end of my own message.

---

* Which is helpful, because it hits a high B at the end of the song, which is a stretch for me on a good day.

THE NEXT STORM

We had a difficult winter,
We had a rough few months,
And when the storms came in off the coast
It felt like they broke
Everything on us at once.
It's easy enough to talk about Blitz spirit
When you're not holding the roof up and knee deep in it,
And the pictures and the papers got ruined by the rain,
And we wondered if they'd ever get dry again.

But I don't want to spend the whole of my life indoors,
Laying low and waiting on the next storm.
I don't want to spend the whole of my life inside;
I want to step outside and face the sunshine.

We lost faith in the omens,
We lost faith in the gods,
We just ended up clutching at the empty rituals
Like gamblers clutching long odds.
And I don't care what the weather man is saying,
Because the last time that I saw him he was on his knees, he was praying.
The preachers and the scientists got soaked just the same,
And we wondered if they'd ever get dry again.

But I don't want to spend the whole of my life indoors,
Laying low and waiting on the next storm.
I don't want to spend the whole of my life inside;
I want to step outside and face the sunshine.

So open the shutters, raise up the mast,
Rejoice, rebuild, the storm has passed.
Cast off the crutches, cut off the cast,
Rejoice, rebuild, the storm has passed.

I don't want to spend the whole of my life indoors,
Laying low and waiting on the next storm.
I don't want to spend the whole of my life inside;
I want to step outside and face the sunshine.
I'm not going to live the whole of my life indoors.
I'm going to step out and face the next storm.

* * *

'Get Better' was the first piece of the puzzle for *Positive Songs*, and demo versions in various states of completion litter the archives I have from that time. Surprisingly, to me, 'The Next Storm' was actually one of the last. I'd forgotten, until I sat down to write this, how late in the day that song came together. In its beginnings, it was a very different song from the version that you might know.

I can remember where the song started. I was sitting in a recording booth at a radio station somewhere in the middle of America, waiting for the light to go red and the live session to begin. As the DJ waffled away about some local news item, I had a rare moment of emptiness in my usually hectic schedule, and I was holding a guitar. Predictably enough, my fingers started wandering around the neck, even before my brain engaged, trying to find new pathways around the strings and the melodies they might contain. After some initial fumbling, they fell into a little pattern that caught the attention of my active brain.

The most standard lick in rock'n'roll rhythm guitar is a little honky-tonk phrase, the origins of which are lost in time, but which was popularised by players like Sister Rosetta Tharpe, Chuck Berry, and indeed Status Quo. It involves playing a two-note chord (a dyad), with the root at the bottom, and the second note rising and falling between the fifth and the sixth – think of the opening of 'Cigarettes and Alcohol' by Oasis. It's an instantly recognisable, timeless riff. I was messing around with playing it in the key of C, a slightly unusual approach, as it's easier to play with the root as an open string, an E or A or D. Somewhere in my reverie, I kept the higher notes the same but changed the root note to an F. That turns the fifth and sixth into a more wistful and suggestive second and third, relative to the F root. I loved the way it took an obvious, swaggering trope and gave it a new feeling of openness and vulnerability. I spent the rest of my brief moment of respite toying with the figure, moving from the F to the C and back again. I was playing quietly, because I was waiting to go on air, and the gentle fragility of the performance became part of the attraction.

Over the next few weeks on the road, I kept toying with the idea, whenever my fingers had a free moment holding a guitar, and slowly the structure of a larger song started to suggest itself. I was particularly taken at the time with a set of imagery that had to do with farming and the weather. I suspect it was borrowed, subconsciously and by a roundabout route, from John Steinbeck's *The Grapes of Wrath*, with its harrowing portrait of the collapse of agriculture in the Oklahoma dust bowl in the 1930s. There was something moving in the idea of honest people, doing their best to remain stoic and work hard with the land against everything the elements could throw at them. In keeping with the rest of the material I was working on, towards the album title, which I already had in the bag, I didn't want it to be a negative piece. It was more a statement of resilience, survival against the odds.

The other mental image that contributed to this song is slightly more bizarre, and indeed is based on a false memory. I was absolutely convinced, without ever having checked, that there was a scene at the end of the film *The Wizard of Oz*, in which Dorothy returned to the farm and the aftermath of the twister, and helped her family clean up the devastation and start to rebuild. I was so sure of this that I drew on the images I had in my head of the scene extensively in writing the verses to this song. I loved the sense of commitment, of American pioneer spirit, in resolving to not let calamity get you down and to start over again. It was only after we'd actually finished the album and I mentioned it to someone else that I learned that I'd completely fabricated this scene; it's not in the film at all. I have no idea why I thought it was, but I'm kind of glad I did, as it informed the lyrics to 'The Next Storm'.

These lyrics took an absolute age to get right. It was one of the slowest births of a song I've ever had. I can vividly picture my notebook open on the piano in my flat, with maybe three lines finished. A few times a day, I'd wander over and read them through again, trying to naturally feel out what the next line would be. They were glacially slow in coming. One upside of that was that there were almost no alterations, edits or corrections; each individual line was eked out like blood from a stone. It also meant that the song lived with me for a long time, and I am proud of the end result. As well as successfully employing the imagery and metaphors I was aiming for, it also includes one of my all-time favourite couplets that I've written – 'Cast off the crutches, cut off the cast'. How's that for a perfectly balanced piece of writing? Well, I like it. And if that's not enough for you, there's even a cheeky reference to Louis Armstrong's 'Jeepers Creepers' – 'I don't care what the weatherman says . . .' Something for everyone, I'm sure you'll agree.

We had a difficult winter
We had a bad few months
And when the wise men told us the worst was passed
We didn't believe them all at once

I don't want to live inside for the rest of my life
We lost faith in the omens

The storm has passed
Summer has come at last
Pick up the pieces
Open the shutters
Rebuild

We know the storms too will come again
We built our homes on the floodplain.

Initial jottings for 'The Next Storm', before I started writing it properly

In time, I had a finished song. The majority of it featured the gentle riff, overlaid with a vocal melody in a low register that accentuated the introspective, plaintive feel of the music. However, in the middle, I added a dramatically different section. As the lyrics reached their climax – 'open the shutters . . . the storm has passed' – the full power of the band kicks in out of nowhere, like they'd been hiding in the wings all along. Everyone playing turned up to eleven,* the Souls drove the message across the finish line, until the riff reemerges from the wreckage at the end, this time feeling hopeful, like the survivor protagonist in the song itself, resolving finally onto a C major chord.

I loved the song, and considered it finished. I worked up a demo version,† and then briefly taught the band the chords for their moment of glory, laid that down once in a soundcheck recording session, and left it there. It was a slightly odd piece, but full of character and melody, and in keeping with the central themes of the album. Job done.

Or not. While we were working through the material I had amassed for us to collectively work on, Tarrant kept coming back to 'the storm song' again and again, insisting that there was gold in them hills. He was adamant that the musical and lyrical ideas in the song were being wasted in this esoteric arrangement, and that we should look at it again and consider some other approaches. Initially, I was resistant to this – the song was done; let it be! But he's a persistent fucker, and in the spirit of exploring all possible avenues when considering the songs, I reluctantly agreed that we should give it a go.

In the event, it was both a lot of fun and a complete musical revelation. Given how complete the original version felt to me, it was like we were working on a cover, rather than an original piece. That mindset was liberating, as it felt like I wasn't in danger of losing the work that I'd become attached to. That was safe and dry; now we could work on other angles. The first thing I did was to completely change the register in which I was singing,

---

* Can you turn a drum kit up to eleven? Or indeed any other number? I'll ask Nigel.
† Which was also eventually released on the *Ten for Ten* compilation.

taking the song back down to its original key of C (I'd been playing the riff with a capo on the fifth fret, putting the song in F). My voice entered a completely different emotional space straight away, bringing much more energy and a stronger sense of defiance to the words. Once the Souls had got their heads around the chord progressions and the structure, we tried a couple of different styles out. It was intriguing, but it hadn't quite found its metre.

Eventually, we tried out an idea that I can best describe as a 'Hail Mary pass'.* I'm not entirely sure where it came from – and we were lost in a rabbit hole of different time signature approaches just then, at Tarrant's suggestion – but I just blurted out the words: 'Thin Lizzy? Let's try it like Thin Lizzy.' I can't say I knew exactly what I meant by that, they're not a stylistically monotonous band, but somehow the Souls figured out what I was trying to say. After some brief discussion, Matt worked out a rolling version of the original riff on the piano, Nigel backed him up with the 12/8 shuffle Tarrant was so keen on, and Ben played ringing open chords over the top of me holding down the basics on the acoustic. The effect was instantaneous: the song had arrived in its finished form. My attachment to the stripped-back solo version evaporated like the morning dew.

I can honestly say that we were within striking distance of the finished version of the song within half an hour of this break-through. The feeling in the room was euphoric, yet still focused – we could see the finish line now. There were a few issues to get around with the new feel, chiefly how to make the middle section of the song land with enough impact now that the band were playing on the rest of the song. By halving the time on the drums, and me switching to electric guitar, we got over that

* Yet more sporting metaphors! Nurse!

hurdle. Once we were in the studio, Butch added one more touch. The last chorus was basically the same as its predecessors. Butch said the chorus needed to come up one final notch to bring the song home, and sent me off into a side room to think it over. Five minutes later I had it – bringing in the crowd backing vocals as a call-and-response, reviving the lyrical and melodic motif of the bridge. The song was complete.

It's one of my more prized songs in my catalogue in terms of the sound and arrangement. I just feel like it's a tour de force, the sound of a band in peak condition, sculpted by years on the road. I'm extremely proud of the musical unit the five of us have built over the years, and, as I've mentioned, one of the aims of *Positive Songs* was to capture the strength and energy of our live shows on tape. I think we succeeded overall, but especially with this song. Out of all the numbers in my catalogue, it's the one that has changed the least over the years, and we've played it a lot. We got it right first time – well, maybe the second.

THE OPENING ACT OF SPRING

Oh the birds are ringing in the opening act of spring,
And I have fallen down and I'm so much worse than I have ever been.
Oh the season's acting strange, and I know that something has to change,
But there is no path I can choose that will not bring somebody pain.

And oh, please forgive me for the things that I must do.
But oh, though I have hurt so many people it was never my intention to hurt you.

Oh the clouds are gathered thick and in my stomach I feel sick,
And I have all this drive and no idea what I should do with it.
But they say there is a calm after the passing of the storm,
So I can dream of going back outside when the rain and thunder's done.

And all the old folk say they can
Tell which way the river's flowing, tell which way the wind is blowing,
By watching careful for the
Signs among the little things, the barking dogs, the birds on wing.
And I am deaf and blind and
I can't say if I can change the patterns that have caused you pain,
For I was raised in suburbs
Sheltered from the sun and rain, far away from subtle season's change.

Oh baby I will read about the buzzing of the bees,
About the grass and snakes and spawning lakes and different types of trees,
And I will find a way that leads from cruel April into May,
And someday soon it will be June and you'll decide to stay.

* * *

As noted, my major creative preoccupation when I was working on *Positive Songs for Negative People* was the idea of going back to basics, rediscovering the beginnings of my thinking about music and reasserting that approach. However, much in the way that Sepultura embraced rap metal around the *Roots* album,* there's a whiff of historical revisionism in the air here. *Positive Songs* is basically an indie rock record with strong folk overtones. A careful examination of my track record will show that, in fact, between Million Dead and my early solo records, there wasn't actually a moment when I was making music exactly in that style, though I was hovering around it. If I'd truly gone back to my own roots, the album would either have been a post-hard-core workout, or else a collection of slightly sarcastic solo numbers.

I was aware of this contradiction on some level while I was writing and recording the material. I suppose I was harking back to the basics of my taste, rather than my own output. I was also, as I've said, trying to capture the essentials of our collective live performance as a band, without getting lost in the trappings of endless extra instrumentation in the studio. All the same, I could sense the incongruity of having the boldest rock songs of my

---

* Come for the thoughts about songwriting, stay for the obscure bitchy comments about nineties metal! Sepultura's 'roots' were classic death metal; they had released four albums of it.

career, songs like 'Get Better' and 'Glorious You', on an album that was supposed to be a return to something older.

More specifically, I spent much of my early career talking about and describing my music as 'folk music'. As I've explained, on a lot of levels that was an ideological statement more than anything else, but there was of course a sonic element to it as well. Throughout all those long, hazy Nambucca weekends, my obsession had been with acoustic instruments and Appalachian harmonies, the music of Laura Marling, Kid Harpoon and Marcus Mumford. At some point in this writing process, I decided I wanted to have at least one song on the album that would incorporate those sounds, and be a true restitution of form.

I was helped along my way with this by Matt Nasir. Matt had started to play a mandolin as part of the live show ever since we'd used one to fill out the sound of the introduction to 'The Way I Tend to Be'. Over time, starting with that song, we had evolved a set of two-man arrangements of my tunes, with Matt on mandolin and me on guitar, both of us singing, that was perfect for radio sessions and shows where we couldn't bring the whole backline and personnel required for a full-band performance. And of course, if you leave two musicians alone together with instruments for long enough, they'll start coming up with new musical ideas – all the more so if one of them is Matt.

Matt is truly one of the most remarkable musicians I've ever met (not to do down anyone else in the band – they're all incredibly talented). The last to join the band, he's the most classically trained member of The Sleeping Souls, but he's also driven by a restless, relentless creative imagination, and an ability to produce new ideas at the drop of a hat. He can also play every bloody instrument under the sun, usually better than I can. Despite the mandolin being his *fourth* instrument (after bass, guitar and piano), he'd mastered it in no time at all. And then, in the green rooms of radio stations across the world, he started messing around with his own compositions, of course.

Morning TV with Matt Nasir on Mandolin, somewhere in America, 2013

As I write this entry of this book, Matt is peering over my shoulder (hi Matt!) and wants it to be known that the mandolin riff that leads 'The Opening Act of Spring' is the very first thing he ever came up with on that instrument. The talented bastard. My memory is of him running it around over and over again in any moment of downtime when we were in duo mode, and me slowly working out the root guitar chords that underpinned it. For a while, it was nothing more than another 'soundcheck riff'. But from such small acorns, mighty oaks of songs can grow. After all, Pantera's 'I'm Broken' started as a soundcheck riff.*

* And again! Also, Pantera were the best metal band of the nineties, hands down.

In time, I realised the riff was catchy and striking enough to form the basis of an actual proper song. I haven't, in my solo career, done much in the way of co-writing (aside from my album with Jon Snodgrass), but that's not because I'm against the idea. At the beginning, there wasn't really anyone else around to write with, and I was so full of ideas (and indeed furiously trying to outline my own creative character), so I wrote alone. As time went by, there were a few moments of natural collaboration with the Souls that crossed the line from arrangement ideas to song-writing – for example, Nigel changed a pivotal chord in 'Wessex Boy' (from a G major to an E minor), Ben wrote the middle-eight riff of 'To Absent Friends', and a piano idea of Matt's runs through the bridge of 'Plain Sailing Weather'. But prior to this song, I hadn't really written a song from the ground up with someone else since the Million Dead days.

It was an invigorating experience for me. We began with the riff. Next, I contributed the verse part (all overlaid with non-sensical syllabic mumbling, for the time being). Matt had a descending figure on the mandolin worked out that fit beautifully over an E chord, which became the start of the chorus; I came up with the second half and the vocal melodies. At some point, I put a capo on my second fret, changing my playing into G shapes (while keeping the key of A, as Matt was using open strings and so couldn't shift his part down), which felt more natural to me.* The bridge section was, as far as I can remember, a straight 50/50 collaboration. The fact that I reach a point where I can't remember exactly who brought what to the table

---

* On the record, Butch had me and Matt both on acoustic guitar, one with capo and one without, standing around a single stereo microphone, creating a lovely folky blend – that's why, on the record, it's hard to work out the chord shapes that we're using.

is, for me, a great sign. The layout of the song worked itself out all on its own. We kept playing the ever-expanding piece in soundchecks and dressing rooms. Before long, Tarrant had stepped into the picture and worked out the rolling fifths bassline. Nigel quickly picked up the vibe with a brushed train beat, and Ben overlaid the second verse and the choruses with a beautiful slender tremolo guitar melody. 'The Opening Act of Spring' was, appropriately enough, given the lyrical subject, a truly organically grown song.

Speaking of the lyrics . . . All throughout the process of the music coming together, I'd been working on the melodies for the tune without thinking of words at all. With each repeated run-through of the song, certain patterns of sounds had begun to solidify, and even, in some cases, evolve into actual words. It's a strange, subliminal approach to writing lyrics, to let your subconscious spill ideas uncontrolled out of your mouth.* In a way, it lets me take a step back and examine my output like I'm a bystander, a third party. At the very least, it can give me an interesting insight into my own preoccupations.

Looking back now, I can happily admit that, from the point of view of subject matter, *Tape Deck Heart* and *Positive Songs* are very much two sides of a coin, a yin and yang, if you will. I was searching for a sense of closure, of escape from the wreckage. As the contours of the words began to emerge for this song, I realised I was putting together the last song I would write for my ex, Isabel. It's an explanation, an apology, a plea for forgiveness and understanding. I don't actually know if she ever heard it – after what happened with 'Anymore', I got out of the habit of asking her opinion about my music.

* A technique apparently much used by Chris Cornell in Soundgarden. OK, OK, I'll stop now.

My stream-of-consciousness approach to this tune also found me using the weather-based metaphors that had come to the fore in 'The Next Storm'; in fact, the line about 'the passing of the storm' always made me feel like these two songs were of a piece, hence them being next to each other in the album track-listing. I had a sense of reaching back again to that MewithoutYou album I mentioned, in terms of the variety and eccentricity of the vocabulary employed here. And no song of mine written without affectation would be complete without a little nod to T. S. Eliot – 'cruel April into May'.

The problem, or the advantage (depending on your point of view) of writing in this direct, uncontrolled way is that you might end up saying very raw and personal things about yourself. Of course, on some levels, that's something I'm actively trying to do with a lot of my words. All the same, I was interested to read back one particular line from this song, as I think it's not a bad assessment of my entire character, for good or ill: 'I have all this drive but no idea what I should do with it'. Looking back over my life, the bits I'm proud of are the times when I have found positive and constructive paths in which to channel my inherent hyperactivity. At other times it has led me down my darkest paths. As to where that drive comes from in the first place? I sincerely wish I knew.

By the time 'The Opening Act of Spring' was finished, along with the rest of the album, I was thankfully in a place where my energies were being put to better uses again. The song feels like a wonderful piece of closure, for everything that happened between me and Isabel, and for everything I'd written about on *Tape Deck Heart.* Looking forward, getting this song and its subject matter out of my system helped clear the way for me to go somewhere entirely other on my next record. But much more on that subject in good time.

JOSEPHINE

I heard the name Josephine,
It came to me in a dream.
And I don't usually set too much store by the things
These things might mean.
But it was spoken with seriousness,
More of a whisper than a scream.
So now I'm waiting on some Josephine
To show herself to me.

I could have been anyone I imagined I could be;
I just needed somebody to wake me from my sleep.
I could have been Napoleon, could have been Beethoven,
Could have been anyone but uncomfortable me.
So come on now Josephine, show yourself to me.

Come on now Josephine,
Give me what I need.
I don't like to be needy but needs must,
I can't stand being the person that I've been.
I'm an impending car crash,
And you're the first one on the scene.
I'm a defeated commander, I'm a half-deaf composer,
I'm a strange name whispered in a dream.

Come on now Josephine, let's pretend it's Halloween.
You come as a car crash, I'll go as James Dean.
I'm Napoleon on Elba, and you're a hundred days in 1815.
I wrote all of these letters to my immortal beloved,
And you're the only one who's ever going to know what they mean.

Come on now Josephine, wake me from my sleep.
I could have been anyone, but I ended up being me.
I could have been wide awake, could have been what you need,
I wish that I was anyone except for just me.
So come on now Josephine, show yourself to me.

* * *

The catalogue of popular song is positively overflowing with songs that use a woman's name for a title, from 'Peggy Sue' to 'Jenny from the Block'. There's an entire *Family Guy* sketch about it. And it's something I have been guilty of myself in my career, with 'Isabel', 'Peggy Sang the Blues' and 'Susannah' (with Jon Snodgrass). Even though those songs are all about real people, I can admit that it is, in fairness, an over-used trope. All I can say in defence of the song 'Josephine' is that it isn't actually about anyone in particular, which is sort of the point.

I also have more than a few songs in my drawer that originated, conceptually, as dreams, the most obvious one being 'I Am Disappeared'. 'Josephine' also literally came to me in a dream, as the song says. I was staying in a hotel by the bridge in Lancaster city centre one night. My older sister lives there and we were having a family gathering; her house wasn't big enough to cater for the whole tribe, so after dinner I walked into town, checked in and went to sleep. That night, I had an intense but vague dream about someone I couldn't quite get a hold of or see clearly. And then, right at the end of the dream, I heard someone whisper the name 'Josephine', right into my ear, extremely clearly. It was spooky. I actually woke up and looked around the room in fright.

The experience was sufficiently affecting for it to stick with me for a couple of days. I didn't know anyone by that name,* so I started researching famous and historical Josephines. Two quickly came up, one of whom I'd heard of – Empress Joséphine de Beauharnais, Napoleon's first wife. The other, who I hadn't known about, was Josephine Brunsvik, Beethoven's secret lover, and the likely intended recipient of a curious letter he wrote addressed to his 'Immortal Beloved'. I am something of a history nerd – it's crept into my lyrics on more than a few occasions – so I was intrigued by all this.

The dream remained with me for some time, and I decided I wanted to sing about it. But I was having real trouble figuring out *what* I would sing, what I was trying to say, what the point of the whole exercise was. It seemed a little esoteric, to say the least, to be writing a song about a woman who I didn't know, who didn't exist.

And then I realised that, in fact, I had stumbled across my subject matter. As I drew away from the wreckage of my broken relationship, I was starting to repair the damage I'd inflicted on myself. Part of that involved me enjoying the opportunities that are available to a single musician on the road. I don't want to be overly explicit in talking about this, as a liaison involves two people, and it's not my place to discuss someone else's business here. At the same time, I don't want to be prudish about it either – in every case, it involved two consenting adults, and I had a

* Or so I thought. A long while later, after the song was out, my friend Josie (ahem) pointed out that, in fact, I did. I'm an idiot.

good time with some great people. Nevertheless, after a certain time, that kind of serial philandering reveals itself to be a profoundly empty way to live. I wanted to connect with someone again, and it wasn't for lack of trying – I'm one of those incurable romantics who finds it easy to convince myself I've fallen in love (and, predictably, that means I found it easy to walk away as well). I felt like I was searching for someone who I hadn't found yet.

With the benefit of hindsight and some small amount of hard-won wisdom, I can see now that this too is not an especially healthy way to approach life and love. Hopefully we all come across someone who completes us, someone with whom we can be our honest selves, but it's a little bit skewed to spend your time actively searching for that, vetting each person who wanders into your path in the hope that they might be 'the one', and trying to force them into some pre-existing template. It's not a very mature form of behaviour. I was certainly guilty of that, and that's essentially what this song is about – the hypothetical perfect other. In the event, I did find someone I'm going to spend my life with. She's amazing, perfect, wonderful, but it didn't happen in the way that I had been expecting it to, at all – which is probably why it works.

That's a story for another time. Back on topic, I started writing the words, one line at a time. Not long into the process, I noticed that I had begun with a very simple rhyme structure – every line the same, an A-A-A-A pattern, in the technical lingo. Something about that appealed to me. Sometimes a restriction in writing is a good thing, it can push you to be more creative within your artificially limited means. So I stuck with it, and it's still one of my favourite things about the song.

I worked hard to capture not only the dream but also my own sense of incompleteness and yearning. Perhaps the fault for not finding my perfect partner was my own. I found myself channelling Marlon Brando's legendary speech in *On the Waterfront* – 'I coulda been a contender. I coulda been somebody.' Hitting my stride, the second theme of the song became my frustration at my own imperfections in life. I was so happy with the phrase 'uncomfortable me' that, for a time, it was a contender for the title of the song,* and indeed the whole album.

The ghosts of Napoleon and Beethoven thread through the song, a 'defeated commander' and a 'half-deaf composer', both of them yearning the loss of their Josephine, their 'immortal beloved'. I also brought in a couplet that I had had jotted down in a notebook for many years: 'Let's pretend it's Halloween / You come as a car crash, I'll go as James Dean'. It had been there, homeless in my jottings, for a few years already, waiting for the perfect moment to present itself, and here it was, finally. It's one of my proudest bits of poetry, even if I did realise, after the event, that I had partially borrowed the imagery (by accident,

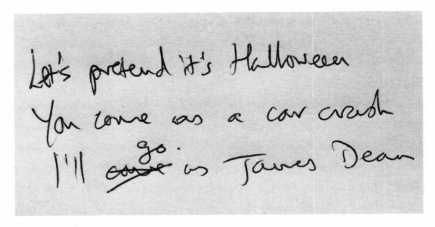

This was hanging around the edge of my notebook for many years

* Of course, 'Josephine' is a better title. On that note, 'Four Simple Words' should, obviously, have been called 'I Want to Dance'. You live and learn.

subconsciously) from the song 'Crush' by Cory Branan. Thankfully Cory and I are old friends; I ran it past him, and he asserted, in his timelessly wise Southern drawl, that 'everything is stolen'. All the same, you should check that song out, if you don't already know it.

Musically, I also delved deep to find the right starting point for the song. In my late teens and early twenties, in between being in a school band called Kneejerk and Million Dead, I had spent a little while experimenting with more electronic music. I was very into a lot of tracks on labels like Warp Records and City Centre Offices at the time. I'd also been hugely taken (like everyone else) with the Postal Service album, *Give Up*, released in 2003. I had an idea about trying to marry minimal electronic beats with guitars and a song-based approach, in the style of Jimmy Tamborello. Unfortunately, I was pretty rubbish at programming that kind of stuff, and my songwriting wasn't up to much either, so after a short while I was back finding my feet in a hardcore band again. But I still have endless tapes of those half-baked ideas, and some of the ingredients still have some nutritional value.

Specifically, I had an old song called 'Soil' that had been based around a slender guitar riff in A minor, high up the neck. The lyrics for that piece eventually evolved into the Million Dead song 'Sasquatch', but the guitar part was on the scrapheap. One day, in a soundcheck when we were working on new mate-rial, and when I had my new toy – an electric guitar! – in my hands, my fingers wandered into those old shapes, and the whole riff came flooding back to me. Shorn, for the moment, of my ambitions towards electronica, I started jamming it around with Nigel, feeling our way towards something like a Death Cab for Cutie song, and the music of 'Josephine' started to emerge.

As the lyrics for the song were essentially already finished, and as I found the melody and the basic layout pretty quickly, the main work to be done was in arranging the piece. And that took for-fucking-*ever*. I probably have more soundcheck recordings of this song than any other, and they are all infinitesimally different from one another. Guitar parts and keys parts swap around, the drums stop, start, splutter and half-time. I suppose there was method to the madness at the time, and in a way I'm proud of our evident dedication to the task of trying all possible alternatives, but it sounds like an endless, shapeless morass to me now, listening back, though there are certain developmental themes that I can pick out.

My guiding parameter for this song was to keep it as something driving and simple in the rhythm section, as a counterpoint to the delicate weaving of the guitar part and the lyrics. This actually led to probably the biggest argument that the Souls and I have ever collectively had. Our creative and professional relationships are multi-layered and complex, and on occasion it can be unclear where the boundaries of authority lie. In the final analysis, this is my project, so I retain a power of veto, but of course, the boys are talented players and arrangers themselves, and have strong opinions about what works and what doesn't. Nigel and I butted heads over the drum parts for this song for a protracted length of time, which, combined with the everyday stresses of being on the road for long stretches of time, led to a major bust-up. Of course, being middle-class Englishmen, it was all conducted with an icy air of cordiality, but it got to the point where Nigel was saying he wasn't sure he was the right drummer for the album, or indeed the band. I was shocked and dismayed that it had become that serious, and after a cooling-off period, we came back to it with clearer heads. We didn't actually settle the exact parts he was going to play until Butch Walker weighed in to the discussion in the studio, brilliantly finding an approach that both split our differences and was self-evidently correct. I'm very glad that Nigel decided to stay with me.

The other major change, as the song evolved, was the birth, growth and eventual domination of the top-line synth part that Matt plays. I was surprised, on listening back, to hear how late in the day that arrived. Actually, there's a clearly empty moment in the way the lyrics fall over the chorus, and after a time Matt began to experiment with filling that with some melodic information. My ears caught on, and I was reminded of my love for the band Reggie and the Full Effect, who combine blissful pop melodies with heavy guitars and huge analogue synthesizer sounds. Working against some of the band's inherent scepticism, we pushed the melody to the forefront of the song on such a synth sound, backing it with Ben's electric guitar, and eventually with 'woah' backing vocals, until it reached the state you hear on the recording. It wasn't part of the initial idea by any stretch, but it grew into a central component of the song, one definitively provided by the Souls.

'Josephine' stands now as one of the weirder songs on *Positive Songs,* not least because it's arguably not really a 'positive' song at all. Nevertheless, it fits into a special category for me – a song that I find quite difficult to explain. On its release, I was bombarded with questions about it, about who Josephine was and what I was trying to say. I found myself unable to answer coherently, and in the end I suppose I just have to put on the song for people to listen to. And, given that we're talking about songwriting here, that seems like an excellent thing to me.

SILENT KEY

On the 28th of January 1986 Christa McAuliffe
Gazed in horror as the O-rings failed,
And she died, and she died, and she died.

For the next agonising two minutes and forty-five long seconds
She called out the truth on a broken radio:
'I'm alive, I'm alive, I'm alive'.

It came as some surprise to realise that
As she lost everything
The world was revealed in a transmission so real
That she understood everything:
You're still alive.

Four thousand nautical miles as the crow flies away
A home-made ham radio in the loft of a Hampshire family home
Came alive, came alive, came alive.

And so the four-year-old amateur operator thus became
The only person to hear Christa's last desperate communique:
'We're alive, we're alive, we're alive'.

It came as some surprise to realise
While he didn't catch everything,
The world was revealed in a transmission so real

That he understood everything:
You're still alive.

And Christa said:

'The darkness up above
Led me on like unrequited love,
While all the things I need
Were down here in the deep blue sea.'

At four years old I heard the truth on my radio,
So now I keep a moment's silence for my Silent Key.

* * *

I've mentioned my first foray into writing character songs, with 'Balthazar, Impresario'. By this stage in my career as a writer, I was both gaining more confidence, and starting to look further afield for subject matter. People often ask me whether it gets easier or harder to write songs as time goes by, and the answer is: both. Once I have an idea to write about and some basic building blocks to work with, turning that raw material into a song is easier, because I'm more skilled at my craft. But finding those initial ideas gets harder as the low-hanging fruit, available to every young writer in the beginning, gets used up. I've written my basic songs about love, travelling, belief and so on. If I don't want to repeat myself, then I have to dig deeper to find new sources of inspiration.

Clive James is one of my favourite writers – more on him with regard to the next album – both as a poet and as a cultural critic. In 1972, he wrote an amazing critical piece on Bob Dylan for *Cream* magazine, in which he argues that Dylan had exhausted his initial, typically rock'n'roll source of material – his 'instinct-ive, unstudied spontaneity'. After a time, simply drawing on the wild musings of your own id becomes repetitive. James argues that Dylan, and rock music in general, needs to find a way of systematising and bringing a sense of discipline to its search for sources of inspiration if it is to continue to grow, progress, or even just have anything interesting to say (and this in 1972!). On a much smaller, less significant level, this comment has resonated with me enormously as I've aged as a songwriter. At the very least, it has pushed me to search widely for ideas for songs, outside the confines of my own solipsistic experience. On the face of it, it goes against the old adage, 'write what you know'. But what you know is necessarily limited; at some point, you have to move beyond that, even if you try to retain a sense of keeping the *emotional* content within your own knowledge and experience.

I started thinking about all of this towards the end of the writing process for *Positive Songs*. That album, and its predecessor, are very much examples of songwriting that draws directly on raw personal experience for its subject. I became aware that I was reaching the end of that seam of ideas, and keen to look beyond them. For the most part that realisation influenced my approach for the next record, *Be More Kind*, but it also made an impact here, with the song 'Silent Key'.

Winnipeg's John K. Samson has long been one of my song-writing idols. His work in The Weakerthans and as a solo artist nears perfection, for me. He has a literary sensibility that is rare in rock music, and his lyrics are some of the few that bear laying out as poetry on the page. He has a great line in idiosyncratic character songs, writing about a man who saw Bigfoot (in 'Bigfoot'), Arctic explorers (in 'Our Retired Explorer'), or even cats (in his suite of songs about Virtute the cat, who I happen to have tattooed on my left forearm). I'd long been toying with the idea of trying my hand at that kind of approach to a song, and thankfully, somewhere along the way, I came up with the seed of an idea.

I cannot now remember where and when it came to me, but one of my notebooks has a hastily jotted down entry on the inside flap of the cover, which simply says 'Christa McAuliffe song'. The Challenger Shuttle Disaster of 1986 hovers just on the edge of my memory. I was four years old at the time, and my mother (who taught at my primary school) certainly says that it was discussed, both after the tragedy and before, not least because

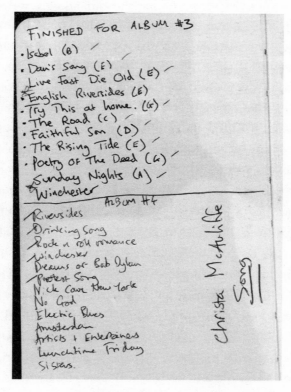

Lists of songs for albums 3 and 4(!), complete with a
note about Christa McAuliffe

McAuliffe, the citizen astronaut, was herself a primary school teacher, included in the mission to engage the youth of America and the world with the Space Program. But I can't recall if my memories of the event are real, or if I entered them into my own record sometime after the fact; childhood memory often straddles the border between myth and truth.

Regardless, as a child of the 1980s, the disaster was part of the fabric of my folk memory of growing up. Sometime many years later, I found myself reading random websites late one night when I couldn't sleep, and stumbled across a piece detailing how the events of that awful day in January unfolded. I hadn't known much about it other than the bare headlines, so I was devastated to read about it in more detail. Investigators believe that the crew survived in the capsule after the explosion, dying only when it smashed into the sea, two minutes and forty-five seconds later. That idea, of the crew trapped inside a tiny space, watching the world they'd so recently left rushing up to meet them through the window, haunted me for a long while. Somewhere in the recesses of my brain, an idea for a song was starting to take shape. I made a note in my notebook.

That note stayed as nothing more than some undeveloped pen-strokes for a long while. I kept circling back to it, running my tongue over the rotten tooth, but I couldn't find the right way into the subject matter. I tried writing from a first-person perspective, but that felt presumptuous. I tried second person, but that had a tone of accusation that didn't make sense. Finally, I settled on a journalistic approach, at least for the first half of the song. All along, I was trying hard to be sensitive to the fact that I was dealing with the death of real human beings, in the recent past, who had family and friends still alive and hurting. No matter how unlikely it is that any of them would ever hear my song, I wanted to make sure that it wouldn't be disrespectful to the dead.

I kept going back to the article I read and couldn't help myself constantly imagining myself in the doomed capsule. I tried to picture what it would have been like, should they have been conscious. And it occurred to me that they would most likely have tried to communicate with the world below. I started thinking about what anyone would, could have said in that situation. I like to think they would have found some sense of peace and acceptance, some understanding, though of course I could never actually know.

(While we're here, I should mention that it wasn't until after I'd finished the song that I became aware of various tabloid hoaxes that claimed that the astronauts had actually radioed back to earth. I have no truck with these ghoulish, exploitative conspiracy theories. I hope it's clear that the song I wrote is a piece of fiction, one that was intended to be respectful. The report into the disaster concluded that the passengers were, almost certainly, mercifully unconscious during their fall.)

While thinking about radios and transmissions, I found myself delving into another obscure corner of the internet, and finding out about the world of ham radios, amateur homemade equipment used for experimental and recreational communication. I discovered an intriguing term, 'silent key', which respectfully describes a ham operator who is deceased.* Immediately I knew that this would fit into the song I was trying to write about Christa McAuliffe. The idea that she had in some way been part of a ham network in her final broadcast seemed apt, and it also brought in the suggestion of a recipient for the message, and thus a potential to involve a first-person protagonist in the song. This would bring it back into emotionally known territory for me as a writer.

* It comes from the Morse code prosign 'SK', which signals the end of a transmission.

Of course, I was four years old at the time, and knew nothing about radio equipment (now or then). But the song is, as I've said, a flight of fancy, and the full imagery started to become clear. I had a picture of young me, fiddling with the dial in the loft of my family home, and stumbling across Christa's final message to the world. There was satisfying bathos in the idea of a small child learning the true meaning of life in such bizarre circumstances, and not quite knowing what to do with it.

Of course, for the song to work structurally, the content of the fictional communiqué had to be weighty enough to bear the load being placed upon it. I reached a point where I had all of the song finished apart from that section, and I remember taking a deep breath, laying down my pen, and thinking that it would take me a long time to craft something good enough. I went to take a shower, and somehow that old trick worked again, and it came to me there and then, fully formed: 'The darkness up above . . .' Christa, and by extension humanity, had been drawn by its quest for meaning to the stars, when in reality the truth was down below all along, hidden in the waters that were about to claim her life.

The musical evolution of the song was a protracted one. Sometimes you can start working with one idea, and over time change it beyond recognition, move so far away from it that you have something completely other, and the original idea remains intact, to be used for something else another day. That's what happened with this song. It all started with a riff, written in a soundcheck in Aberdeen, that isn't even in the final song, and which I fully plan to use again in good time. The band and I kicked the idea around, letting it branch out in all different directions. A second motif arrived – originally written in open G tuning on an acoustic, but later transposed into the key of E in standard tuning and put onto my electric, to fit with the first piece of the puzzle – which eventually became the basis of the finished piece. The feel gradually emerged as being something inspired by Weezer, specifically their masterpiece record, *Pinkerton*, an essential album for anyone interested in rock music, pop melody and songwriting. The song is characterised by a woozy reliance on flattened thirds that right themselves (shifting from a C to a C# in the main riff over an A root, descending down the scale in the outro section). It took a long time for us to settle on the structure, but the work was good once it was done.

Recording the song with Butch was, for the most part, an easy process – he's also a huge Weezer fan, so he knew what I was aiming for. There was one final element to get right, however. Christa's final lament, the finale of the song, had to be right, and I had long since decided that this meant it had to be sung by a woman, someone who could properly inhabit her voice. During the endless process of recording demos, we had various friends stop in and lay down a vocal for the version at hand – Nigel's Norwegian then-girlfriend Alyssa Nilsen and my Australian pal Emily Barker both did a wonderful job. However, for the album proper, I wanted to look further afield.

One of my conditions was that I thought it would be appropriate for the singer to be American, like Christa. Various names came up in conversation – my own ideas and suggestions from the label – friends and famous people alike. Given that Butch has worked with her in the past, Taylor Swift was briefly mentioned, but the idea didn't go anywhere – Butch didn't feel right asking, and of course, even if it had come off, it would have overshadowed the song and possibly the entire album.* We

* The label got a bit excited about this and it started a rumour about the whole thing that I'm happy to put to bed here.

actually left the studio in Nashville in December with the issue unresolved, the part unsung. Fortunately, early in the new year, Xtra Mile began working with an amazing singer from Colorado called Esmé Patterson. She has a voice to break hearts through the ages, and after catching one of her London shows, I knew I'd found the singer I needed. She was happy to be asked, and I got her into a studio for an afternoon to finish the part and thus the whole album. She did a wonderful job; the moment when her voice arrives in the song remains one of my absolute highlights on *Positive Songs*.

THERE SHE IS

I have wandered through the dark,
Through the dirt — I was hurt —
And in the end I came back to the start,
And I stumbled — Lord knows how I stumbled.
I slipped on myself, no help from anyone else,
I feel in love, and I was humbled.

There she is — isn't she everything?

Down at the bottom, I found the things I'd forgotten,
And despite all I've done, I can learn, I can learn,
And this time, I'm going to hold onto them.
I'm going to forgive myself, and then ask for forgiveness,
Crossing my fingers and toes, because God only knows
I need this, Lord how I need this.

Isn't she everything I need?
I needed someone who'd believe me,
I needed someone who wouldn't leave me,
I needed her.

There she is — isn't she everything?
And I will give, I will give anything.

Anything you need,
I promise you I will believe you,
I promise you I'll never leave you,
I need my girl;
There she is.

* * *

On my travels around the world through the years, I've had many flattering and touching conversations with people who enjoy my music. People have said the most wonderful things to me about how my songs have touched their lives, and I am constantly humbled by the experience. One particular breed of this type of interaction has long given me pause for thought. More than a few people have told me that they have used one of my songs at their wedding. My initial and vocal reaction is to be humbled and grateful – what a wonderful compliment. I'm usually struck, quietly, by a second, more troubled thought – 'which fucking *one*?' Up to a certain point in my career, essentially all my songs about affairs of the heart were, in my view, unhappy ones (with the possible exception, as discussed, of 'Isabel'). That says quite enough about my own romantic ineptitude, and of course, in my view, a song means whatever the listener chooses it to mean, so it's all good. Nevertheless, it was a strange position to find myself in, contemplating a couple pledging their eternal union to a song like 'The Way I Tend to Be'.

Thankfully, in recent years, and with my seventh album, *Be More Kind*, this has changed. I've found my partner for my life, and that has naturally come out in my songs. Sitting down to write in the aftermath of finding some kind of peace for myself was a pleasurably different experience, and I was able to delve into what is, for me, new writing territory: the happy love song.

There are a few on the new record, proudly reflecting my newfound stability. 'There She Is' was the first of the bunch that I finished, and it also lit the way forward for me stylistically.

With Jess, the love of my life, in Rome, 2016

A few years ago, Jess (for that is her name) and I were on holiday in Italy, having a lovely time. We stayed in various different spots, and we finished the trip with a few nights in a hotel in Rome, seeing the sights. We were at that wonderful transitional moment in a relationship, where the initial excitement starts to wear off a bit but, because it's serious, it changes into something deeper, a sense of long-term communion and partnership. I woke up one morning in the hotel room before she did and, looking across at her sleeping face, I was filled with a sense of love and peace. I know, I know, this sounds like some hippy shit, but it's true. Seized by the perfect beauty of the moment, I started turning some phrases over in my head, phrases that came with a melody attached to them – as ever, an excellent sign – and before long I was on my way to knocking out an entire song in one sitting. I'd love to tell you that I finished it there and then, that'd make a better story, but the truth is she woke up as I was working on the second verse in my head. I told her to go and get breakfast and leave me alone to finish capturing the idea, which she generously agreed to do. When she came back, I played her the idea as I had it. It was a sublime moment for us both. Again, I'd love to say that I left the song untouched from that moment, but it did go through some revisions over time. Ah well.

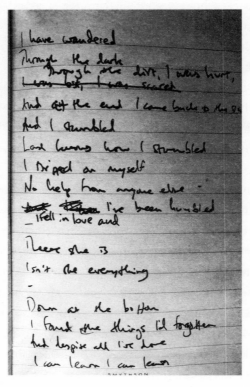

The very first pass, written in the hotel in the morning

Aside from the surge of passion running through me that morning, the chief inspiration for the song came from music we had both been listening to the day before on our drive to Rome. In some isolated Italian gas station, I'd picked up a CD of 'Motown Hits' to play in the car. On pressing play, we were both amused to discover that it was a collection of cheaply re-recorded versions of the famous tunes, rather than the originals, presumably to get around some publishing issue. As low-budget as the renditions were, it was reassuring to discover that the strength of those classic songs shone through, and it was still a great listen.

One song stood out from the pack, and I'm sure it's one you know – 'Stand by Me' by Ben E. King. Not only did the ersatz version still pack a heavy emotional punch, I was also struck by the power of the simplicity of the song. Verbally, it's a lyric that is militantly stripped back, almost elementary, with no dramatic vocabulary or imagery. It just says what it needs to say in the most direct way possible. Engaging with that kind of language is a risky business, as it's easy to stray into territory where you end up not saying anything at all, but if it goes well, it makes for a classic song. 'Lean on Me' by Bill Withers is another great example. The song is also musically striking. The legendary introduction is underpinned only by a minimal guitar line, but it occurred to me, as we drove, that perhaps even that wasn't required. You could sing that first verse a cappella and the contours of the melody and the accompaniment would be instantly clear. That's how strong a song it is.

Of course, deciding to try to write a song like 'Stand by Me' is a crazily hubristic idea, and I don't want to sit here and compare my work with something so completely timeless. All the same, I drew inspiration from its structure and arrangement for 'There She Is'; I wanted the opening verse to be something that could stand alone if ever needed. I also began by borrowing the rolling rhythm, as well as keeping the structure and the words as stripped back as could be. All of which made it an easier thing to imagine and construct while still lying down in a bed next to someone who was asleep.

That initial burst of creativity left me with a verse[*] and a chorus, a melody and a chord sequence. I didn't want to add much more to it, but there was obviously some more work to do before it was a finished piece. Once I was back on the road, I set about recording a demo on my laptop. After the process for *Positive Songs*, which had been collaborative from the start and had involved the Souls working on the songs with me when they were still half-formed, I wanted to take a different approach to any new ideas I had. So it was that I fired up GarageBand and started laying down the building blocks of the song.

I set up a loop for the basic syncopated rhythm and set it running through the song. At the start, I had intended to keep it as simple as that, but while I was working on it I stumbled into a massive musical breakthrough. The loop suggests a slow, wandering half-time feel. Somewhere along the way I added a second rhythm track, a counterpoint that was built around a massive backbeat on the two and four. Suddenly the whole song shifted up a gear and leapt forward into completely new territory. The approach was still minimal, but for the first time in my creative career, I was working with not one but two drum loops at the same time. This was a bold and exciting move for me.

The inspiration for this move came from a number of different ideas that had been quietly coalescing in my head. We had spent some time on the road with a Canadian band called Arkells. Not only are they wonderful, talented people, but their music hit me

* Complete with reference to 'Substitute' from *Love Ire & Song* – 'I stumbled . . . I fell in love . . .'

hard. It's intelligent but unashamedly pop. Pop always has the residual feel of being a dirty word for me, given my punk rock adolescence, but they helped show me that that doesn't always have to be the case. And while they use live instruments, they were not afraid of working with loops and synthesizers on their recordings. One day, in soundcheck, they were working out how to play a song called 'Passenger Seat' live – they'd put it together in the studio and had never actually played it as a band. That kind of blew my mind as an approach, and sent my brain spiralling in new directions.

I'd also recently finished reading a book by Simon Reynolds, called *Rip It Up And Start Again*, which was a history of the post-punk movement in the 1980s. I read books of music history incessantly – it brings my two passions in life together – and I'd set out to fill a gap in my knowledge, as for the most part my taste has run from '77 punk through American hardcore to Nirvana and nineties indie. While reading I was, naturally, listening through to the bands mentioned in the text, and in the process massively widening my awareness of that scene. The early eighties were a very exciting time for music, technologically speaking, as bands like New Order and Human League began to use the new machinery available to them, like samplers and sequencers. Their first basic steps into that world felt fresh and exciting to me, and again, it made me start thinking of different logistical approaches to arranging and recording songs.

As the time for actually going into the studio with my new material came around, I found myself in talks with Josh Block and Austin Jenkins as producers. Josh and Austin used to play together in the band White Denim,* but had jumped ship to work

---

* Who, small world, had briefly been tour-managed by Tre, my tour manager, once upon a time.

as producers for the soul singer Leon Bridges. Having thus established themselves, they were looking for other people to work with, and the label hooked us up. The first connection came because I was, for a time, idly contemplating trying to make a soul record myself. That idea didn't last long (probably for the best), but our conversations continued, until, in the summer of 2017, I found myself at Niles City Sound studio in Fort Worth, Texas, beginning the process of making my seventh album.

I had decided to use a radically different methodology for this session. Whereas with *Positive Songs* we had set up as a live band in the studio and attempted to capture the energy of our shows, this time I stripped everything back to basics, and went down the route suggested to me by Arkells and my post-punk explorations. Part of that was bringing the members of the Souls out to Texas one by one and working on their parts in isolation. I'd placed a moratorium on the band and myself on working on the new material outside of the studio, instead working up the arrangement ideas that I had on my laptop. That process had accelerated my experimentation with loops and beats. In the studio proper, we built each song from the ground up, piece by piece, with me overseeing the whole sound and keeping an eye on the destination I had in mind. One of the advantages of this is that it meant the parts we laid down served the song alone. If you work out an arrangement in a room with five musicians, you tend to come up with a version that has five separate parts, naturally enough. Doing it this way around, it meant that the parts that we recorded were just what was required for the song, and nothing more. Sometimes that meant we had fewer than five ideas running at a given moment; sometimes it had many more. But I put all considerations about how that would play out in a live context out of my mind, letting the songs dictate the parts, just as Arkells had shown me.

So, with 'There She Is', we began with the drum loops. Nige laid down the basic, Motown part, with floor tom and claves, and then we copied and pasted that through the whole song. Then he played against that with a full kit from the second verse forward, building the groove. Percussion and cymbals came later. At every stage we had all the parts separated, which gave me and Josh and Austin the ability to quickly experiment with different layerings and combinations. It was a hugely liberated creative approach, drawing a lot from what I'd read in the post-punk book, and also from what I knew about David Byrne's technique on the early Talking Heads records. It places rhythm at the heart of the process, which was new for me, and it took me to exciting new places.

Once we had the rhythm tracks in place, I laid down the basic electric guitar part, using a chorus pedal to give it a real 1980s vibe. Once Matt arrived, we worked through a huge pile of old analogue synthesizers, settling on a venerable Roland Juno for most of the padded ambient sounds. Tarrant held down the bottom end with a simple but rich bassline, and Ben added twinkling guitars over the top, each musician playing to their own strengths under my direction.

Between the early versions of the song and the studio, I'd made a few changes. First of all, I'd dropped the key, from C to A major. That made it feel more natural and comfortable for me to sing, and was also a tacit recognition of the fact that, as I get older, my voice is changing, my range dropping, as is only natural. I had also added another section to the middle and end of the song. For this I finally managed to employ a guitar riff I'd had lying around for a very long time, and which had found a temporary home on almost every song I'd been working on for this album, so keen was I to use it. There's a snippet of it in Ben Morse's *Get Better* film, where I enthusiastically hammer it out under some half-formed lyrical ideas about a game of chess. That was one of many, many dead ends, but the part finally landed here, used both for the 'everything I need' bridge section and the huge play-out at the end.

Speaking of the play-out, I knew the song had to reach a climax big enough to justify the timelessness of the themes I was working with. I wanted the looped rhythm of the song to break down, and be replaced with an enormous beat in the style of an old Phil Spector record. Josh and Austin took my idea and ran with it, eventually setting Nigel's kit up in the middle of an empty warehouse space adjoining the studio and getting him to play the beat in there, microphones all around the room to capture the endless natural reverberation. We layered huge guitars, distorted bass chords and string parts over the part, and even added a horn section at a later date to bring a final extra melodic line to the song. The vocals we layered up with doubled parts down the octave, a great trick that really thickens a performance out in a way that isn't immediately noticeable to the untrained ear. Eventually, I was satisfied that the sound coming out of the speakers matched the grandiosity of the emotions that had inspired the song.

'There She Is' was something of a breakthrough moment for me at this point in my career. Somehow, I felt I had successfully gone back and anchored myself in the very basics of my ideas about songs, while at the same time pushing myself as a recording artist far into unknown territory. It was the first song that I fully conceived for the album, and it pointed the way forward for most of the rest of *Be More Kind*. And it also finally puts a song in my arsenal that really would work at a wedding.

BLACKOUT

You were watching your favourite show when the TV died.

The biggest powercut in your neighbourhood since 1989.

A blackout in the centre of town but

Down in the suburbs, where it first went out they've been asking

Asking the question:

Are you afraid of the darkness?

I'm afraid of the darkness too.

In the hospital, on the critical ward,

Too long a breath between the break and the backup of her life support.

One system failure and it stopped her heart;

One power vacuum and we're coming apart.

We should be asking, asking the question:

Are you afraid of the darkness?

I'm afraid of the darkness too.

We're all caught in the blackout,

Trying to feel our way out.

Wait for the morning, I'll be waiting for you.

Meet me in the middle, meet me in the middle,

Bring a burning candle with you.

Meet me in the middle, meet me in the middle,

I will be there waiting for you.

I was in my comfort zone, I was singing selfish songs,

I'd been taking for granted everyone understood how easy trouble comes.

But it's not enough any more.

We can't just turn around and close the door on a world

That's asking uneasy questions.
We should be asking ourselves uneasy questions.

* * *

If there's ever a time in a career when you have the right, the opportunity to take some risks, it's probably on album seven. I believe that artists have a duty, in fact, not to repeat themselves and to move forward. Of course, I'm aware that, as a writer, I don't reinvent the wheel; I'm not Karlheinz Stockhausen. But within my own idiom, it's not just that it's fun to push boundaries; I think it's something I need to do. Working with new sounds, new styles and new technology was important to me for *Be More Kind.* And in the spirit of pushing the boat out, I also decided to try sitting down with Iain Archer to work on a couple of songs together.

Iain was a friend of friends; we hang out in the same circles in London. He's written for and with a cornucopia of great acts, from Snow Patrol to James Bay. We got to talking about song-writing one evening and, after mulling it over for a long while, I thought it would be interesting to try writing with him collaboratively, just to see what happened. It's a situation he is very used to, professionally, so he was gentle in helping me overcome my caution and inexperience. As I've said, I'm not opposed to writing with other people by any stretch, it's just something that I haven't had much time or opportunity to do, apart from with the Souls and Jon Snodgrass. In the event, Iain's approach was more that of being a coach for my own process. We spent a few sunny afternoons in his writing studio in north London kicking ideas around, and most of the time the process involved me coming up with an idea, and Iain pushing me to make it better. We came out with a few songs for this album from those sessions. I don't regard them as any less 'my' songs, and Iain definitely pushed me out of my comfort zone – exactly what I was aiming for.

Alongside stylistic eclecticism and working with another writer, the third plank of my self-inflicted discomfort was to tentatively dip my toe back into the waters of writing about politics. I'll have much more to say about that in due course; broadly speaking, I was interested in writing about the way we interact with each other, especially the people with whom we disagree. The growing polarisation of our political discourse is hugely worrying to me, and I think that we all need to focus on our common humanity as the certainties of the world we inhabit start to crumble. If I may be so bold as to make a prediction, I suspect that the period of 1989 to 2016 might be seen by future historians as an idyllic holiday (for Western societies) from the full force of history. The rise of the internet, social media, our confusion of anger with wisdom, and the absolute disaster that is the notion of 'fake news' as an argument, has left me feeling like we're all stumbling around in the dark.

I wanted to get this feeling of confusion and breakdown into a song. Chatting about it with Iain, we came to discuss the New York City blackout of 1977 (we'd both recently watched a documentary about it on TV). We talked about how, despite the explosion of violence and looting that accompanied the power failure, there were some shining moments of human compassion and connection in the darkness.* We tried to imagine how we would have behaved in that situation. Clearly, we had stumbled on the central metaphor we needed.

We worked on the music at the same time as the lyrics. Almost

* And the birth of hip-hop was hugely accelerated by all the, uh, liberated DJ and audio equipment.

every song I've ever written as a solo artist has begun life as a sequence of blocked chords. This time around, I came at it with something more like an actual riff. I've long been a fan of the tight, funk-influenced guitar work of bands like Gang of Four and XTC (and indeed Dire Straits). There's a particular sound, of an electric guitar being aggressively finger-picked, that feels really good to my ears. A great example of what I'm talking about is, of course, the opening riff for 'Blackout'. It's built around hammer-ons and slides, with percussive slaps on the strings in between chords on the two and four of the bar, which suggests the feel of a backbeat on a snare drum. It's also unusual for me in that not only does it not start on the root chord of the song (something I do all too often), but it doesn't even contain that chord, A major, in the introduction and the verse, at all. It's a riff that feels somehow off-centre to me as a result, and I really loved that vibe for the song.

Of course, being me, I then offset that effect by dropping a massive, unashamedly pop chorus, opening with the missing A major. It's a case of tension and release, and I was trying to emphasise both parts of that equation. The verses are written to feel tense, uncomfortable; the chorus is wide open and huge. It fits with the lyrics, a sense of unease about the world, followed by the release of being able to openly admit the problem, to ask the uneasy question about our collective fear. And then the song eventually moves on to a post-chorus section that brings it all together with the beginning of a suggestion of how to move forward: by meeting in the middle, and bringing a light to each other's darkness.

The rough demo version of the song that Iain and I laid down stresses this vibe in its arrangement. On that recording, the verses are completely solo, apart from a lone kick drum; the choruses explode into a wall of sound. As with the early versions of 'There

She Is', there was a clear commitment to using beats and loops with the song, from the word go. However, with 'Blackout', I would find myself pushing that idea as far as I could make it go.

The other great thing about making your seventh record, aside from being able to throw caution to the wind creatively, is that you can take your time. I had been in a hurry to get *Positive Songs* recorded and released, and we'd toured it relentlessly. Contemplating my next move, I felt more relaxed, and decided to take my time in planning the recording – not least because I knew I would be trying to do lots of new things, and I wanted to make sure I got them right.

As mentioned, I had been talking with Josh and Austin for a while about making music together. There were other names on the table for the album as well, though, and I wasn't ready to put all my eggs in one basket straight away. Fortunately, working again with Polydor, I had the financial backing to be choosy and to take my time. After some back and forth, in March 2017 I flew to Texas on my own to spend four days in Niles City Sound studio, for a trial session. It felt luxuriant to be able to work like that, and I'm also extremely glad about it. I was unsure whether or not I would be able to convincingly pursue the musical avenues I was interested in, and I didn't know if this was the right team to help me with that. So I arrived in Fort Worth feeling both adventurous and nervous.

I was always intending to record the album with The Sleeping Souls, but going out ahead of them on a scouting mission was useful for me. I wanted to take more creative control of the arrangements on this record, to let the songs dominate the decision-making process, and to keep my ideas bold and undiluted. I hadn't played with Josh (an excellent drummer) or Austin (a sublime bass player) before, so we set up cautiously in the live room of their studio to attack a song. I had chosen 'Blackout' for us to work on. They had heard the demo Iain and I had made, but I had already mentioned that I was planning on taking the song into wildly different musical territory.

Jamming the song around with those two was an absolute revelation. Playing with people I was unfamiliar with was a great way of shaking loose of my habits. I knew that the Souls were perfectly capable of playing any style I could think of to throw at them, but the shock of the new really opened me up. I began with the finger-picked riff. Josh immediately fell in behind me with a solid dance beat. The most exciting thing for me was when Austin began feeling his way to a slinky, off-beat bassline that perfectly complemented the guitar part, alternately weaving around it and locking in behind it.

With Josh Block and Austin Jenkins in Texas, March 2017

In just playing that verse, I could tell that I was succeeding in my aim to push my boundaries. Music history is littered with bands talking the talk about how their next record is going to be 'radically different', and in the event it turns out they just used a different guitar amp or something, while keeping everything else predictable. It's a revealing moment, in its way, potentially highlighting the gap between the musicians' ambitions and abilities. I didn't want to fall into that trap, so I was absolutely focused on making sure that I was in new territory. The opening of 'Blackout' that we worked out that day made me feel confident about the whole project.

Once we'd established the groove for the song, the rest of it fell into place quite easily, though with constant surprises in store. For the chorus, Austin held down the root notes, while I switched up to a high funk part in the style of Nile Rodgers of Chic (again, completely new for me). Once we got to the second chorus, I suggested messing around with some synth sounds. Before long, I'd discovered the arpeggiator function – a digital algorithm that plays sweeping arpeggios of whichever notes you hold down on the keyboard. More new sonic textures came in the form of retro-sounding electronic hand-claps and sub-heavy kick drum triggers. I extended the original riff into an actual guitar solo. And for the final verse, chorus and play-out, I allowed myself to revert to type a little, bringing in a heavy electric guitar part (inspired, specifically, by the extra guitar line that lands in the last chorus of Foo Fighters' 'February Stars') to thicken the mix.

The session was driven by a dedication to the idea of sonic adventurism and novelty. I was also obsessed more generally with rhythm and the idea of danceability. For a few years now I have been doing DJ sets. That's a slight misnomer: what actually happens is, a club or festival pays me money to show up with my laptop and play indie and punk songs that I like, one after the other. There's no beat-matching, no real skill other than trying to read the room and keep the party going. It is, I have learned, considered customary for a musician playing a DJ set to drop at least one of their own tunes. I tend to finish with 'Four Simple Words' (not least because it gives me ample time to pack up, finish my drink, and get ready to go home). One thing I noticed on all those late nights was that I didn't really have anything in my catalogue that sounded like a song you could dance to in a club. Playing my tunes in punk and indie discos is all well and good, the crowd know what they're getting, but the sheer physicality of hearing a proper dance tune over a club PA got me thinking. I wanted to have a song like that. A lot of it comes down to 'four-on-the-floor' – underpinning the song with a solid kick drum part that runs continuously through the piece. So, in working on 'Blackout', I mentioned this to Josh, and he made sure that the architecture was in place for the song to work in a club setting.

After four days, we had a finished piece. Listening back to a rough mix over the studio speakers, I felt exhilarated, and slightly naughty. Was I even *allowed* to make this kind of music? Obviously, the answer is an emphatic 'fuck yes'. I knew then that Josh and Austin were the right team to make the album. I headed home to finish working on songs and gather up the Souls. When I played them what I had worked on, I was relieved to see that they were nothing so much as excited about the new direction I was heading in.

When we got back to Texas together later in the year to work on the album proper, we re-recorded 'Blackout' from scratch. I wanted the song to be a little faster, and I shifted the key up, with a capo on the second fret, to let my voice shine out a little more on the higher notes. Of course, I also wanted to bring the skills of the Souls to bear on the song as well. While we didn't radically alter the arrangement that Josh, Austin and I had come up with, we were able to draw on the kind of musical connections you can only get with close to a decade on the road together. The version that we finished for *Be More Kind* is a tougher, leaner beast.

Once the album was done, I lobbied the label hard to make 'Blackout' the first single. I felt like it was important for me to put my best foot forward, and to open the campaign with the boldest statement of sonic intent that I could. This song is probably the most off-reservation track on the whole record, and reactions from the general public were mixed, as I'd anticipated them being. Some people embraced my new approach immediately. Some people outright hated it (and weren't shy about letting me know). Some people were just a bit confused by it, as far as I could tell. It's difficult to say with any certainty how this song will be perceived in the long run, as we're now at the point in this book where I'm writing about things that have happened within the last year. The way my audience reacts to my songs changes over time as they become more familiar. Whether or not 'Blackout' will find its place on my career retrospective playlist in twenty years' time is hard to say. And, of course, it doesn't matter a damn. The experiment was a success.

1933

'Stop asking musicians what they think,'
He slurred softly as he poured himself a second drink,
And outside, the world slipped over the brink.
'We all thought we had nothing to lose,
That we could trust in crossed fingers and horseshoes,
That everything would work out, no matter what we choose.'
The first time it was a tragedy, the second time it's a farce.
Outside it's 1933, so I'm hitting the bar.
And I don't know what's going on anymore.
The world outside is burning with a brand new light,
But it isn't one that makes me feel warm.
Don't go mistaking your house burning down for the dawn.
If I was of the greatest generation, I'd be pissed,
Surveying the world that I built slipping back into this.
I'd be screaming at my grandkids, 'We already did this!'
Be suspicious of simple answers –
That shit's for fascists (and maybe teenagers).
You can't fix the world if all you have is a hammer.
Aren't you ashamed of this? I surely hope that you are;
Living in a society that's maybe heading for Mars,
While down here we still have a shower of bastards
Leading the charge.
Outside it's 1933 so I'm hitting the bar.

* * *

I grew up listening to punk rock records and immersed myself in the world of anarchism. After a few adolescent years of going on street protests and attending book fairs, I got pretty disillusioned with that whole scene, with all its self-indulgence and crankiness. A few years later, I got deeper into reading about economics and history, and lost myself in a rabbit hole of classical liberal political philosophy for a while (as noted in discussing 'Sons of Liberty'). Then I had my run-in with the *Guardian* newspaper in 2012. I will absolutely shoulder my share of the blame for that kerfuffle. I put the points I was trying to make across badly, but I was also being attacked for apostasy, the worst of all sins (as well as being pretty heavily selectively quoted). Various people had made lazy assumptions about my opinions and seemed, bizarrely, to be personally affronted to discover that they were wrong about me when they finally deigned to check.

The upshot of this was twofold. On the one hand, I took the time to re-examine my views, and especially the language in which I chose to express them. These days I'd say I'm driven by the idea that, as a society, we're terrible at educating ourselves about the philosophical underpinnings of our socioeconomic system, and at defending it. No form of human organisation is perfect, obviously, but the liberal societies of the West in the last century or two have done a historically impressive job of creating and spreading wealth and freedom, and I think that all people across the world deserve those things. And I'm also interested in trying to discuss and refine those thoughts, rather than just shouting them at people on the other side of the aisle (an image that doesn't make a huge amount of sense, actually, because I'm reasonably sure I'm a centrist at heart).

The second outcome of the whole affair was that I was very much not interested in talking or singing about politics for a few years thereafter. One of my reservations about the whole 'protest singer' thing is that it completely overshadows any artistic considerations. I want to write songs and talk about music much, much more than I want to talk about politics. I felt good distancing myself from that scene. I also need to be motivated to write about something, I need to have things to say on a given topic. It wasn't just my own hurt that stopped me writing political songs before 2016, it was also the fact that, looking back, the world of Obama, Cameron and Miliband wasn't all that bad. Some of my more traditionally protest-singing friends already had their outrage dials set to maximum before things changed, leaving them with very little room to express themselves when they did.

And what a change it was. Of course, the roots of what's happening in our politics stretch far back, arguably to the birth of the world wide web and, later, social media. But 2016 seemed like a watershed year to me, even as it was happening. Of course, there was the Brexit vote in the UK, which completely shocked the entire political commentariat and upended a lot of assumptions about the way our system works.* And then there was the US presidential election race, for a lot of which we were actually on tour in the States. In August we were driving across the country playing shows with Flogging Molly, and I was genuinely shocked to encounter vociferous pro-Trump voices at punk rock shows. At the very least it showed me that I didn't fully understand what was happening there. All of this started pushing me towards writing songs that were engaged with the world again. After two

---

* I'm a Brexit agnostic, for the record. I had very smart and compassionate friends on both sides of the divide, so I kind of sat it out. That said, I think we can all agree that, at the time of writing, our political class has collectively demonstrated its utter uselessness since the vote, and I'm pretty worried about where we're heading.

albums on the subject of affairs of the heart, it felt like time to look outwards again.

The song '1933' grew out of this. At some point in that crazy year, I read an article somewhere that tried to make the case that the 'alt-right' were the new punks. My initial reaction to that was the fury of the slandered. Thinking about it in more depth, though, it helped me clarify my thinking about some things. Many youth subcultures, especially punk, place a premium on the idea of rebellion. But rebellion is a morally neutral concept; it completely depends on what you're rebelling *against*. Living in a society that is doing a reasonable job of establishing socially liberal norms is a wonderful thing, but it pushes those who wish to rebel merely for the sake of it into dark and unpleasant political territory. So maybe the original article had a point, but not perhaps the one the author thought it did; punk makes sense as an act of rebellion in the right *context*.

The second thing I was conceptually wrestling with was the American nativist movement that supported and was encouraged by Donald Trump. Many people immediately reached for the Nazi metaphors, but, as someone who likes to consider themselves a history nerd, that sets alarm bells ringing for me. Nazi analogies are far too commonplace in our discourse (which says a lot about the way we teach history in our schools, incidentally) and can often be unhelpful. I don't think Trump is Hitler (and I haven't said that anywhere, for the record). It's a more subtle connection than that, as I see it. I believe that any political movement that promises national renewal as its core concept, as a panacea for society's problems, needs to be treated with extreme caution. I would have thought that a brief wander through the history of the twentieth century could teach anyone that. Apparently, though, the inoculation seems not to have been 100 per cent effective.

And finally, as I hope all this vague pontificating has demonstrated, my core feeling about politics and society in this mad post-2016 world is uncertainty. I genuinely have no idea what's going to happen in the future. We could be on the brink of a world-historical catastrophe, or this could be a blip in our long march to progress. I don't know, and nor does anyone else. I started thinking about ways to communicate all these ideas into a song. And that's actually quite hard to do. Most political songwriting is powered by extreme self-confidence and self-belief. To be in a band like Rage Against the Machine or Anti-Flag (both excellent bands, by the way), you have to be extremely sure you're right. Doubt doesn't really enter the picture in a song like 'Killing in the Name' or 'Kill the Rich'. In a way I admire their conviction, but it's not a mental universe I can honestly inhabit in the here and now. So I kind of stumbled into the idea of trying to write political, fist-pumping anthems on the subject of being unsure. Not the easiest thing to pull off.

The song begins with a line I'd had in my back pocket for a while – 'Stop asking musicians what they think' – and I love it because it's serious and sarcastic at the same time, and it's also my get-out-of-jail-free card. I do actually think people should stop assuming that celebrities have some insight into the workings of the world, any more than anyone else.* And I don't think that songs are always the right place to get into the nitty gritty of policy proposals and so on. Most importantly, though, it's a striking opening. First lines matter.

From there the lyrics (hopefully) work through the ideas I've outlined above. I referenced a quote from Marx (not my favourite philosopher, but always an engaging wordsmith), on how history

* Sean Penn, for example, certainly has no fucking clue about anything, at all.

repeats itself, 'the first time as tragedy, the second time as farce'. I pinned the chorus of the song to a mock-triumphant slogan: 'I don't know what's going on any more.' I managed to get the phrase 'shower of bastards' in there, much to the confusion of not a few American listeners, unfamiliar with British idiom. And the central theme of the song wraps it all up: 'don't go mistaking your house burning down for the dawn'. Just because it's warm and light (or rebellious or transgressive), it doesn't mean it's good news.

A draft of '1933', in need of some edits

The title of the song is taken from the lyrics. Having said that I think Nazi comparisons are overly simplistic (and subject to Godwin's Law – whoever brings up Hitler first in an argument loses), I'm aware that calling the song '1933' is provocative, if not self-contradictory. Again, I'd plead for a subtler reading of my intentions. The song is called '1933', not '1939' or any other later more calamitous year. Between 1933 and the *Götterdämmerung* of 1945, there were a lot of decisions taken, choices made, across the world, that could have gone another way. I don't believe in historical inevitability – that's a cop-out. If there are analogies to be made between Germany in 1933 and America now, the lesson we should learn is that there is still time for us to change how things work out – and we should.*

For the music of the song, I wanted something suitably aggressive and direct. I was keen to have one song on the album that would be a bit more in the punk world than the more electronic stuff I was experimenting with on 'Blackout' and 'Common Ground'. I started with a melody and chord sequence I'd had lying around for a long time, which had had the beginning of some words attached but which hadn't gone anywhere.† I repurposed the music and laid the new, political lyrics over the top. The basic contours of the song were clear quite early on, but the feel and arrangement took a lot longer to get right.

The first demo I have of the song is a vocal and guitar performance, as usual. It's notably slower than the finished thing, which makes it feel less urgent, more lackadaisical. With each successive demo, the pace ratchets up a little. At the same time, the full band arrangement started in quite a flowery, complex place. We recorded the song in Fort Worth in the summer and took the

---

* Also, 1933 was the year Prohibition ended, making the line about 'hitting the bar' something of a joke. Geddit?

† It was going to be a song about seeing Joseph Grimaldi's ghost running down Clerkenwell Road, which I still think is a good idea; I just haven't found my way into it yet.

rough mixes home with us. Tarrant had laid down a bassline in the style of Bruce Thomas, bass player for Elvis Costello's band, The Attractions. In and of itself it was an excellent thing, but after a while I realised it was too dispersed for the vibe of the song. Similarly, Matt's keys parts needed to be stripped back. The pace still needed to come up. There was an over-the-top harmonica solo in the middle. The song wasn't right yet.

Unusually, I was able to schedule a return to Niles City Sound later in the year, in October, for another couple of weeks. That break was a godsend for us, as it allowed me to mull over where the album was sitting and where it needed to go for a time. Normally, you're in the studio for a set time, lay out what you have, hope you get it right, and that's it. To be able to step back and then return to the project was a great advantage. When we returned, we re-recorded '1933' from scratch; I think we'd all felt it wasn't quite hitting its mark, not least Tarrant, despite his excellent bass part on the first version. In fact, in the interim, we had been working the song over in soundchecks, on tour with Jason Isbell in the USA, much in the way we had with the material on *Positive Songs*. We drilled down into every single component of the song, making sure it was as lean and hungry as could be. If we were going to have a punk song on the album, it was going to be fucking *punk*. The drums were tighter, faster and simpler. The bass just hammered the root notes with a low grizzled sound. The guitar parts shifted from open chords to power chords. Finally, the song started to feel mean and aggressive enough to carry the weight of the lyrics.

The final touch was suggested in the studio by Matt. We were listening back to the song, and Matt started humming the last line of the song as a call-and-response, staggered against the main vocal. It filled a gap in the song that we hadn't noticed was even there before, and it brought the climax of the piece up to yet higher levels. And once we got the Souls around a microphone in the live room, it made me think of nothing so much as Sham 69; the icing on the cake. I was pleased that we'd managed to get the most traditionally punk-sounding song of my career* on the album on which, overall, I veered furthest away from that musical territory. It was the first song we released from *Be More Kind*, and it instantly landed with my audience. The only complaint I have is that people still keep asking me, as a musician, what I think.

* Alongside the middle part of 'Four Simple Words', of course.

MAKE AMERICA GREAT AGAIN

Well I know I'm just an ignorant Englishman,
But I'd like to make America great again.
So if you'll forgive my accent and the cheek of it,
Here's some suggestions from the special relationship:
Let's make America great again,
By making racists ashamed again.
Let's make compassion in fashion again,
Let's make America great again.
Well I've been fortunate to go round the continent,
From California through the Midwest to Providence,
And I've mostly only encountered common sense,
Hospitality and warmth from Americans.
But I wish it was a bit less significant,
The program and the name of the president,
Because it seems to me the truth is self-evident:
You fought our king to be independent.
Ellis Island take me in,
Everyone can start again
In the shining city on the hill
Where nobody can be illegal.
Let's be a friend to our oldest friends
And call them out when they're faltering,

Remind them of their best selves and then
We'll make America great again.

* * *

I challenge anyone to stand up against my love for the United States of America. I'm hugely passionate about almost all aspects of the country (perhaps not the sports, but that's true of every country, for me). Growing up, I think I had a pretty standard set of pre- and misconceptions about the place, fed by a steady diet of American films, punk bands and critics. I first visited New York in 2004 when I was in Million Dead, and realised quickly that I didn't really know anything about the place at all. I've been fortunate to spend a large chunk of my time on the road in the USA since then (it's a huge country that's into rock'n'roll music, it's natural to tour there a lot). I find the place endlessly fascinating. I think it was Stephen Fry who commented that, for every one general statement you can make about America, you can find the opposite to be true as well. There is considerably more than a lifetime of travel and learning to be done.

Of course, back home, there's a strong strain of Euro-centric, armchair anti-Americanism prevalent in a lot of the corners of society I've inhabited – in the universities, in the punk scene and so on. Once I'd started to get to know the place, or at least to understand how little of it I knew, I spent a lot of my time over the years in bar-room arguments about this, in which I would continually fight America's corner. Of course it's not perfect, politically or otherwise, but the American Dream remains a land-mark achievement in the way humans think about their societies and the opportunities naturally due to every individual person, when considered in historical context.* I think it's hard to argue against the proposition that, on balance, America has been a force for good internationally in the last 200 years (often by example more than through its own actions). I strongly believe that the American Constitution is one of the most powerful liberal statements in history. In short, with the obvious provisos about the darker moments of her history, go Team USA.

And then there's Donald Trump.

As someone from the other side of the pond, Trump's rise to power is borderline incomprehensible – and I say that as someone who has done his best to understand all corners of the American psyche, and who has spent more time outside the coastal city enclaves than most Europeans. He's just so self-evidently corrupt, amoral, self-interested and, let's be honest, thick as mince. If one of my ill-informed anti-American friends was to draw up a caricature of the stereotypical dumb American, and presented Trump, I'd protest that it was so far-fetched as to be silly. And yet he is, apparently, for real. Throughout 2016, as he inexorably rose through the ranks of the Republican Party, I watched in continual disbelief, certain that at some point some semblance of reality would kick back in and send him crashing back down to earth.

By the time he'd won the nomination, I'd given up making predictions about what was going to happen. On that summer tour with Flogging Molly, I remember walking through a student housing district of Columbus, Ohio, and seeing Trump flags on quite a few of the houses. That blew my mind and got me worried.

---

* Incidentally, a small political bugbear of mine. The fact that something or someone fails to live up to an ideal doesn't invalidate that ideal; it just means you need to try harder. This seems screamingly obvious to me.

As the tour went on, I started adapting my little speech that I usually do in the final section of 'Photosynthesis' to talk about this. I spent time carefully phrasing what I was trying to say. I began by admitting that I was, of course, an outsider, but one that came to the conversation with much affection for the country. I said that the America I had fallen in love with over the past decade and more was better than a failed real-estate mogul in an ill-fitting suit. To my surprise and sadness, this was met, night after night, by a small but vocal section of the audience shouting, 'Fuck Hillary!' For the record, I'm no particular fan of the Clintons. I've read Christopher Hitchens' magisterial takedown, and I think she was self-evidently one of the worst candidates in history – after all, she lost to *Trump*. All the same, the tolerance for the idea of the morally bankrupt orange con man as president that I encountered at what were, at least nominally, *punk rock* shows, shook me. The experience led me to write the song 'Make America Great Again'.

Let's address the elephant in the room: the title. It's clearly a piece of deliberate provocation, but that technique has a long and respectable history in punk and in culture more broadly, from the Dead Kennedys to NOFX's *War on Errorism*. I wanted to take that stupid, smug phrase and repurpose it. In actual fact, I think America is pretty great as it is, taking the broad geographical and historical view. And I certainly don't think it will be improved by ahistorical nativism. After all, the USA is, in point of fact, a nation of immigrants. You can be in favour of building walls and restrictive border policies, and you can be in favour of harking back to the American past, but you can't do both at the same time. My idea in using the title was to annoy people who take that piece of lowest-common-denominator sloganeering seriously (as well as to subvert them when they were wearing those stupid hats – hey, you like my song! Nice!). In the event I was kind of in a hurry to get the song released, as I was sure someone else was going to have the same idea and beat me to the punch.

I like to think that the song as a whole goes beyond this baiting of die-hard Trump supporters, though. The second verse addresses the increasing imbalance in the division of powers at the heart of the American system, the creeping imperial overtones of the presidency, a tendency amplified by presidents from both sides of the aisle in the last few decades. It shouldn't matter quite so much who the president is; he's meant to be an employee of the people, not a monarch – Americans famously fought against our king because of his overbearing authoritarianism. And the song also celebrates one of the best moments in US history, in my view – the open door immigration policy of the nineteenth century, best represented by Ellis Island. The fact that, even today, so many people want to get to the USA should be seen as a compliment, not a problem. It's still the shining city on the hill for a lot of people around the world, and that's a vote of confidence. How tired I am of Americans casually commenting that they live in a 'police state' or whatever. No you fucking don't, and lots of people actually do, right now, not far away. Have some perspective! Sorry, rant over.

The idea for the song was that of a simple piece of political statement, and I wanted music that would be powerful and direct to back that up. In fact, I wanted it to be a pop song. If you're going to annoy people by writing about politics, why not go the whole hog and piss off the musical purists at the same time, right?

I have long had ambitions to have a song in my repertoire containing what I think of as a 'guitar shop riff' – one of those easy-to-play figures that every snotty teenager in the store starts playing sooner or later as they try out guitars they're never actually going to buy. Something like 'Smells Like Teen Spirit' or 'Enter Sandman'. I know, I know, that's a hugely ambitious statement, but why not dream big? I came up with what felt like such a riff, four barre chords played raggedly on an acoustic in a lilting, stumbling rhythm. This was the keystone of the song, right from the start. And given that I was already in the head-space of working with loops, it was an obvious move to record a few bars of it and lay it out through the whole song, building the other components around it. I wanted the riff to sound rattling and low-fi, like something from Beck's *Odelay* album.

Against this, I programmed a beat that accented the rhythmic pattern of the guitar. The whole thing is off-kilter, with nothing on the beat until the third, snare-heavy count of the bar. Adding percussion and other drum loops to this gives the whole piece a rolling groove around the thudding central motif. As with the guitar, I treated each new part as a layer, generally leaving it in the song once it had been introduced, so that the piece built up over the whole song. Once we get to the bridge, I had Nigel play a looser, jazzier part against the main beat, in the style of DJ Shadow's classic *Endtroducing* work. And in the basement of the song, I had the bass slamming down the root notes in time with the basic beat and then sliding down the neck, like a soundwave peaking and falling on a meter.

The top floor of the song is characterised by massive analogue synthesizer sounds. With each pass of the song, I tried to make them bigger and more monumental. I wanted the choruses to sound enormous, like an iceberg falling into the sea. And I also wanted to treat the vocals in an unusual way. I have generally shied away from double-tracking vocals in my recording career – it's a slightly artificial sound, to my ears. But that was sort of the vibe I was going for here, so in the event I sang the song *five* times over, panning takes left and right and layering them on top of each other until they created an otherworldly, ethereal whole. Once again, if I was going to step out of my comfort zone on this song, I might as well take a running jump.

I finished a comparatively slick demo of the song and presented it to the label and my producers. The label were extremely sceptical, both of the lyrics and the musical approach, but Josh and Austin immediately saw what I was trying to do, and how to help me make it better. We reconstructed the parts I'd come up with in the studio, but made them better, slicker, groovier. With Nigel's help we added more layers of rhythm; Matt kept digging out extra ideas for weird, blippy synth lines. At some point, Nigel suggested that the song could handle a key change towards the end, in keeping with the cheesiest tropes of mainstream pop music – Ben referred to it as the 'stool-kicking moment', as in when the boy bands stand up, kick their stools away and sing the final chorus in a higher key. I worked out the chord changes (something I'm not usually adept at; changing keys makes my head hurt), and it sounded great.

In between the first and second session in Fort Worth, I also realised that the song needed a few lyrical tweaks. Firstly, I added a line to the end of the bridge, which I borrowed from a comment John K. Samson made on stage in Los Angeles at a show where he was opening for me.* John quietly commented that we should remember that no individual can be illegal, in and of themselves. That resonated with me, and went into the song. Secondly, the original draft of the lyrics had me trying to make 'racists *afraid* again'. Something in that didn't sit quite right, it felt overly aggressive. I don't actually think punching people you disagree

---

* I know, I know, it's fucking ridiculous.

with is particularly smart.* I'm glad I changed the line to 'ashamed'. Finally, in earlier versions, the last chorus had simply been a double repeat of the lyrics, and that felt like a missed opportunity to me. There was space for me to really emphasise the message and intention behind the song one more time: 'Let's be a friend to our oldest friends, and call them out when they're faltering.' I still believe in the enormous potential for good in the USA; it's just that they're kind of fucking it up right now. The duty of friendship, when your drunk buddy is making a fool out of himself at the bar, is to politely but firmly suggest that they get a cab home and sleep it off.

When the album was done and we began working up a promotional plan, the label was still a little unsure about 'Make America Great Again'. My counter-argument to this was to say that, seeing as the song was on the record, we had to be bold about it. It would be much worse to make that statement and then sit on it like we were embarrassed about it. So eventually I convinced them to release it as the second single from the album.

Naturally, the label were keen for there to be a promotional video to accompany the single, and I knew I had a good idea for that (one I'd come up with over a few beers with Ben Morse). In March 2018, a few months before the album release date, I was in Texas again, Austin this time, for the South by Southwest festival. I had five busy days in town, but there was one free afternoon in the middle, and I put my plan together. I decided to bypass the label's scepticism altogether and simply shoot the video myself on my phone. The idea was simple enough for that to work. All I had to do was to buy a ridiculous suit. This I managed

---

* Everyone that I know personally who has posted on Facebook about the merits of 'punching Nazis' looks like someone who'd lose a fight.

to do, though not before the tailor in the store made me drink a shot of tequila with him at midday, saying he wouldn't sell a man a suit unless they'd drunk together. That derailed my day somewhat. A few hours later I found myself on the pavement, dressed like a moron (complete with Stars 'n' Stripes bowtie), holding a whiteboard and asking random strangers what their favourite thing about America is. It's one of the best videos I've made, in my view, and it cost almost nothing to make. It reinforces the message of the song, while also gently undercutting any of my sense of self-importance. And, as with everything else about this record, it placed me far outside of my comfort zone; I don't usually ask strangers weird and probing questions.

The video and the song dropped in April. I was braced for the reaction; I knew some people were likely to really, really not

Dressed like an idiot for the 'Make America Great Again' video

appreciate it. And I was right, though surprisingly the initial wave of negativity had more to do with my use of synthesisers than the politics. I was also tickled to discover that almost no one in the USA has heard of the 'Special Relationship' (the supposed close connection between the UK and the USA which, it turns out, we're much more worked up about than they are). I got a few angry emails from people who felt attacked by the words. That was inevitable, of course, and I went into the whole thing with my eyes open. All the same, feeling yourself to be insulted by a song that is, in essence, an anti-racist anthem might, perhaps, say more about you than it does about me . . .

The next phase, of course, was to play the song live, and that has brought its own challenges, not just on the technical side of things (Matt and Nigel did a great job of building some sample pads to play the extra parts that we didn't have enough hands to perform ourselves). The very first time I performed it in front of an audience was in New York in December 2017, when I flew in for one day to do a secret set opening for The Hold Steady at Brooklyn Bowl (something of a dream come true, though I also learned that flying to New York and back in under forty hours is a young man's game). I was nervous as to how the audience would react, but thought I might as well give it a go. In the event the crowd went crazy when I got to the second line of the chorus, after an uneasy introduction. That was exactly what I'd been hoping for. Since then, we've had more mixed receptions outside the namby-pamby liberal bubble of NYC (I jest, sort of); I've played it everywhere in the US, from Alaska to Texas. I feel like I have to put it in the set for the time being; again, to write a song like that and not play it seems like a cop-out to me. In the UK people just seemed a bit confused – after all, the song isn't really for them. For the most part people have appreciated the sentiment of the song. My favourite reactions are when I get talking to people who identify themselves to me as Republicans or even Trump supporters, but say they can see where I'm coming from. That kind of reaching across tribal lines is precisely what I was trying to achieve with *Be More Kind*, so it's been wonderful to see that in action.

BE MORE KIND

History's been leaning on me lately;
I can feel the future breathing down my neck.
And all the things I thought were true
When I was young, and you were too,
Turned out to be broken,
And I don't know what comes next.
In a world that has decided that it's going to lose its mind,
Be more kind, my friends, try to be more kind.
They've started raising walls around the world now,
Like hackles raised upon a cornered cat,
On the borders, in our heads,
Between the things that can and can't be said,
We've stopped talking to each other,
And there's something wrong with that.
So before you go out searching, don't decide what you will find.
Be more kind, my friends, try to be more kind.
You should know you're not alone,
And that trouble comes, and trouble goes.
How this ends, no one knows,
So hold on tight when the wind blows.
The wind blew both of us to sand and sea,
And where the dry land stands is hard to say.
As the current drags us by the shore,
We can no longer say for sure
Who's drowning, or if they can be saved.

But when you're out there floundering, like a lighthouse I will shine.
Be more kind, my friends, try to be more kind.
Like a beacon reaching out to you and yours from me and mine,
Be more kind, my friends, try to be more kind.
In a world that has decided that it's going to lose its mind,
Be more kind, my friends, try to be more kind.

* * *

Finally, then, we come to the last song I'm going to write about for this book. I chose 'Be More Kind' as my finale for a number of reasons. It's the title track of my current album as I write this, so it's clearly something I'm trying to put forward into the world. Ideologically, it says most of what I want to communicate with my audience as succinctly as it can. More importantly, for our current purposes, the recorded version represents what I regard as the pinnacle of my abilities and achievements as a writer. But the song began as something much more simple, a finger-picked folk song that harks right back to where I started, and it still stands up in that presentation. So, here it is, 'Be More Kind'.

Clive James is an Australian writer, poet, critic and broadcaster who has spent most of his life based in England. Anyone around my age tends to know him primarily from his TV show of cultural criticism, in which he was endlessly witty and perceptive. It was only comparatively recently that I discovered the other strings to his bow. In 2011, it was announced that James was suffering from terminal leukaemia, and didn't have long to live. In reading an article about this, I was surprised to see mention of his work as a writer, and started reading some of his poetry. I was immediately mesmerised by his talent. Then he started to write new poems, about facing the end of his life. They are works of rare beauty and wisdom. In particular, he wrote a poem called 'Leçons de Ténèbres', published in the *New Yorker* in 2013, which featured the lines 'I should have been more kind. It is my fate / To find this out, but find it out too late.' I was knocked sideways. For someone of James's emotional and literary stature to make such a statement at this moment in his life was no small thing. It was a matter of weeks before I had begun working on a song of mine using his phrasing.

Instinctively, I reached for the most basic, honest guitar playing I could think of, a simple picking pattern borrowed, in my own library, from the songs of John K. Samson.* The guitar part feels ageless. The chord sequence was a straightforward one, for the most part, though even at this stage in my life of wandering around the elementary chords on a guitar, I was able to stumble across a weird chord that I still can't fully name (it's the second one in the verse; it features both a B and a C clashing together, it doesn't make much sense, but it feels good). I made use of the major second chord (an F# major here), another nod to John's melodic sensibility. The structure is also uncomplicated: verses, choruses and a bridge exactly where you'd expect them to be.

For the words, I did my best to put down exactly how I felt about the world around me going mad. I suspect that the revolution in the way we communicate with each other that is social media lies at the heart of our problems. It's an accidental machine for dehumanising our opponents. When you argue with someone online, you argue with a cypher, a symbol, not an actual person, and that removes many of our cultural barriers to awfulness. People say things to each other on Twitter and the like that they'd never say in person – or at least wouldn't have, until the internet normalised that kind of poisonous rhetoric. Any amateur

* The lyric in the verse about a cat is a nod to this influence.

historian will tell you that the moment any society starts to regard its adversaries as less than human, serious trouble follows soon after.

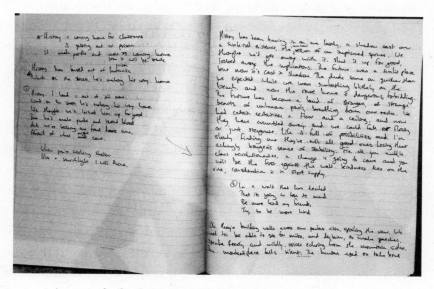

A prose draft of 'Be More Kind', checking I was on course, philosophically

Online sociality also leads us to wall ourselves off into echo chambers of agreement. Everyone is guilty of this, myself emphatically included. We seek out information and opinion that reinforces our pre-existing opinions. We decide what we will find before we look. Both sides of the divide start to outlaw things they don't agree with – whether it's words and ideas, or the movement of people. Somewhere in all of this, we are losing the ability to disagree with each other like adults. And disagreement is the central fact of any society composed of humans.* If we don't

---

* Any ideology that posits an end state in which there is no disagreement is either childish, totalitarian, or usually both.

work out ways to disagree with words, we will necessarily do so with force instead, and, despite the cocksure bravado of people from the extreme wings of the political spectrum, that's really not something to look forward to.

In short, somewhere along the line I decided to write a bona fide message song. It's something I've usually shied away from, or at least attempted to shroud in defensive clouds of sarcasm or vagueness. But at some point in your life, you have to put your money down for something you believe in, and for me, this is it. It's not a song or a sentiment that I could have formulated at an earlier point in my life. It's taken me a lot of learning, reading, experience and fucking up to get here, but in essence, I think that Clive James is right. Kindness, consideration for your fellow human being, is the thing that comes out in the wash at the end of our lives, for almost all of us. The content of our arguments will mostly fade over time; the way we handled ourselves while we argued will be remembered. No one knows who's waving and who's drowning, so best to try and save each other.

A small technical aside here. A trick I often use while writing words that are meant to carry some serious weight is to stop and step away from the poetry for a moment. I put whatever I have so far aside for a moment, and try to write out my point in full in prose, without the constraints of metre or rhythm. Whether it comes out as a single paragraph or several pages, it's a great way of clarifying what you're trying to say. Afterwards, you can compare it with the actual lyrics you've written and see if they measure up, philosophically. It can also get you out of any writer's block dead-ends. I did that a lot with this song, it felt important to get it right.

I finished a folk song, and then set about turning it into something more. I was deep into the world of beats and loops by now.

The main musical guide for the way I went about building this song up was the work of Arab Strap, the criminally underrated Scottish indie band, who spent much of the 1990s beautifully weaving acoustic instruments and programmed beats together into achingly perfect tapestries of sound. After some initial messing around with ideas in a soundcheck with the Souls, I went back to my laptop. I brought in the four-on-the-floor beat (though I knew that this was unlikely to be a song anyone would actually dance to), and added layer upon layer of tight rhythmic percussion, until I had a bed of sound that, if listened to solo in the studio, reminds me of nothing so much as Berlin techno. I loved the contrast between that and the folkiness of the guitar.

On the demo I had used a simple analogue synth to fill out the sound as the song progressed, but in the studio, I asked Matt to write a string arrangement. I had been expecting him to come up with something simple that mirrored the pads I had laid down, but he came back with something much more orchestrated. At first I wasn't sure if it was right for the song, but once we had a string section in the studio, I knew he had given me something wonderful. The violins soar between the lines of lyrics, the cellos hold the middle of the song down perfectly. Over the top, I was able to sing the song in a gentle, vulnerable voice, leaving behind my automatic association of effort and volume with sincerity, and letting the words deliver the weight of the song on their own merits.

After we had left Fort Worth for the last time, I took the sprawling mess that we'd recorded back to London and handed it over to Charlie Hugall, a London-based producer, to mix it into a coherent whole. The work he did in making the album make continuous sense was invaluable. He also suggested some additions to some of the songs to fill out sonic gaps that we had left open. For this song, we tracked some extra piano, some backing vocals, and a whole extra layer of rhythm for the bridge and final chorus, adding yet another level of depth and complexity to such a deceptively simple piece of writing. And, blissfully, I know the song still works if you take all of that away and strip it back to the folk song it started as.

At the end of a couple of years' work on writing, arranging, recording and mixing, I am able to listen back to this song with an immense sense of pride. I can finally say to myself without fear of hubris that I am a songwriter of some skill. It's a real piece of art, something I can unambiguously stand behind in public, point at, and say, 'This is mine, I did this, and I think it's pretty good.' It makes me feel, here at the end, that I am qualified to write a book about songwriting. Which, after nearly 80,000 words, is something of a relief.

CONCLUSION:
TRY THIS AT HOME

Let's inherit the earth, because no one else is taking it.
Come on, do your worst before the moment's passed.
In bedrooms across England and all the Western world,
There's posters and there's magazines but the music isn't ours.

Because we write love songs in C, we do politics in G,
We sing songs about our friends in E minor.
So tear down the stars now and take up your guitars,
Come on, folks and try this at home.

Let's stop waiting around for someone to patronize us;
Let's hammer out a sound that speaks of where we've been.
Forget about the haircuts, the stupid skinny jeans,
The stampedes and the irony, the media fed scenes.

Because the only thing that punk rock should ever really mean
Is not sitting around and waiting for the lights to go green,
And not thinking that you're better because you're stood up on a stage.
If you're oh so fucking different then who cares what you have to say?

Because there's no such thing as rock stars,
There's just people who play music,
And some of them are just like us,

And some of them are dicks.
So quick, turn off your stereo,
Pick up that pen and paper.
You could do much better
Than some skinny half-arsed English country singer.

* * *

What have we learned, on this rambling journey through (my) songs? A wag might immediately answer: 'That you don't know what you're talking about, mate.' And given the supremely personal approach I've taken to my subject, I'd be essentially defenceless against such a reply. But I like to think that if you bothered to pick the book up in the first place, let alone finish the damn thing, that you might have some affinity for the music I make, and that you might even have learned something along the way.

The one song I haven't written about yet is the one the book itself is named after: 'Try This at Home'. Fear not, intrepid reader, this was the plan all along. And actually I'm not going to go into it in the same detail I have with the other works I've examined here. My point is a broader ideological one.

I came up with the title before I had a song, and it's a slightly snarky nod towards my old friend and inspiration, Billy Bragg. Bill put out a great record in 1991 called 'Don't Try This at Home'. I know, I know, he was making a different point entirely, but all the same, the title always struck me as somehow being the antithesis of the punk spirit. A punk zine called *Sideburn #1* published a hand-made poster in 1976 featuring three crudely-drawn chord boxes, showing an A major, an E major and a G major. They were labelled, 'This is a chord, this is another, this is a third', and underneath, in underlined block capital letters, it simply said: 'NOW FORM A BAND'. That's more like it.

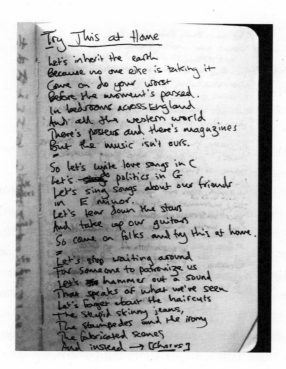

Try This at Home

Let's inherit the earth
Because no one else is taking it
Come on do your worst
Before the moment's passed.
In bedrooms across England
And all the western world
There's posters and there's magazines
But the music isn't ours.

So let's write love songs in C
Let's ~~sing~~ politics in G
Let's sing songs about our friends
in E minor.
Let's tear down the stars
And take up our guitars
So come on folks and try this at home.

Let's stop waiting around
For someone to patronize us
Let's ~~its~~ hammer out a sound
That speaks of what we've seen
Let's forget about the haircuts
The ~~stupid~~ skinny jeans,
The stampedes and the irony
The fabricated scenes
And instead → [Chorus]

A first draft of 'Try This At Home' from my notebook, 2008 or so

The essence of punk as an ethic, as I understand it, has always been democratisation. Music, and by extension art and self-expression more broadly, shouldn't be the preserve of some elite, whether they're aristocrats or the educated. We all have something to say. They say that everyone has a book in them (and Christopher Hitchens added that, in most cases, that's where it should stay, the card). A song is a simpler, more direct thing than a book, and I do believe that everyone with any small amount of musical ability has something good to say inside them. At the very least, they have the right to try.

Historically speaking, punk was born in part because of the disconnect between popular music and its audience. Kids at home in suburban England could find no meaningful connection with the complex, sprawling pomp of the music of the mid-1970s charts. So they rose up, seized some battered instruments, and did it themselves: they tried it at home, and some of it was really, really good.

I mentioned earlier in this book that I've always centred my music on the idea of myself as someone leading a congregation in song, rather than a figure on a stage* willing everyone else to shut up and listen to my art. When music becomes a collective activity, its power multiplies exponentially, and it becomes something worthy of longevity and passion. There's something very important in the idea in folk music that a song isn't really the property of its writer. As it's recorded and sung, it becomes public property, part of the community. That's how I like to think of a good song, and hopefully some of mine might fit into that category for some people.

From time to time, people contact me to ask permission to cover my songs. While I appreciate the good manners that represents, I think it's a redundant question. Play any song you know, any way you like, change it, speed it up, add a verse, change the chords, change the key, make it your own. That's how I think we should all approach songs and songwriting. The music is out there, waiting for you to reach up and grab it. Try it at home.

* And rarely a lone figure at that. At this late point in the manuscript, I'd like to highlight one more time the contributions made to so many of these songs by Ben, Nigel, Matt and Tarrant, The Sleeping Souls. They have influenced and shaped all my work in the time we've been playing together, and have brought the songs to life on stage and in the studio in a way no other group of musicians could have done. Thanks, boys.

ACKNOWLEDGEMENTS

Writing this book was a much quicker and more enjoyable process than it was for its predecessor. That's mainly down to the guidance and encouragement of my editor at Headline, Richard Roper, so I'd like to thank him first. Of course, almost nothing in the book would have turned out this way without my manager, Charlie Caplowe, and The Sleeping Souls – Nigel Powell, Matt Nasir, Ben Lloyd and Tarrant Anderson – along for the ride. Special props to Nigel for fact-checking my recollections.

Thanks to everyone at Xtra Mile Recordings, and the other labels I've worked with over the years, for giving me a chance to make this whole songwriting thing into my living.

Thanks to my publishers – Mick Shiner at Pure Groove and Hugo Turquet at BMG – for helping me look after my catalogue.

Thanks to the producers who documented these songs – Tristan Ivemy, Ben Lloyd, Alex Newport, Rich Costey, Butch Walker, Josh Block and Austin Jenkins.

Thanks to my partners in writing, Iain Archer and Jon Snodgrass.

And, saving the best till last, thanks to Jessica Guise, the love of my life, for putting up with me, as a writer of songs, of books, and as a partner.

PICTURE CREDITS

INDEX